CLASSROOM DISCIPLINE

An Idea Handbook for Elementary School Teachers

SECOND EDITION

Dorothy M. Rogers

The Center for Applied Research in Education, Inc.
West Nyack, New York

Library of Congress Cataloging-in-Publication Data

Rogers, Dorothy M. (Dorothy McKellar)
  Classroom discipline.

  Bibliography: p.
  Includes index.
    1. Classroom management—United States—Handbooks,
manuals, etc.   2. Elementary school teaching—United
States—Handbooks, manuals, etc.   3.   School children—
United States—Discipline—Handbooks, manuals, etc.
  I. Title.
  LB3013.R58   1987   372.11'02   86-29969

ISBN 0-87628-011-4

About the Author

Experienced in urban, suburban, and ethnic neighborhoods, Dorothy McKellar Rogers taught, tutored, and substituted in various Illinois and Massachusetts schools at both the elementary and secondary levels. The first edition of *Classroom Discipline* included ideas derived from her own teaching and from interviewing other teachers in the Evanston, Illinois, schools. This edition carries more techniques and information gathered from further extensive researching and from interviewing, conducting a selective but nationwide survey of administrators, and from conferring with discipline seminar participants.

Her writings and innovative ideas appeared in such publications as *Teacher* (formerly *Grade Teacher*), *The Instructor, The Christian Science Monitor, Travel-Holiday,* and the in-flight magazine, *Frontiers.* At the time of her death in 1986, Mrs. Rogers was still actively involved in education as a board member of American Dance Heritage, a nonprofit organization headquartered in Wellesley, Massachusetts, which conducts a fine arts enrichment program for schools.

Foreword

The decade of the 1980s will surely go down in history as the period of American education's greatest reform movement. A deluge of national studies and reports floods the academic landscape. One, *A Nation at Risk*, suggests that American education is awash in a sea of mediocrity. Others are less pessimistic, but all insist on the need for reform.

Whether significant reform will take place is a matter of conjecture. It is far easier to criticize and to suggest change than to bring it about. To use a surfing analogy, will we "hang ten" and ride the wave to the beach, or will educators, politicians, and the public fall off the board, while the wave loses its energy, washing peacefully up on an unchanged shore? Successful surfing is difficult. It calls for agility, balance, and perseverance. The same can be said for significant educational change.

Curriculum has been a major focus of the reform movement. What should we teach, and how should we teach it? Legislators throughout the country have been raising high school graduation and college admissions requirements. They are insisting that schools spend more time teaching the traditional subjects of English, history, mathematics, science, and foreign language.

Lengthening the school day and year, more credits in core subjects, more testing, and higher teachers' salaries share the spotlight with curriculum reform. The implication is that if we do all these things, the quality of education will improve. Graduates will achieve a higher degree of literacy, will be better problem solvers, will be able to think intuitively and critically, and will maintain American leadership for a sane, equitable, and just society. These reformers assume that we can mandate better schooling just as the FAA regulates higher safety standards on the airlines.

Opponents of regulatory change label this approach the "quick fix." They raise questions of content. What elements of American history should be taught? How should we treat minorities? How should we deal with non-Western perspectives? Are we moving toward the potential tyranny of a national curriculum?

Another school of thought in the reform movement is epitomized by Theodore H. Sizer (*Horace's Compromise: The Dilemma of the American High School*) and John I. Goodlad (*A Place Called School*). Both call for radical change. Restructure schools. Increased standardization will lower standards, not raise them. Standardized solutions, new regulations for solving school problems, will not work. Each school must be shaped by its own constituency of students, teachers, and parents. School units should enroll no more than 500 students. More time in school will do little to improve learning if class time is not used more effectively. More is not necessarily better.

The school reform movement of the eighties is not characterized by consensus and consistency. A cacophany of voices fills the air. Shrill voices call for instant legislative action while others talk of evolutionary change projected for 1995 and beyond. But in all the clamor, the single most important element of successful schooling is lost—the individual teacher in the elementary school classroom. It is here that the education seed is planted and takes root. For five, six, or seven years it must be carefully and skillfully cultivated and nourished. Only a healthy seedling with a well-developed root structure can flourish and grow strong enough to bear fruit. Without such treatment the plant will surely wither and die or be lost in a field of weeds.

That is what this book is all about. Sensitive teachers who recognize and accept the individuality of each child are the key to real educational reform—teachers who recognize and respect the human rights of children as people.

Even these teachers, however, need to acquire a number of specific skills and techniques. Although some of these skills may be intuitive, others can be learned by sharing the experiences of other teachers. The late Ronald Edmonds, in his research on effective schools, concluded that at the core of good schools are common sense notions; that if the faculty believes in its task and in the kids, all children can learn.

This book is a compilation of strategies and tactics used by some successful teachers to develop a classroom atmosphere conducive to learning for all—an atmosphere in which each individual's rights are respected and no person's opportunity to learn is sacrificed for the sake of the group.

When we have such a climate, when we are teaching respect by example in classrooms throughout America, then and only then can we expect real education reform.

The reader is not expected to approve or accept all the suggestions offered. That an idea has worked for one teacher does not guarantee that it will work for another. Teaching, like learning, is a highly personal process. However, if the reader garners just two or three thoughts which will lead toward better classroom practice, the effort has been justified.

> Gregory C. Coffin, Ph.D.
> Director
> Urban Schools Collaborative
> Northeastern University

About This Handbook

Teaching is a fine art, and part of this art is refined control in the classroom. Knowledge of what constitutes good classroom discipline evolves from two origins: guided instruction and discovery. The first includes reading tomes and scholarly articles, attending university lectures, and melding these ideas into a sound personal philosophy of education. And discovery? This often overlooked aspect is, or should be, an ongoing process, a widening awareness of effective strategies that work well for the individual teacher. Experience brings a cache of strategy ideas. A repertoire of techniques can be augmented through timely suggestions from a colleague, a master teacher, a kindly administrator, or the printed page.

The suggestions in this second edition of *Classroom Discipline* are a combination of traditional approaches and ideas as fresh as wet paint. The book can be used in various ways. First, as a reference guide. Let's say we're faced with a specific problem, such as a grousing student or class. As we read the section on constructive protest, the various ideas should stimulate our thinking into a solution which uniquely fits the immediate scene.

Second, the material can be used for polishing teacher performance. If we choose a topic such as "changing subjects" and concentrate on improving transitions for a week, results are bound to appear. Trying different approaches, we can refine our style, adjust to student reactions, and finally discover which implementations are best for us.

Third, portions can be used in planning a six-week campaign. By combining fresh combinations of strategies from different chapters, we can, for instance, hone group discussions.

Dealing With Everyday Incidents

Sometimes a tadpole, as Mark Twain would call him, does things "just 'cause"—like barefooting around town . . . mimicking a screeching cat . . . short sheeting a camp buddy's cot. Most minor school incidents occur for a similar "just 'cause"; they are simply a part of normal growth. A child's buoyancy is precious and natural, but it must be channeled.

In recent years our efforts to help students acquire self-control have been tainted with an infusion-of-meaning mania concerning everyday happenings. Some experts' intended guidelines have been transfixed into revelations from Olympus; other sound behavioral premises have been warped into psychobabble. Since the vast majority of behavior incidents are normal to growing up, we can exhibit our normalcy, our genuine insight, by viewing them as normal rather than ". . . *personality* is defined as an analytical constant, based on the hypothesis that internal, systematically organized cognitions and effective relationships influence many overt behaviors in a relatively stable manner."

Since less than 15 percent of American classrooms and schools can be accurately classified critical problem arenas, *Classroom Discipline* addresses itself primarily to the first 85 percent—the relatively normal classroom and its normal inhabitants, their problems, and how some have been solved, others alleviated. The book includes several chapters on morale building and concrete, proven strategies for promoting individual self-confidence and *esprit de corps*. It also provides several chapters on mundane control problems, together with specific techniques that humane, excellent teachers are using with success in today's classrooms.

Creating a Good Classroom Climate

Discretion in selecting and applying the ideas in this book is the vital contribution of each individual teacher. Ethos is the essence of a natural classroom control, and the right blend of components for an outstanding climate is difficult to convey either in lectures or print. A good example is, of course, priceless. Often a superb teacher comments simply, "Discipline is not a real problem," without analyzing it further. The personality that enables a teacher to find authentic rapport with young people is usually modest; yet such teachers have made this book possible.

Complementing Formal Training

Every certified teacher has taken psychology, but many never had a course in classroom management; fewer still in conduct management. Others had good training years ago; almost everyone needs refresher ideas. Some teachers did their practicum under splendid tutelage. And others? Well, there still persists a widespread lack of precise collaboration between colleges and public schools. Then too, experienced teachers find it neither cost- nor time-efficient to lumber through night school courses rehashing theory to ferret out nuggets of pragmatic strategies.

Nationwide, numerous college graduates are teaching in public and private schools on temporary certifications; they need realistic suggestions while they are completing statutory requirements. When we consider that 40 percent of teachers now entering the field will leave within five years, coupled with an upcoming shortage of teachers due to school population growth, the number of temporary certifications will probably increase. Teachers reentering the field after long absence, reassigned high school teachers, and teacher aides should find the techniques and strategies in this book an invaluable complement to their previous training.

Sections of the book provide an excellent springboard for inservice sessions or university seminars on discipline. Most participants are wary of mentioning their immediate student conduct problems to mere acquaintances, some supervisors, or visiting brass; plucking and examining strategies and topics from print keeps the discussion tone above the pale of personalities. Clearer thinking and more candid comments should be a natural result.

A Final Word

From the potpourri of suggestions, your imagination may weave clever composites to meet your immediate needs. Certainly, given examples can be copied, per se, if the approach fits snugly. But, better still, let's hope *Classroom Discipline* prompts fresh and original discovery!

Dorothy M. Rogers

Acknowledgments

I wish to thank the following teachers, administrators, and professors who were generous in sharing their experience and ideas with me:

Jerry Abern
Helene Abernathy
Michele Abrams
Ron Amend
Corene Anderson
Elizabeth Arras
Ron Barnfield
Leo Benson
Ann Bevan
Kathryn Blair
Charlotte Bond
Marjorie Bredehorn
Judith Brostoff
Jean Buck
Elise Burkholder
Richard Cande
Gretchen Carr
Paula Clark
Norma Core
Lynne Courtemanche
Yvonne Davis
Eddie M. Ellis
Kathryn English
James Eliot
Betty Fisher

Clara Floyd
Mary Flynn
Edith Ford
Brenda Foss
Barbara Friedberg
Cathy Freeman
Mary Garrity
Martha Gauger
Ronald Gearing
Jackie Gerth
Bonnie Gillespie
Ethel Grays
Betty Hall
Mary Hunter
Barbara Huntzicler
Lyn Hyndman
Mary Jenkins
Suzanne Jewett
Irene Kantner
Ruth Khowais
David R. King
Wendy Klein
Jean Kixmiller
Myril Landsman
Phil Lapalme

Susan Larsen	Liam Roomey
Ann Lavers	Pat Rousselle
Edna Lehman	Edna Saewart
Mary Lenahan	Gary Sanders
Caroline Lewis	Ruth Ann Sayre
Jody Mack	Shirley Scullane
Hester Meeder	Judy Segal
Marilee Mercer	Trudy Selz
Eleanor Metzger	Joy Simon
Charlotte Meyer	Virginia Sinclair
Virginia Milne	Edward Smail
Dorothy Muldoon	Janet Smucker
Ann Murray	Irene Spensley
Nicola Narcisi	Dan Stefanilo
Eunice Neal	Candas Sullivan
Helen Newell	Charles Thomas
Avian O'Connor	Jean Thorsen
Edward O'Reilly	Susan Tourigny
Edward Pearson	Stuart Vincent
Margaret Payne	Sarah Weingarten
Alita Reicin	Mildred Werner
Bessie Rhodes	Susan Wheeler
Anne Richter	Carol Wilkinson
Judy Ritter	Alice Wimberly
Ernest Robbins	Carol Yoder

. . . and to the many others who shared their techniques and strategies with me at discipline seminars, in faculty lounges, and while we were breaking bread. Would that I had written down all your names; I surely remembered your ideas.

Contents

One

ENHANCING TEACHER CONSISTENCY IN CLASSROOM CONTROL

Dominie is a Scottish word for *pedagogue.* Aye, it's a canny term, for it skirts dominion and domineer. A domineering teacher thinks from a heavy personal sense of her own authority, ability, and accomplishments; but a teacher with true dominion (call it understanding self-confidence if you prefer) draws a strength from the inner poise of knowing her own unique identity, and from wise aspirations, humility, and gratitude. Paradoxical as it may appear, the sounder her sense of dominion, the less tempted she is to domineer. Surely, children feel the difference before the first word is spoken.

In this chapter we will consider various aspects of helping teachers maintain a more even tempo and a better climate in the classroom. If strategies and techniques, formulas and campaigns, are the leaves and flowers on a shrub, control consistency is the root system which is nourished in the soil of a teacher's philosophy, her balanced life, her integrity, and skill.

As she grows professionally, she must prune strategies judiciously and clip techniques so that her control methods complement a unique teaching presence.

No one learns on a paper keyboard; no one masters sonatas merely by reading the score or even understanding the music theory and patterns behind them. Practice, practice, practice is the only way to become a pianist.

Teachers may study Glasser and Kounin, Dreikurs, and T.E.T., understand them and in part agree with them, but the only way teachers learn effective group control is by practice, mild experimentation, errors, and more practice. Just as a musician goes over and over a difficult passage until it's right, so teachers need to concentrate on specific, tricky areas, work on timing and intonation. This chapter also discusses facets of a healthy perspective, professional bearing, reducing emotional swings, concrete strategies for corrections, and eight suggestions for starting a year.

Though visions of cherubims and celestial trumpets, all on our side, may cavort in our minds, let's remember the actual post is called schoolteacher. Even if parents are fumbling and muddling—still, in the final analysis, rearing their offspring is their job, right, and privilege. Surely, humility's first requirement is that we avoid taking ourselves too seriously. Earnestly, ever so earnestly, we may believe we are pointing to salvation's road through education, but our words, actions, beliefs, are not that salvation itself. It is fortunate that children are marvelously resilient, and have spontaneously shed, and will continue to shed, many consequences due to our mistakes.

Along with staying calm and relaxed, nurturing gratitude is great for strengthening mental poise. Since the word gratitude is an antonym for complaint, let's consider some school world pluses.

Compare the computer terminals, overhead projectors, plethora of films and filmstrips available, copiers, and books of today with the equipment of forty years past. Rare is the school board that is stingy in authorizing supplies. Although in some large cities the distributing of materials can baffle: one building may receive thirty-two overhead projectors and across town another may get delivery of all the blank transparencies . . . but that's not the point. The tax dollars are being spent.

Salaries have come eons from school-marm-boarding-around-the-village days. When one computes the total time, hours and days, that teachers are required to be in school and then divides into a yearly salary, teachers are not among the huddled masses. (See Figure 1-1 for some interesting data.) Indeed, per hour expended, many are ahead of their administrative colleagues sitting behind big brown desks.

Focusing attention only on cash income when comparing teacher salaries with other professionals or with blue collar labor contracts tends to tunnel vision. Too many vital aspects of employment remain peripheral. Let's use one example, a grave-diggers local . . . there are psychic and status reimbursements to be considered in teaching.

Again, most administrators and principals genuinely try to be fair, considerate, and supportive. A good school climate is of utmost importance to them. Finally, try recalling your early training: informally watching favorite teachers' styles, formal sessions at seminars and universities. Most of it was enjoyable.

PROFESSIONAL BEARING

Teachers are indeed professionals, but in matters of grooming and clothing, what happened? Evidently many faculty members assume style is pointless or that super casual clothing, no matter how dated, will put children more at ease, making it simpler to establish friendship. But, our body language changes with our attire—and our attitudes are likewise influenced. Managers and professionals usually dress according to their role.

Airline pilots project a military officer cool-in-a-crisis aura and then blend in the down-by-the-hollow, Chuck-Yaeger folksiness when using the public address system. Nurses' garb announces hygienic crispness; they rely on personality to convey nurturing warmth. Dentists and pediatricians dress for success and the image of success.

No one's advocating men teachers start wearing vested, pin-striped suits to school; teaching is not, after all, an internship for joining the state bar. But, jeans, battle fatigues, and

Figure 1-1

DEMOGRAPHICS—SELECTED DATA

FIGURE A
PERCENT OF ALL TEACHERS HOLDING
GRADUATE DEGREES, 1963–1983

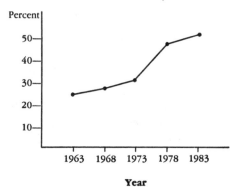

FIGURE B
PERCENT OF ALL TEACHERS HAVING TEN YEARS
OR MORE TEACHING EXPERIENCE, 1963–1983

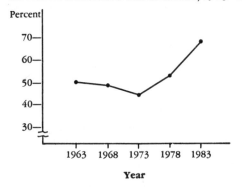

The percent of all teachers holding *graduate degrees* has increased from 25 percent in 1963 to 52 percent in 1983. The percent of all teachers having *ten years or more teaching experience* showed a slight decline between 1963 and 1973 (from 51 to 44 percent) but in 1983 the percent of teachers having ten years or more teaching experience is at an all time high of 69 percent.

Research has consistently shown that teacher training and experience are positively related to student achievement. In addition, training and experience are the *only* two teacher characteristics rewarded on the single salary schedule which is currently the compensation system used in virtually every school district in the United States.

The evidence in Figures A and B indicates that the current teaching force is the most experienced and best qualified in history.

Source: National Education Association, 1983

duck blind boots miss the mark, regardless of current reverse chic. (Neither men nor women faculty should, in spite of similarities they might feel they perceive, wear green berets. The symbolism is bound to offend someone.) Some East Indian dresses are stunning, but usually they don't underscore a professional profile.

The clothing we wear is a centuries-tested mode of announcing our station in life and what we think of ourselves. Many education administrators rate appearance as the second most important factor among their best teachers. Here comes an elementary point on consistency: we want students and parents to respect us as competent, even outstanding, professionals; let's inform them nonverbally that we are. Apparel projecting our role is *not* a hindrance in developing warm rapport with students.

A notch more formal dress and better grooming have a marked effect on students. A teacher wearing a dark blazer exudes a more authoritative appearance than when she is wearing an Irish fisherman's sweater—or, far worse, an ancient, pilling acrylic. The blazer silently announces to the class her manager or leader responsibility; it clarifies expectations. Wearing more businesslike clothing establishes a subtle division, a good one, for the teacher struggling for better classroom management.

Certainly, students living in poorer neighborhoods encounter few adults who dress as professionals. Well-dressed teachers, reassure, by example, that reasonable affluence does follow a good education. Youngsters love clothes, and they notice them. But, do they really expect a faculty as informally turned out as they are? Not anymore than they would expect a teacher to consider wearing a propeller beanie!

Since your dress, personality, and talents add to your distinctive style as an individual, why not use your same inherent taste to develop your unique fashion in teaching? No one needs to be a character to put character, a flair of the slightly off-beat or panache, into a teaching approach and demeanor.

One teacher claims he's not a kindly shepherd who patiently leads a reluctant flock over rocks and rills, dales and hills. He says he's closer to being a sheep dog, and he plans to nip the heels of his lambs when they frolic. He adds that sheep dogs are alert and affable. They bite only to keep their charges from danger.

Lip service to "caring," "loving," "individual differences," abounds, but if we carry this philosophy full course, we must include teachers as well as students. While thinking about your own professional style, mentally picture and feel the classroom climate you hope to create and toy with various adjustments. Let's keep in mind that a well-stated classroom, organized and attractive, is an expression of the teacher's thinking. But above all, balance is a keynote, and balance is a goal.

CLEARING YOUR THOUGHTS

Many of today's teachers try to separate, in their thinking, the child's naughtiness from the child. Often they ask themselves: Why did he pull this last one? Do all the kids around him do the same thing? Is it a pattern or becoming a pattern, or is it a fleeting impulse? Before any correction is attempted, several more questions need answering. What is the teacher's motive for wanting to cope with this gaffe? Is it to teach a lesson? What kind of lesson? That learning-goal-distractive behavior doesn't pay off? Does the teacher want to get even for the nuisance of being interrupted? Is the teacher easily annoyed today?

Every Behavior Incident Involves Emotions

The emotional climate while administering correction is more important than the exact technique used. Please allow involved students a few moments to calm down. Wisely, you can spend this time pinpointing your own emotions. Before you speak or act, clear your thought. Ask yourself:

1. Why do I want this child to obey? Really? No other reason? The more precisely you can level with yourself, the more adept will be your resulting actions and words.

2. What do I expect of him, exactly? Mentally spell it out.

Would I have expected this of him yesterday? Will I expect this of him tomorrow?

Deciding wisely what is best for individuals within the context of the group is a master key to classroom harmony. Often, individual rights versus group rights is an imaginary dilemma. The two are not necessarily at loggerheads, since every child must learn to live in organized society. If he doesn't learn from those who are concerned about his welfare, he'll be forced to learn from those who are indifferent, sometimes brutally indifferent.

Another question which sometimes mushrooms into a needless harangue is "the immediate versus the long-term welfare" of the pupil. Nonsense. It's not necessarily an either/or proposition. Always consider that it can be a three-forked decision point, the third answer taking in both now and later.

Common humanity should prevent us from labeling a child as hopeless. Honesty will bring times when we must admit failure in handling a student, sometimes total failure. Thousands do every year. As the French say, *C'est la vie.* Eternal damnation is not a twentieth century doctrine; such failures need not be forever.

If you have an impossible student in your class, one whom you don't handle well and in your heart, you can't like, try working a trade with another teacher. Take one of her impossibles. You may want to tell the students that you're trading like a team trades ballplayers, and you sincerely hope that each child will be happier, and will perform better, under the next coach.

On Valentine's Day It Would Be Natural

So many teachers feel unappreciated; they recognize the priceless worth of their contributions but their best efforts go unnoticed. Sending your children's teachers small, pretty corsages with friendly enclosure cards would be a gracious move. Corsages are not in great style, so why a corsage? Cut flowers would stay on her desk all day, unnoticed except by the class. But courtesy dictates wearing a corsage, so when the teacher goes to the office, lunchroom, or through the halls, others will see it and probably comment.

An Excellent Teacher Never Gets Angry?

Nuts. Of course she does. That is, unless she's a masochist or a martyr. Next, how should it be handled? If a teacher expresses anger without any nuance of insult, she is on safer ground. Thus, if she expresses herself candidly, "I am extremely provoked . . . irked . . . frustrated . . . disappointed . . . enraged," rather than, "How could you do something so stupid?" there will be fewer fences to mend later.

A Diploma, a License, a Certificate

Teachers' professional education and backgrounds are usually semiobscured. How about other professionals? They display their diplomas, licenses, certifications, honors where the world may view their credentials. Some professionals are required by law to exhibit them. Lawyers, dentists, psychologists, doctors, surveyors, engineers, interior decorators, architects, all frame their precious parchments, tap a nail, and up they go.

Since this tradition has never developed among teachers, a single individual would be hesitant to hang his credentials in the classroom; but if a few colleagues did likewise, a different light would be shed. The display would make a good nonverbal counterfoil, especially in neighborhoods where a militant minority seems intent on putting teachers down. Many taxpayers are acutely alert to school district costs, but they are quite unaware of the faculty's financial investment for years of study. Displaying a few parchments makes a nice left-handed reminder.

A subtle, yet effective, presentation would be a group display of the entire faculty's diplomas in the window case near the office. Mounting it, let's say, just before an Open House. Parents everywhere welcome knowing their children's educational welfare is in skilled hands.

SYSTEMATICALLY WORKING ON
CONTROL CONSISTENCY

Most teachers are wonderfully aware of how a child can improve his analysis and attack skills in reading during a year. He is intelligently guided and works day by day, notch by notch. Take a cue from your skill in teaching reading: although you work on particular vowel and consonant combinations, you never lose sight of the real goal, reading comprehension. In the same manner you can systematically polish your own skills in classroom control. Analyze your performance. Too much fluctuation? Is it from day to day, or from child to child? Or both? Focus your attention on one aspect at a time.

Let's say you decide to narrow the fluctuation between students. You want to treat them more equally. *First,* list several trouble spots annoying you: (1) Incomplete supplies, no pencil nor paper, (2) Roaming with insipid reasons, (3) General group dawdling, (4) Eruptions of loud talking. *Second,* concentrate on improving your finesse piecemeal, untangling one knot at a time: attend to other problems as you have been, but on the focal snag try various techniques and approaches. Also notice how differing background factors influence the effectiveness of a particular strategy.

Where are you going to discover these strategies? A few are listed in this book. Or, offhandedly introduce the topic of an isolated nuisance, say roaming, at lunchtime; certainly your colleagues have encountered the same annoyance. Pick their brains. Another avenue is to ask your vice-principal. Many times a supervisor welcomes being asked; your opening the topic removes the implied criticism that accompanies his broaching the subject. If you're reluctant to expose your weakness to him, select a time when your class has accomplished something outstanding. Tell him about their feat and then weave in a question about one particular control problem. Consider his advice and all the ideas, water them with your imagination; a few more will sprout.

Third, remember the rule of three to five in learning. Alertly drill yourself on overcoming a focal problem for three, four, or five days, according to your classroom results. *Finally*, tackle the next item on your list and employ the same experimentation and self-drill. Or, you may use the term auto-reinforcement if that word turns your crank.

A good information lode on the class's reaction to minor snarls is having each student write a letter or compose two lists. Let them name three things they like and three things they dislike in the room. Lists may be signed or unsigned. These compilations yield many useful facts about your control methods without getting openly into personality discussion.

TEACHING SELF-CONTROL
COMES WITH THE TERRITORY

"Most discipline problems stem from a weakness in the teaching." We've all heard the adage. True? Yes and no. The implication is poor lesson planning or presentation; occasionally this is a major factor. But an almost ever-present factor is dominant: few teachers were advised to *positively* and *concretely teach* conduct standards. In classroom management courses, theory and platitudinous generalities usually are considered sufficient. The result? Many young, idealistic teachers enter the classroom without a heat shield. Dismay ensues.

You'll reduce much of your tension, resentment, fatigue, exasperation, frustration, discouragement, and disillusionment if you learn to *expect* to teach some form of student self-control as long as you plan to stay in teaching.

If your group arrives well-behaved, enjoy the luxury of helping them acquire refined consideration of others, more tact, and better camaraderie; but plan to devote the time. Obviously, with less fortunate students, you must adjust to emphasizing more basic aspects of behavior. Expecting to invest time and energy on developing self-control and courtesy with every class you have, keeps matters in balanced perspective. Accepting conduct training, a hidden curriculum, as a normal facet of teaching helps you overcome a sense of imposition—the feeling that conduct training is an unnatural extra chore foisted improperly on you by a small, but dedicated number of rascals.

Multitudes of upper- and middle-class children have responded well to the following explanation: In all groups there must be control, or there will be chaos. Others can impose it, outside control. This type of governing force comes from members of a group or an authority. Or an individual can impose limits on himself, inside control. (Your talk may well include verbal descriptions of military codes, tribal customs, unwritten rules in corporations, as well as training regimes of athletic champions.) Tell the class the control type will be entirely their choice. It can be personal self-control or by teacher authority or by the group. *But control there will be.* You'll respect their decision as long as they abide by it. Incidentally, many, many inner city classrooms have students who are ready for responsibly making this decision for themselves.

Over and over and over again, with different teachers in different schools, I asked questions about establishing a good learning climate, routine procedures, and conduct training. Each teacher, without exception, emphasized the wisdom of stressing expected conduct standards and routine methods for the first several weeks of school. Voluntarily, they added that time spent in establishing basic control will be rewarded many times over with happier students and far more learning accomplishment.

Not once, even with the strictest teacher, did I hear the old saw "don't smile until Christmas." Nor did they proffer advice to really zap the first student who causes serious disruption to make an example of him. They were all addressing the other direction: solid guidelines, reasonable limits, and goal-oriented activity.

Then I would weasel in my question once more, "But wouldn't it be wiser to plunge into interesting projects first, and work on conduct control as the need arises?" The answer was "No." The teachers were unwilling to change priorities. May I add that these professionals are not old curmudgeons? Nor are they rigid personalities; they are well-rounded, excellent teachers.

Their guideline suggestion on the time span needed to weld a group varied from two to four to six weeks, depending on the neighborhood. One seventh grade social studies teacher in a good suburban school advised me that she spends most of a daily forty-minute period for two weeks on self-government tactics, room procedures, and school customs. Her orientation includes a building tour; even though students know the premises, they like this. A training lagniappe: she has them learn the first and last name of every classmate and the names of some students in other rooms. This last she handles with a bingo type card. The only academic progress she attempts is developing group discussion rules and manners; for this she uses news clippings the youngsters bring from home.

It's rough to be thoroughly consistent in handling mischief and unruliness. If a teacher is in high spirits, or if the child is a good student, it seems natural to be lenient. The reverse is true, too. However, a child sees only the immediate act, not an overall attitude, achievement level, or other mitigating circumstances: throwing an eraser is throwing an eraser in his book. All concerned, faculty and students, need guidelines beyond personality. Firm rules, enforced by an adult with a flexible attitude, give youngsters a feeling of security. They know what's expected of them and what to expect. Your flexibility shows up in your one-to-one talk, your firmness and fairness in your actions.

When you must correct a child, relate the deterrent directly to the offense. Your comments will have greater impact if your actions are patently clear and logical to the student. Examples: for imposing on another's time, impose on his free time; for lacking personal supplies, have him inventory some art materials for a coming project; for chattering too much, isolate him so he can talk to nobody but himself.

List of Drastics

Sometime while you're curled in an easy chair before a glowing fireplace, warm, comfortable, purring, analyze your school world as it pertains to classroom control. One time-honored way is to make two lists. The first records, in ascending order, remedial or relief steps open to you. The second is a list of common annoyances in your room. Then develop a third list, a carefully considered combination of nuisances and correction steps for first, second, and third offenses. For instance, in some suburban classes children getting out of their seats is no real problem, and any teacher can well afford to ignore it or treat it lightly. In some urban classrooms, however, roaming can rapidly become rampant; a teacher must be firm or she will have chaos. Take a look at Figure 1-2.

First of all, simply composing the list will clarify your feelings and intentions. Naturally, any teacher who has good judgment is going to use common sense in applying these decisions, making exceptions in rare circumstances.

Figure 1-2

Example

Remedy or Correction

ignore action	phone home
stand near child	dismiss from class
speak to child	send for parents
change child's seat	see social worker
scold child	contact student council
talk to child in the hall	see principal
assign simple punishment	put child on probation
keep child after school	suspend child
deprive child of after-	expel child
school privilege	
send note home	

Misdemeanors

gum chewing	tardiness from recess
eating	"forgetting" homework
loud talking	running in halls
insolence	horseplay in assembly
sharpening pencil	making foolish noises
	etc.

Teacher Reaction

	1st time	2nd time	3rd time
gum chewing	_____	_____	_____
eating	_____	_____	_____
loud talking	_____	_____	_____
running in hall	_____	_____	_____

Interviews with many skilled, pragmatic professionals brought splendid suggestions on practical ways of modulating teacher consistency in classroom management. They are:

Fussin' and Frettin'. You've had a major upset in your life or a severe disappointment. Or you don't feel well physically. Certainly all year you've been giving students sympathy in their darker hours; perhaps it's your turn to collect some return consideration. Plainly tell children that you're out of sorts today, and you might snap when ordinarily you wouldn't. They'll be grateful. Usually, they'll let up on their antics—surprising, but true.

Ever Hear a Noisy Teacher? The kids call it yelling. Make a checklist with the trouble areas. Code it with initials so you may leave the slip openly on your desk. For example: R.V. (raised voice), S.T. (sharp tone), Sc. (scolding). As you progress through the day, check mark each time you slip.

Garbage In . . . Garbage Out. Computer programmers have their own jargon. A favorite saying is "garbage in . . . garbage out," meaning, of course, if poor materials are fed into computers, poor results are the product. Sometimes when you have students who are impossible to please, who are bored with anything and everything, you might weave this phrase into one of your spiels. It does help.

One Teacher Almost Flunked. Evaluate *yourself* every time you issue report cards. Compose a list of salient points, such as: (1) Clear lesson goals, (2) Explicit, *brief* directions, (3) Supplies ready, (4) Positive comments, (5) Calm attitude, and (6) Controlled voice. Add others which seem important to your growth. Tape a few hours of your teaching and listen to it. Grade yourself each time a related item occurs. If this task seems monumentally boring, beware!

Keep Right on Spouting. You or the class stiffen, or even worse, freeze when the principal or the district office brass walk into the room? Leave your door open so your teaching or the industrious, controlled buzz of worthwhile activity may be overheard while the room is unaware of an audience. Your principal must evaluate your work; it's part of his job. Of course, he wants to know your best.

Hearken . . . to the Soft and Pleasant. Testing one, two, three—testing for your best and normal speaking voice is easy with a tape recorder. Place it with a trusted student and ask the student to switch it on several times during the day for ten or fifteen minutes. Neither you nor the class is to know when it's on. Later, review the tape. Is your voice "the mirror of the soul" you'd like the world to admire? Or, more bluntly, would you want your principal to speak to you in the same tones?

Best Friends Do Confide. Ask a colleague to visit your class during his free period and take notes on your classroom presence. A friend can direct your attention to weak spots in your teaching, obviously giving you the opportunity to eliminate them quietly and privately. After all, the front office doesn't need to know every little thing.

Teacher's Too Busy for Students

Yes, we all know of times when a teacher simply must write at her desk while students are present. The monthly report is due early afternoon on the last day; the district office demands statistics by 10:00 and it's now 9:30; the building office sends around next month's film order at the last minute. One effective way to handle this dilemma is having a prepared tape of your voice for emergencies. It's surely more pleasurable to prepare a tape than to grade sets of written busy work. Another mode is to run a Best Row contest.

One Teacher, Two Voices. Children love poetry. Like music, poetry must be heard to be appreciated. Who has the time? Always, it seems, more pressing items jam the docket. Prerecord poems from a reading text . . . as you record, add personal comments when you tell students to turn the page. Place a cluster of students around a table; each child has his copy of the text. If the table is close to you, you may tap your room rascals to sit there while you're working. These tapes may also be used on low volume in one corner of the room while you're presenting a live lesson in another.

Mayday, Mayday, Mayday. A Best Row contest is good for thirty to forty minutes, no more. Elicit best row qualifications from the class and list them on the board. Inform students you'll be keeping a tally while you complete work for the office. Periodically you'll look up, and the best row *at that moment* will get a point. About midway they'll want to know who is winning. Be careful. To keep all rows competing, the standing of the contestants should be an unknown fact or it should be a tight race. The prize? The glory of winning—a wrapped candy —extra computer time.

EIGHT RECOMMENDATIONS FOR
STARTING THE YEAR

Interviewing literally dozens and dozens of outstanding teachers crystallized in my thinking the following conclusions. I offer them as a summary indicating the teachers' general opinions and advice for establishing a natural, good climate in the classroom. The basic premise preceding this is that the teacher has good lesson plans, a full complement of supplies, and her paperwork, including seating chart, in good order.

1. Consider the training period for establishing conduct guidelines as an important investment: dividends will be returned during the year and the earnings ratio will be splendid. Your shakedown cruise for fixing methods, procedures, and class rules should last the first few days. Use inviting lessons, which in most cases will cover a refresher and review of last year's achievements, but don't worry about grades. If you do issue marks, make them a ✓+, ✓, ✓-, 0 on the systems you're teaching.

After completing orientation, start the year's studies in earnest, and simultaneously, concertedly, and positively, teach conduct standards. This should last for two, four, or six weeks, depending on the neighborhood and the history of this class. Often it's wise to review for the class a few of the regulations for the teachers: preterm orientation meetings, hours-in-building rules, building and district meetings, extra duty roster, and lesson preparation time. The unspoken moral: everyone has duties and must abide by rules.

2. Set standards and goals for students, especially emphasizing those covering chatter and discussions. Make six or eight rules, no more. Usually students enjoy making suggestions for these. Put many, many ideas on the board for two reasons: one, the ideas, and two, so students will genuinely feel they've been heard.

3. Teach—actively teach—the rules. Any effective approach is fine, but make sure you do more than just hang a list on the bulletin board.

4. Use the eloquence of example. Express salient qualities yourself, particularly those in which the group needs improvement.

5. Balance every complaint with a compliment. This is an invaluable aid in avoiding discouragement—or becoming a scold. When you must correct a student, compliment him (or another child) on an unrelated good feat.

6. List student antics that irk you. Don't worry whether they *should* bother you; if they annoy you now, jot them down. Then, your compilation completed, split it. Make two lists. The first could be entitled "Requires Attention" and the other "Temporarily Ignore." Revise lists after a fortnight and again at month's end. Growing students change and so do teachers.

Requires Attention	Temporarily Ignore
Fighting	Gum chewing
Out of seat	Messy desks

7. Keep misdemeanor and its sanction related. You're well aware of the connection: make sure students see a pattern or relationship. Students like teachers to take action correction, to "do something." In addition, have a brief, remedial talk with the offender.

8. Initiate a custom of calling children's homes regularly. About six calls on a Friday will cover the average class in a

month. A good report gives parents two days to praise and reward or, for a negative account, two days to work on correction.

CONCLUSION

True dominion, sometimes called healthy self-respect, lifts a teacher's outlook above the shortsighted ego trip involved in being domineering and brings equipoise to speech and action. Since domineering personalities usually feed on self-righteousness, remedial steps involve learning to appreciate the rights and individuality of others. Genuinely so, not just lip service. Gratitude does much to dispel a self-centered attitude of entitlement; this, coupled with humility and wise aspirations, helps to dissipate feelings of frustration and futility and to bring a sense of balance to the scene.

Repeatedly, teachers advise students who want improved recognition to begin the change within themselves, to take small, consistent, persistent steps. Many faculty members yearn for an improved public perception of their professional accomplishments and abilities; more dignified dress and grooming is an excellent first step to improving the profession's image. A well-stated classroom, organized and attractive, is another; it's an indication of healthy pride.

A key to an effective classroom climate in discipline matters is an ability to decide wisely what is best for the child *within* the context of the group. Individual and group rights are not inherently in conflict; after all, each child has the need and right to learn group living.

Here it is, one more time . . . Clear your own thought of emotion before you handle a behavior incident.

Just as some may have musical genius or a natural ear but nobody becomes an accomplished musician without practice, so some teachers have an innate rapport with students and classes, but even they must hone their skills if they are to be really outstanding. And a key is practice, subtle experimentation, and more practice.

Quietly polishing control techniques with systematic diligence is a clever way to improve teaching results; it adds noticeable time and energy to a teaching day. A teaching day and classroom day are not necessarily terms to be equated, though often so used. Since training students in conduct goes hand in hand with classroom teaching, why not sharpen your analysis incisiveness, enlarge your technique repertoire, and add a patina to your tact?

Two

IMPROVING COMMUNICATION AND COMMITTEES

Silence, thoughtful silence, is the first requirement for the "feast of reason and flow of soul" (Pope), which makes for richness in conversation and discussion. Brevity and restraint on a teacher's part reflect effective disciplining and marshaling of her thinking. Good educators listen, and listen again, to their own better judgment before they speak.

Progressive footsteps show yesterday's best is not enough for today's best. Much is known about expected avenues for students' growth. But the best teaching of all is example. What paths are we, as teachers, taking into the golden sunrise of learning? Basically we have a good grip on subject matter and are aware of good instructional methods. Constantly trying to improve our succinctness and tact in communication keeps us in a daily growth pattern essential to fine teaching. The accompanying sense of progress will protect our early enthusiasm, our freshness, and help us avoid a pitfall fate common to many

21

splendid, experienced teachers—going to seed. It retards frustrated stress and burnout.

No espionage system ever devised has outclassed the mole communication network which children set up intuitively when danger threatens their common good. Often not a word appears to be spoken, but the message spreads. Thus, we don't have to teach them to communicate: we must teach them how to reach us in a form we understand, at our present level of interest.

Distinct communication problems are taken up elsewhere. This chapter addresses itself to promoting the flow of information and the exchange of ideas. Even the present discussion is confined to several elements which are of focal interest only to the practicing teacher: controlled whispering, recitation, class discussion, informal and formal group techniques, individual constructive protest, and finally, some splendid suggestions and plans for committees.

CONTROLLED WHISPERING

No one need explain the advantages of allowing students the freedom of talking quietly among themselves, at least intermittently. An easy working climate does all that educators claim for it in stimulating learning, but children also need to feel background stability.

First, decide the best decibel level for your room. Second, *expect to systematically train* students into accepting and respecting this level. It is far better than correcting or scolding them into it. Use short, specific lessons or training periods. Third, set up a student monitor arrangement, both for self-government benefits and to relieve you of holding the line. Finally, for the sake of their encouragement and your balanced outlook, express appreciation, silently and aloud, for notches of improvement in individual and group self-control.

From time to time you'll be faced with a need for refresher training sessions, but take heart. You well know that even in all-adult groups the chairman must rap his gavel and call, "Order, order."

Here are some excellent, proven techniques that are being employed successfully by some widely admired teachers.

Whisper, Whisper

Children need practice in learning to modulate their voices. Start with four training sessions of five to ten minutes each over a period of two weeks. Repeat later in the year if the original lessons seem to have faded.

Directions: Children mingle and whisper to others. If you or a chosen person can hear what they are saying, they must drop out of the game, go to one side, and stand patiently.

Stage Whisper, Real Whisper

Ask them if they have ever heard of a stage whisper, and if they know the difference between a stage whisper and a real whisper. Give examples of each and define the terms. Then every day for two weeks have them practice five minutes of whispering into each other's ears.

Monkey See, Monkey Do

Stand close to noisy children and whisper when you correct them for loud talking. Tell them they are to use the same volume you are using. A teacher who stands a distance away from a student and calls, "Be quiet, Jonathon!" adds considerably to the noise herself while simultaneously setting a bad example.

Author's note: There's another sound reason for this approach. A teacher standing at a distance and calling attracts the attention of the class. If the loud talker is rebellious, he may try to defy her as a face-saving device before his classmates.

A Flea in My Ear?

Make a loud SSSSS sound. Explain that whispering at a distance sounds almost like this. If you, as teacher, can't hear anything more of what children are saying than SSSSS, they're not talking too loudly.

Soft As a Morning Breeze

Students' desks touching one another reduces children's desire to talk. Yet, when they need to converse, they can keep their voices very low. Group the desks in clusters of two or four. Consider students' personalities and choose complements: quiet/noisy, dawdling/diligent, quick/slow learner.

We Monitor Our Own Chatter, Thank You

Arrange children's desks in clusters of eight. During homeroom and free periods one child in each group is monitor. Youngsters like this, and they seem more amenable to being corrected by a cluster mate than by an adult.

Challenge Change? Chair Change

Having two different seat assignments for different types of lessons crystallizes student understanding about the degree of conversation permitted in each. Use one seating chart for lab work or committee sessions and another for lecture and silent reading sessions. If you have two sets of chairs, better still.

Stop . . . Proceed With Caution . . . Go

This noise level control device is effective when the group is operating properly. Use three colored cardboards: red, yellow, green. Red means no talking. Yellow means discreet communication such as asking a neighbor for an eraser or a question about the assignment. Green means general quiet conversation. Mount the cardboard conspicuously on a bulletin board. Yellow is used most of the time.

Take Two

Turning lights off signals everyone may stop working and enjoy a talk break. Allow quiet chatter for about two minutes, never more than three. Switching lights on signals a return to business as usual. Perhaps tell your principal ahead of time about this practice; your room might seem disorderly to him should he stroll past.

Trooping the Colors

Training develops a sense of appropriateness concerning whispering or when to leave seats. The following technique is a great transition step from a teacher-controlled classroom to a self-directed one. After everyone has performed the role of messenger, the class will understand the rules well. When students are sure of what's expected of them, you can eliminate the yellow card entirely and each child can bring his own red card to your desk.

Directions: (1) Create the post of room messenger. This heady station in life is rotated on a scheduled basis, perhaps half a day for each child. (2) Issue two colored cards to each student, say yellow and red. (3) Students hold up yellow cards to signal the messenger for pencil sharpening, a dictionary, map, or new worksheet. Students hold up their red cards when they need the teacher's help. The red cards identify a row and seat number or a student name. The messenger leaves red cards at your desk, and you will help as soon as possible. Meanwhile, students are relieved of time-wasting, holding-up-the-hand and may return to tasks they can accomplish independently.

10, 9, 8, 7 . . .

When introducing this, a teacher often hears, "Gee, that's fair," or "Fair enough," from young voices. It's a great device for reinforcing the whispering level best for your room. The students enjoy this challenge of numbers, and it seems to shift focus away from the teacher herself.

Example: The youngsters are doing desk work, committee planning, or working on projects, and are getting too noisy. Stop all activity. Tell them they're too boisterous, and you are going to have a countdown. Put a ten on the board. Explain that they may converse quietly, but every time you must check the entire class, a small group, an individual, or there's an unidentifiable cat call, you'll simply lower the number. If the number reaches zero, you'll have your own blastoff, and in the process they'll lose a special movie, an extra gym, or whatever. If it's a treat the class really anticipates, they'll do a splendid job of monitoring each other.

Once Accomplished, You Can Do It Again

When pupils are working at a satisfactory noise level, tell them so. Compliment them mildly. *Caution:* Compliment them simply and matter-of-factly, so they'll continue at the same pace. If your praise is profuse, they overreact, and everyone starts chattering. Sometimes, when the class is a trifle noisy, tell them, "Tuesday, you were perfect in holding a level of self-control. Let's go back to it."

As you can see, the common thread in each of these last methods is two-ply: reasonable expectations and explicit standards.

HANDLING RECITATIONS

"Silver tongues and airy phrases" aptly describes much that passes for thoughtful classroom discussion. Beyond content, other aspects of classroom discussion that usually need improvement are an increase of active participants, and the length of time they are genuinely interested in the proceedings. Real assimilation of oral topics is difficult to measure, but an experienced teacher can feel it—that's part of the art of teaching.

Discussion time claims to be communication time, and good communication requires three fundamental elements. The first is *understanding*—understanding the facts being presented and the background and attitudes of those being addressed. *True* communication requires a giver and a receiver. The second essential is appropriate *vocabulary*, understood and accepted by both sides. The third essential is *sincerity*, the honesty of straight thinking and speaking.

The pivotal point in the art of discussion and recitation is individual questions, intuitively worded. Usually, of course, one starts questioning on specific, vivid topics and leads into deeper meanings for patterns. Later, when you want to emphasize a point or summarize, raise your voice a bit. Better still, lower it noticeably. If you're concurrently training students to take notes during discussion, alert them to this voice cue.

One exceptional social studies teacher has developed a three-level question strategy for his heterogeneous classes. Reading assignments are in different source materials. He prepares lists of three question types, A, B, and C. He addresses a question on facts to a slow student: When and where did the Civil War start? He directs a question involving simple reasoning to an average student: Why do you think it started at Fort Sumter? And he asks superior students questions involving underlying patterns: Why were both sides so trigger-happy?

Thus poor readers can close the gap somewhat by learning to listen attentively. Class notes are extremely important, since test questions are taken from discussions rather than readings. Of course this method takes lots of careful teacher preparation. His freedom to question spontaneously is somewhat curtailed, but his discussions stay on target and his classes finish the year knowing something about American history.

As a professional, you sense when to follow the script and when to ad-lib. Even so, unstructured divergents don't always unfold intelligently. They may just get floppy. Even more important—well-prepared questions, not too rigidly adhered to, strengthen your aura of being in control, imperceptibly, but surely.

When a student conducts a discussion, insist he have a central theme and a prepared reservoir of questions and provocative comments. Obviously, he'll feel more self-confident, and responses from the group will be better.

Following is a review of a few guidelines in the methods and art of class discussion:

- Lead from the known into the unknown.
- Use lively illustrations and examples, lots of them.
- Center discussion among the students.
- Discussions are at their best when students spontaneously respond to another student's remarks without reference to the teacher's views. Genuine thinking and learning are occurring.

- Really welcome good answers beyond the ones you had in mind.

Individual teachers regard the following strategies as valuable aids.

Mystery and Suspense . . . Who's Next?

Add a sharpness, which no teacher's choice could bring, by letting the first student choose a classmate to recite, read aloud, or answer a question. The group's responsibility in calling the order encourages them to keep the place in a reading class or while correcting math papers. Unruly classes respond well. Younger children delight in it; having such great power over their own destinies is a treat. A success always, and you can see why: it capitalizes on the children's natural interest in each other.

Directions: Establish these ground rules. (1) A boy must call on a girl, and a girl must call on a boy; children are usually shy about making the crossover between sexes. (2) Ask each child to select two or three classmates ahead of time: this eliminates a hemming and hawing choice decision which impedes or loses good tempo. (3) Every child has a first turn before anyone has a second.

The Bloke Keeps Blurting Out

When a student persists in speaking out of turn during a discussion, don't scold. It ruins the free flowing climate you're trying to build. Don't let him ruin matters, either. Try, "Jim, please learn to raise your hand," and in the same breath, "Sally, would you give us the answer?" Calmly and casually said, the switch points to self-control, the order of the day. Repeat this technique a number of times and the class will respond well.

Help Uncorner Him

Ask a fumbling, embarrassed student, "Would you choose someone to help you with the answer?"

The Yarn Goes This Way and That Way

A discussion group sits in a circle and only the student holding the ball of yarn speaks. When she finishes, and while still holding the string end, she rolls the ball to another who has raised his hand. The second student answers the question or makes an intelligent comment. When he finishes, he rolls it to another with an upraised hand, but he continues to grasp the yarn string at the point he received it to show that he has participated.

A Baker's Dozen

An ideal number of students for incisive, nimble discussion is twelve to fourteen. Several shorter sessions with this size group yield more than does one long discussion with the whole class, that is, other factors being similar. Seat your students in the most primitive communal form, a circle. Around a round table is even better.

She May Not Always Be Right

Rarely tell a student bluntly, "You're wrong." Instead try, "That's close" or "You're in the right ballpark, but . . ." and break off the sentence. For an impossible answer, "That's an observation good for another time."

FORMAL GROUP DISCUSSION

True group discussion is a miniature seminar. It compares with an aimless, top-of-the-teacher's-head, impromptu recitation period about as a mountain lake at sunrise compares with a muddy quarry. Geographically speaking, both are the same—a hole full of water, and sunshine with perhaps a breeze. But the tarn has clear, fresh water and depth with oblique light rays sparkling on the ripples. Likewise a well-prepared discussion has depth, springing ideas, and sparkling insights in constantly shimmering change.

Conversation often is most charming in its spontaneous moments, but then conversation is informal communication with informal or immediate goals. The old-fashioned classroom recitations, question rack and prescribed answers, is at the other end of the pole. Modern class discussion must draw from both to be outstanding. Some established fund of information and ideas, facts and findings, must be blended with fluent ex·pression of the participants' reactions if they're to gain new insights.

Youngsters love immediacy. "Let's discuss it. Right now!" Sometimes impromptu exchange is not bad, but often students merely rehash trite, parroting comments on a subject. If you hold out and insist on thoroughly preparing the soil, they won't recognize a difference, but you will. They'll simply find school more of an adventure.

Discussion Dynamics

An elementary definition of group discussion is problem solving by several people talking and thinking together. It is not a ramble through the woods. Every good discussion has some basic characteristics:

1. It must include everybody present.
2. The fundamental premise is a common problem and the participants must be interested in a solution.
3. Discussants must be informed with facts, general information, and ideas.
4. It is based on objective thinking toward the problem, the participants, and one's own ideas.
5. Thinking should follow the pattern: define, analyze, examine, evaluate.
6. Always, the group leader must remember he's the chairman.
7. Good listening is necessary.

This basic pattern applies at any maturity level. Does this seem beyond your young students? It isn't.

At any age, a group discussion leader, either teacher or student, has special responsibilities. First, he must clarify the objectives . . . What is it we want from this discussion? Although the leader may not announce it, he has mentally worked out essential ideas and components in a logical order. And finally, his concluding remarks should recapitulate for everyone the salient ideas they should have garnered.

Even Genius Needs a Guideline

Distribute Figure 2-1, or an adaptation of it, and let the students examine it. You'll probably want to review the points with them. Then have the scheduled discussion and afterward, have the class fill in the evaluation sheet.

Figure 2-1

Discussion Evaluation Sheet

                                                          Yes   No

1. Was there an attempt to focus the discussion on a problem?
2. Did leader end discussion with a concluding summary or remark?
3. Was an attempt made to draw most of the group into the discussion?
4. Do you feel you did your share in participating in the discussion?
5. Did you get anything out of it?
6. How would you rate the discussion in terms of the standards we have set up? Circle the number which tells your view. (Number 5 represents the highest score.)

              5   4   3   2   1

Further comments or suggestions:

An Old, Old Chestnut

But, it works. Explain to your class before the discussion that you'll speak to unruly characters once or twice. No more. After that, if you must speak to anyone for being disruptive, you'll write his name on a card and reckon with him later. If it's natural and convenient take the blank card to the student's desk so he may watch you write his name. Why it's more effective this way I don't know, but it is. Usually this student will shape up for the balance of the period. If, in the interim, he's made valid contributions, why not let him go without much comment?

TEACHING CONSTRUCTIVE PROTEST

Little children protest. They yowl. Bigger ones bite. Then it's away to school, and there we often neglect showing them suitable ways to protest against abuses, or seeming abuses, of adult power. The ratio of students to teachers and administrators is marked, but from a child's viewpoint the vast privilege the faculty has is even more marked. Sometimes, indeed, the privilege is abused.

All students need safety valves. If children have no release, nor voice, they develop a burdened feeling of resentment which we call oppression. Four typical reactions to oppression are: (1) apathy, (2) hostility, (3) conforming and voicing objections, and (4) confrontation. Since apathy stems from oppression of the spirit, it indicates the most severe reaction and the greatest feeling of hopelessness. In the long run it's often far more dangerous than confrontation because it's more deadly and self-defeating.

In most circumstances conforming to established requirements and voicing objections civilly, but firmly, is the most reasonable and mature reaction. It is a *learned* skill, involving developed traits of self-assurance, patience, and perspicacious persistence. Boys and girls acquire a sense of touch and timing in voicing objections when they hear parents describe this approach in handling incidents in their adult affairs. Obviously, if a child lives in a one-parent home, he's going to overhear fewer adult conversations and reasoning; thus, often kids who need guidance the most are denied it.

Someone must teach children how to object intelligently, since the grooming for tomorrow's reasonable protesters and responsive citizens starts today. And learning to disagree *respectfully* with authority takes children time. Disagreement without letting tempers flare is a fine art, even for adults.

Usually, when interviewing teachers for this book, I talked with them in their classrooms. Thus I had the advantage of being exposed to the climate of each room. Considering this ethos I submit the following as being some of the best ideas I heard on the topic of constructive protest training.

Teacher, You Goofed!

Make mistakes with obvious facts. Misread the clock. Call students' names incorrectly. Turn off lights at an inappropriate time. Give a story a faulty ending. Automatically, the kids will correct you. Choose the most pointed or tactful correction and discuss it with the group.

In the Caribbean There Are Voodoo Dolls

Carefully select a target topic. It must be debatable, of peak interest, and not too emotionally charged: bedtimes—weekend curfew—fashions and makeup—ball teams. Structure a practice session using role-playing. For additional practice, have a child take his parents' viewpoint and support it, especially if the youngster disagrees with it.

In My Considered Opinion . . .

Ask students to write you a letter when they feel you've been unfair. It may take several invitations before they feel free to commit themselves. Make it crystal clear that the writer will not jeopardize his relationship with you by expressing his feelings honestly. Signed letters are preferred, but unsigned ones are respected and valued.

You're Nice, But Ugh, That Other Teacher

Every teacher has heard students grousing about school, classmates, room rules, or another teacher. Naturally, within her own bailiwick there's no problem; she's free to resolve matters as she desires. When it concerns other teachers or administrators, professional etiquette requires treading a narrow path. Ethically, she must not undermine them. Humanely, she must remain the child's friend. Silently, she may agree with the student, but this won't alleviate his plight.

Try being a friend of the court. Have a short, sympathetic talk with the complaining child. Establish your feelings in warm, general terms, but explain that he must iron out his problem with the irksome teacher herself. Suggest he make an appointment with her. You could, to bolster the child's courage, walk with him to the teacher's room but have him go in by himself.

Gathering the Gripes

Keep a slotted gripe box—decorated if you like. Any child who feels matters are amiss writes his comments and drops them in the box. Never, never divulge the writer's identity if the slip is signed. Unsigned slips are acceptable. Many teachers suggested this strategy.

If I Were King

Each child writes a letter describing the classroom he likes—general atmosphere, kind and amount of freedoms, type of teacher. Invite new ideas and suggestions. Assure and reassure students that you will keep the authorship confidential. Then the group can think and talk about which ideas will work, and why, in a class discussion. It's amazing how many students recognize the importance of being courteous and soft spoken—for others, anyway.

Mr. Gallup or Mr. Harris

Five or six times a year have the class write letters to you on their current progress. Remind them—new ideas for almost any changes are welcome. Reaffirm—everything in each letter is private, so no one needs to plead the Fifth Amendment.

CONSTRUCTIVE PROTEST
AND REPORT CARDS

Intertwined with constructive protest is an understanding that responsible reasoning is needed before one arrives at opinions. Since report cards are a highlight in each student's life, they provide an excellent vehicle for teaching him how to arrive at reasoned opinions, or how others arrive at their conclusions.

Several more dividends come from including the student's viewpoint on grades. Foremost, it reminds teacher and pupil that grades are a symbol of learning achievement along a prescribed line and their source is in the achievement, not in any person. Of course, you know that no student should regard grades as a bleak token of predestination, but most children need clarification on this point. A graphic consultation lesson can do wonders: a teacher consulting with a child teaches him in vivid terms that the establishment does act from reason and that speaking up can pay off.

I Think, She Thinks, We Think

Three days before official report cards are issued, have children make informal cards. List important subjects on the board. Ask the children to copy each one, give themselves a grade for each subject, and give a reason or reasons why they feel they've earned the grade. They must tell why they arrived at their evaluation; if they don't, the estimates are nullified. These papers are a great guideline in completing printed cards.

The Perfect Triangle

Inform children that any objections they have to report card grades are open for a three-way conference: teacher–parent–student. On the appointed day talk to parents privately for about ten minutes and then invite young Mr. Protester to join you. If it's a borderline decision, why not yield? The student is learning to voice objections through authorized channels; this experience could be crucially important in strengthening his courage to speak up and out.

COMMITTEE WORK

"Three, helping one another, bear the burden of six"—so goes an ancient Persian proverb. And three students, working as a cohesive committee, probably double the learning accomplishment over working individually. It's more fun and it can be an adventure!

Tossing a copious quantity of student ideas into a hopper is almost a must in preparing for good committees. It's self-evident that ideas generate ideas and activate other ideas. When the atmosphere is teeming with ideas, enthusiasm and intelligent learning activity come bouncing along a few steps behind.

When the topic is chosen, the hour has arrived to set framework rules for reaching specific goals. When committees are thriving working units, they are nearly always a trifle noisy. If your committees are too circumspect—beware. Usually four of five units will develop about as they should. And the fifth? Well . . . If a negative scene develops, here is a suggestion from an experienced teacher. It might fit your needs.

The Fifth Column

The class is doing great except for one committee which is a disorganized, disorderly mess. Steps to take: (1) Review goals and project rules with them. Make sure that the members clearly understand what is expected of them. Leave that committee and circulate in the room. (2) If garbled noise and foolish activity persist, warn the unruly youngsters. Then leave again. (3) If you must return a third time, tell the group to sit quietly with their hands folded. After a few minutes let them relax. Later when you have small groups and one is troublesome, you'll need only to take the first step and then if trouble continues, ask children, "Do you want to sit in silence?" Generally, you'll find even this group will monitor itself well.

Proof—Step One

Occasionally, during committee work or a play rehearsal, a child is isolated for impeding progress. Shortly, he pleads to reenter the group. Often it's questionable whether he's ready, yet it's hard to say no. You might tell him, "It requires less self-control to work alone than in a bunch. If you can manage two rows of your unfinished math assignment quickly, you'll have earned your right to again attempt group work because you have proved your sincerity and self-control."

Turkey Day Is Coming

Talents and work habits are, of course, of primary importance in assigning committees or teams, but catering to student preferences is considerate and usually adds to the effectiveness of small groups. Figure 2-2 can easily be an added influence in teacher selections.

Where There's Bait, There's a Hook

A cage of small live animals will hook children's interest every time. This device is an excellent way to ease into partner or committee work and to teach necessary rules as a byproduct. Directions: Borrow a cage of white mice, lizards, gerbils, or other critters for a few days. On arrival morning announce to the students, "These mice will be here for only a week. (A definite time limitation adds piquancy.) You are invited to watch them before school, but on the bell tone—back to your seats." Then permit a few students to stay.

Figure 2-2

ROOM 103

We are getting ready to form work groups to put on a Thanksgiving pageant. Will you please list five children in the class with whom you would like to work:

1. _____

2. _____

3. _____

4. _____

5. _____

However, explain they can't just watch while their classmates are working diligently. So ask the watchers to list ten facts they observe about the animals; they may quietly discuss the mice. Rapt interest carries the day. The naughtiest elf will do nothing to jeopardize his ringside seat.

Use Your Head, Save Your Feet

A good plan is half the battle. Tell the students that the staff of Room 103 will sit in the general's tent and plan strategy. Elicit committee project ideas from the entire class. (Your staff and army are exactly the same size. I can guarantee the students won't notice this dual function of your troops.) Analyze the following points and put the list on the chalkboard:

1. Goal of this project   1. _____
2. Research—approach   2. _____
         —method   _____
         —equipment   _____

3. Mechanics of sharing sup-   3. _____
   plies and equipment   _____
4. Chairman's role—di-   4. ___discuss orally___
   rector of traffic, not
   the driver
5. Compose a schedule of leader rotation if project is a long one.

When the above basics have been established, divide the class into committees. As a general rule avoid launching committee projects during the first weeks of school. Welding the students into a cohesive single group is more important.

Potpourri of Talents

Balanced committee units are stimulating and make the project workable in its entirety. Consider these facets when you make selections: Place in each unit (1) a clever child and (2) a slow one, (3) a long attention span child and (4) a short attention span student, (5) a diligent worker and (6) a goof off. It helps if children are naturally compatible; if they're not, switch them quickly and quietly.

Form Your Own Form to Perform and Inform

With a little advance preparation, you *can have* method without madness, the madness of riveting so much attention to detail that one loses the vision of things to come. A solid work schedule for committees or lab sessions helps students retain a sense of direction, hone their ambitions, and accurately evaluate their accomplishments. The following form was developed by an experienced home economics teacher. With adaptation, it readily lends itself to other subjects. Obviously, she distributes this prior to the lesson and usually students complete the forms together under her supervision.

I. Items or products from the counter.

II. Supplies I will use from the kitchen.

III. Utensils or tools I will use and return to counter.

IV. Needed utensils or tools already in kitchen.

V. List of jobs we must do to accomplish our task:
(Teacher announces this to class, "These may be listed and numbered later in the order that you feel would be best to follow. Use the back of the sheet so you can have a detailed listing and so you will understand exactly.")

VI. Time plan:

Class begins _____   Class ends _____
Cleanup starts _____   Product complete by _____
Judging done _____   _____

VII. The storage arrangement which I have made for this lesson is:

VIII. Evaluation of this laboratory:
A. The best part of this lab is:
B. We still can improve in these things:

Now for a few departing words of counsel from several experienced teachers about initiating special committee projects.

Plan your skeleton program. To sell your package, use intriguing thirty-second and sixty-second commercials for a week or ten days ahead. Feed these tidbits to the students innocuously and systematically. Then, if you don't have enthusiastic volunteers on launching day, delay it. If the class undertakes it halfheartedly, you'll probably have more than one committee not functioning well. Later on, try introducing it again; there can easily be a 180-degree change in attitude within the class.

CONCLUSION

Lively, targeted communication in moderated tones adds zip, zest, zeal, to learning. Children are not raucous; they simply need *training* in learning to vary their indoor voices and their outdoor voices, gym voices and library voices. The first need is to establish reasonable, predictable whispering standards and then to teach systematically through practice sessions rather than to correct or nag them out of erring ways.

Then it's on to better classroom recitations and discussions. Oral busy work is not as traceable as written busy work, but it's hardly an improvement. Improving one's skill in the art of group discussion is an open-ended task, but it can be a satisfying adjunct to any teacher's daily duties—at any age, anywhere. And think of the added hours of genuine student learning. Formal group discussion provides the discipline of having a well-defined goal. It is a special method in itself.

Vitally important, but often downplayed in this era of educational reform, is the opportunity to actively and constructively teach students how to intelligently protest when their ire is aroused or their sense of underlying justice is offended. Again, this should be tackled small step by small step to insure protecting a balanced approach and outlook.

Finally, the chapter concludes with some brief suggestions and plans for committee and lab work. If you try any of these strategies, I hope they will give your work fresh impulsion.

Three

SOLVING PROBLEMS WITH ORAL AND WRITTEN COMMUNICATION

Children continue to be interested in each other, with or without adult approval. Sometimes they talk at awkward, wrong times. Moreover, they can express unwelcome ideas in even more unwelcome, vivid language.

This chapter deals with a few communications problems and offers some workable techniques for alleviating them. A noisy room interrupts the smooth transition from one subject to another; surely, the teacher must have the group's attention. Since talking out of turn, individual and collective, is a major factor in about 80 percent of classroom disruptions, a new importance is thrust on correcting this failing. The other problems of swearing, lying, tattling, name calling, rudeness, and yes, even notewriting, are quite minor in relation to their time cost. Obviously, these related weaknesses do subtract from a good climate.

Not the university pundits, nor the curriculum coordinators, nor the principals, nor the prophets sitting under banyan trees, but outstanding, adept teachers themselves, told me repeatedly this major rule: Trouble of every type can be prevented by starting each school day with good momentum. They advised being systematic, getting materials ready the afternoon before, if necessary. Twenty minutes' prior organization brings huge returns, more like a stock split than stock dividends.

Listen afresh for the pattern and content of children's speech. Brevity is the hallmark—except when they decide to tell you a longwinded story—one which you don't particularly want to hear—that will be all tedious details and no plot—with plenty of repetition—and an extra flashback or two or three that aren't needed—and then the storyteller takes a deep breath and . . . Finally, you say, "I just remembered, I have an important errand."

A child may have similar feelings about a longwinded teacher, but students can't, even politely, cut off educators. So you see that if a teacher is prone to "much speaking," it presents a genuine communication problem for students. Many of us find it so difficult to keep stories, friendly talks, directions, and reprimands degassed.

Is there a perfect reprimand, a perfect correction? I believe there is and one for every predicament. How does one find it?

Obviously, the first step is to listen. Hear out the child's reason for talking or acting as she did. Then offer your response or correction in a friendly voice. The perfect chiding refines and sharpens the erring one's perception of a mistake and simultaneously strengthens his understanding of a right or better way. Old-fashioned squelches are out—*a good rebuke makes its point without offending.* A perfect verbal correction can be brief. Indeed, like wit, brevity adds to its effectiveness.

Words, however, may need reinforcing by sanctions. Brief withholding and then restoration of a privilege, repeated if necessary, is a time-honored approach.

NOISY ROOM: CORRECTION BY
COMMENT, SIGNAL, AND ACTION

Lilting speech and a knack for introducing fresh flourishes always enhance a teaching personality; *precise use* of current slang, witty quips, and topical comments adds piquancy. New phrases surprise and snag attention; simultaneously, these remarks reduce any for-the-3,000th-time-be-quiet-and-listen tone that can creep into the voice. Happily, talented, sparkling expression is not limited according to our genes. Almost everyone can develop the skill.

More humor, hmmm? And whimsy? And what, do tell, is a good source for all this charm? Try writing a different witty quotation from some famous man on the board daily. Or, perhaps pick up a small public speaker's quip book and cull it. These quotes, building toward imagination and lighthearted fun, can alleviate the notion many children have that goodness and hard-working people are both quite naturally dull. Quotes that openly moralize are out: students get plenty of character building remarks from other times and sources.

Some admired teachers suggested the following techniques for the ever-present task of attracting the group's attention.

Shhh, Your Favorite Teacher Wants to Speak

Start softly, "I've got a secret." A few kids will listen. Try again, "I've got a secret." A few more will respond. The third time you will have the class. Then tell them about your dog's best trick, a well-loved gym teacher's favorite dinner, your tame rhino, whatever.

Shhh, I Hear the Good Fairy

A good fairy whispered in your ear and you want to share it. Repeat. Inform children she told you her plan: she will travel around the room and tap each good boy and girl. When they've been tapped, pupils are to signal you by sitting up alertly. You could add, "Once upon a time the fairy not only tapped everyone, but she gave one child golden shoes." Watch them check their own feet, no one else's. Primary level.

Is There Anything Simpler?

One quietly outstanding teacher suggested her most effective device. Put your finger to your lips and smile. That's it. That's all she does.

Perk Your Ears, Little Flock

Whisper directions. You'll have to repeat two or three times, but keep on whispering . . . even to the "OK, go ahead with your work."

Shhh, One of Us Is Out of Step

Ask the class, "Am I crabby today, or are you unusually noisy and slow to listen?" Students like this approach and respond well.

Some strategies in Chapter 8 under "Making the Transition Between Subjects" are also helpful.

In attracting a class's attention spoken comments seem most effective when there's a small twist in wording and a variety of segues. However, a symbolic action or an audible nonverbal signal gains strength when it's a recognized token.

One suggestion: Try several different types of both and let your class vote on their favorite. (It's one more step in building an "our room" climate.)

Churchill Used a V

Teach a hand signal that means "your quiet attention, please." Then set the guideline that when you, the room president, or a discussion chairperson raises his hand with the signal, everyone is to be quiet. Again, when students contribute imaginative ideas for creating such a signal, it becomes theirs as well as yours.

According to My Watch

Hold up your wrist and obviously study your watch. At the same time announce, "It's now 10:32. How long will it take to get everyone's attention?" Keep on looking at your watch. One child will nudge another. After initial training the class responds quickly. Later, you'll need only to raise your wrist.

Tinkle, Tinkle, Little Bell

As archaic as it may first seem, a tiny bell is effective when the room is noisy. Warning: Don't use the bell as both a subject transition signal and a noise reminder.

WHEN ENOUGH IS ENOUGH IN A NOISY ROOM!

Quite abruptly the room is becoming a circus without a ringmaster. The contagious ripple of yapping, squirming, fiddling, and mild horseplay rather than studying often suddenly zaps a normal classroom. Regardless of what some learned educators may proclaim, the most glowing lesson this side of Chinese scholars' heaven would not still the turbulence. Here are a few suggestions for early restoration of order.

Fluster Is a Mild Word for the Condition

Your room is in turmoil and requests for order are totally ignored. Ask several tumultuous students each to write a letter. This may be addressed to an esteemed homeroom teacher or— in serious cases—to a principal or vice-principal whose approval they need. Each student explains his reasons *why* it's not reasonable to expect him to obey directions or to return to on-task goals. As these few start writing, the entire atmosphere of the room reverse-ripples into tranquility—usually. Deliver the letters, or not, according to student and class demeanor during the time until the next bell signal.

Room in Purgatory

Keep three or four seats vacant near your desk. Ask the persistent mischief-maker to bring his books and sit near the throne. Obviously, he's then easy to watch and close enough for you to extend encouraging remarks. If he redeems himself, he may return to his regular seat the following day. Generally, allow him no more than three days to repent and purge himself —then send him to your school's limbo. Do notice, teacher, that by inference, heaven is defined as an assigned seat in your class.

It Can Be Done Without Mirrors

Occasionally, a teacher cannot turn her back and write on the board without cat calls or a minor mêlée erupting. Several options are open. Often she can have students write various points. But any teacher is wise to develop the skill of writing on the board while standing obliquely. Since often her writing emphasizes a discussion point, the teacher can also engage the attention of known imps (and others) by asking them to spell particular words. Let's say the topic is the Cheyenne Indians, she could comment, while writing, "Charley, as we know the Cheyennes lived in present day Wyoming. Can you tell the class how to spell Wyoming?" If this type of oral inclusion is repeated, the class realizes the teacher's attention has not been diverted from them.

One teacher tackled the problem and simultaneously astonished her students: she learned to write on the board while facing the class. Really, it didn't take that much practice and surely her students will always remember her unique skill.

More Than One Way to Skin a Cat

Surprise can be jolting. Sometime when the group gets too noisy, try this. Instead of asking everyone to sit down and be quiet, abruptly request, "Everybody in the room, stand up and watch me."

Life Beyond the Pale

Consider this strategy if you have four normal classes and one that's . . . well, use your own adjective. Plan treat periods for the four: outside speakers, ethnic food sampling, show music listening, what have you. Give the fifth group a long, dull writing assignment on those days. If you could locate a documentary film on "The Various Uses and Functions of a Phillips Screwdriver," better still. Word will spread and soon the fifth class will come to you grousing. Explain your reason for partition and inform them that when they change, you will include them on gala days.

Ball One, Ball Two, Ball Three

During a silent period students start talking. First offense: have them tell the class what they were talking about. Second offense: have each write a 100-word page explaining not only the conversation, but why. Third offense: have each write the same type of page, and you read it to the class.

Don't Fight 'Em, Join 'Em

Occasionally an entire group will decide to heckle a teacher on a given signal—say, coughing at 2:05 sharp. End the contest by coughing along with them.

Disaster Has Struck

Perhaps conditions have gone from wretched to total chaos and you have lost all control of the room. Tell your class to stand and to stand still. Choose a girl to be minute-counter by watching the clock. Inform the group it will stay after school one minute for every minute it takes them to become calm. If bus schedules preclude keeping them after school, check with your principal about infringing on their lunch hour.

Though this arrangement is not fair, it may be the fairest thing you can do when circumstances make individual culprits unidentifiable.

Taxes Are High These Days

Taxpayers are required by law to pay assessments for public schools and they want their money's worth; they want teachers to teach. Explain to the class that the school board hired you for a specific job. During school hours the students' deportment must allow you to teach without unreasonable distraction. If their conduct interferes with your duty, then you will keep them after school to fulfill your obligation to the bill payers. If you do resort to this step, it will be done at your convenience.

How long will these sessions be? Here's a suggested pattern. The room is noisy at 8:56. Write that time on the board. Stand quietly until you have order. If it takes until 8:58, put a number two on the board upper corner. Repeat during the day whenever necessary. If time totals fifteen minutes, keep them after school.

In this event, no athletic or religious training obligation excuses an individual. Remind students you will be most happy to talk to displeased parents about your decision. Usually, one after-school session handles the problem for the entire year. Following that, all you'll need to do is write the time on the board, and the room will calm down.

NOISY INDIVIDUAL: CORRECTION BY COMMENT, SIGNAL, AND ACTION

When correcting a noisy child, it's always wise to remember his basic aim is a place in the group. Emphasize, with genuine conviction, the reality of his *special* place. Of course, you would not threaten, belittle, or in any way jeopardize that place.

Occasionally, the kindest action you can take is to isolate the noisy one swiftly, but remind him his vacant niche is awaiting him. Since you're not trying to humiliate him and you're trying to teach him more mature self-control, he should have the dignity of a chair or stool, certainly something more than his haunches, to sit on.

Frequently, children's out-of-turn talking can be lessened or eliminated by simpler steps—some are almost incredibly simple actions. First, the teacher may try just looking at him and shaking her head no. Or, without using facial expression, she may walk over to the child and stand nearby while continuing to address the group. If this doesn't stop his whispering, she may want to touch his shoulder. (It is especially effective for repeat offenders if the teacher walks down an inside aisle, where teachers don't often walk.)

Another simple approach is to interject a quiet reminder. For instance, she might be talking about Argentina and saying, "The Falkland Islands are inhabited by 85,000 Englishmen, none of whom were born there . . . No, Sarah, cut it out . . . and several hundred thousand sheep, all of whom were born there." Here the important feature is to use the same voice tone for the whole sentence, no inflection at all for the interjection.

Many good teachers claim they always offer a chatterbox a choice of alternatives. Example: "Do you want to quit talking or shall I give you an assignment during your free period?" Or, "Which do you prefer, to change your seat or to stay after school?"

Perhaps this is the moment to mention the reactions of students whom I interviewed on the subject of discipline. *Without exception* they approved of the teacher who "did something," who didn't just understandingly counsel them— or lecture. Since this doesn't mesh with the recommendations of many school psychologists, the only solution I can see is to compromise and do both. Have a chat with the child and then assign a simple penalty, so that you have "done something" in his viewpoint.

Here are some suggested comments which splendid teachers considered appropriate when students are talking at inconvenient times.

We're Waiting

Often it's very effective to say, "We're waiting," in a soft, friendly tone.

A Marked Man

Using your index finger only, make a large X on a chattering boy's back. Tell him, "Now you're a marked man." It works, he'll stop talking.

Learned Inquiry by Colleagues

Say with mock seriousness, "I know you two are discussing esoteric customs of ancient wise men, but unless you assume a more scholarly posture, I must ask you to stop." Usually, kids will smile and return to their tasks. Or, they'll try stroking their chins and shaking their heads gravely. This is a cue to nod approval, adding, "That's impressive, but not impressive enough . . . back to your fractions, Charley."

The Burden of Being Macho

Literally for a few boys only, but a teacher with a blarney touch can expand the applicability. Tell lads, "You probably don't realize how far your heavy, masculine voices carry." They'll know they're being flattered, but they'll love it and cooperate.

Capricious Clown Capers

Take him aside and quietly tell him, "If you clown, I'll scold. If you think your mugging and other antics are so delightful that the class won't notice my scolding, go ahead and entertain them." (This approach was offered by a teacher who has been nationally honored for his ability to inspire young people.)

. . . And the Bait Was?

Whispering students have their heads together. Ask them, "Have I ever told you about the big fish I caught?" Put your hands between their heads and pushing their heads apart, say, "It was this long, no longer." Greatly appeals to most roughneck boys.

Let's Confer in the Hall

That's it . . . no more! When an obstreperous student has interfered too seriously and you elect to have a private discussion, proceed firmly but with caution. If you two are at a distance, the whole class is an audience. Thus, going to his seat in your normal walking cadence (and down an inner aisle if it makes sense) and telling him quietly that you two will step out in the hall is a first point. Seriously consider taking his wrist and leading him out. Particularly with younger students defiance is a thin shell and during the chastisement they erupt into crying. Wiping his face with a damp paper towel and letting him take a drink of water has an ameliorating touch. Then, when you return to the classroom, have him precede you. The reason? More than one child, red-eyed and humiliated, has made faces at the teacher behind her back as a face-saving device in front of his classmates.

A Silent Signal

When Sandra is reciting and Patti interrupts, one teacher looks at Patti, shakes her head, and simultaneously raises her own hand as Patti should have done. If Patti's interruption has caused a break in Sandra's words, the teacher then says, "Sorry, Sandra, please continue." If Sandra's speaking was not broken, the teacher says nothing.

In the Footsteps of Emmett Kelly?

Since a student clown's aim is to get the group's attention, ignore the antics while they are happening, if possible. Then, when the class is passing, stop the clown for a private chat. You might suggest ways he could get positive attention, real esteem, to replace his half-baked, misdirected efforts. For example, if the child has any flair for drawing, have him draw three clown faces, each with entirely different makeup—and then post them.

Meet Another Loud Mouth

To help both children, assign a very noisy student to work with an equally boisterous child about three years his grade junior. The older child is absolutely amazed that anyone so small can be so noisy.

Congress Has a Gag Rule

But this is a classroom and that Jackie's mouth is never, never closed. A masking tape roll is in your desk drawer, but resist the first temptation. Safer action: cut two pieces of tape. Write anything from "prithee fair maiden/no prittle prattle," to "cut the yak/Jack." Wrap her thumbs or apply a piece to each hand. Students are surprised, amused, pleased, and usually cooperate very willingly. Do be alert to change your wording each time you use this device.

Your ID Card, Please

Warn unruly students. Then ask for ID cards. Explain you will keep them until noon. If they settle down, you'll return the cards. If they don't, you'll drop the cards off in the office (or their homeroom). After all, most of us have been stopped for a minor traffic infraction and then let off with a warning.

Yon Is Main Office!

A normally well-behaved student has been slipping. Private chats and calls to his home have not revealed the cause(s). Have him stay in at recess; however, since you must attend to an office errand, ask him to meet you at a bench near the office. Mention no names. Make no threats. If asked, tell him the bench would be a comfortable, quiet spot to discuss your differences. The message gets through immediately and most students will want to avert the apparent next step.

THE CURSE ON 200 SENTENCES

For decades upon decades educators have been sniffing with disdain at the idea of assigning students the task of writing 100, 200, or 500 sentences. Yet many otherwise excellent teachers and administrators continue to issue these sanctions. Perhaps the major reason for their disregard of the curse on 200 sentences is that no one has demonstrated a better way which does not involve noticeably more time; often their schedules are incredibly tight with high priority items the day a youngster decides to act the scamp. Intuitively, perhaps, teachers recognize that the argument against the sentence-writing penalty is not total. In a few aspects there exists a case for sentence writing.

I respectfully submit that sentence writing in moderation does not have the pernicious influence of other less traceable sanctions often used in correcting children. To name one, nagging. To name another, using a shrill or intimidating voice.

Through the centuries English advocates and magistrates, engaged in legal trials among a most law-abiding people, have emphasized the urgency in reaching for an underlying sense of fairness. Equally important, according to their thinking, is the swiftness and sureness of correction, not the severity. And it is commonly conceded that the English highly cherish individuality in all walks of life.

As you noted, the key points above are: sense of fairness, swiftness and sureness of penalty, and a respect for individuality. Now let's tie these in with the sentence-writing summons. In assigning a moderate sentences penalty, it's relatively easy for an extremely busy teacher or administrator to be fair, and, equally important, to seem fair in the student's eyes. Also, she can attend to a problem situation immediately when it should be attended to, for she knows this mode will not detract time from other high priority duties.

The next point: the assignment is definite, and it requires energy and action on the child's part. It is an action that expunges. He has now paid for breaking the rules and *he* knows it. He does not owe a debt of gratitude to an "understanding" teacher whom he may or may not like, and who may or may not like him.

The case against the sentence-writing task is all too apparent, for it incurs the dullness of rote and foolish repetition. In some good climate schools a teacher need never resort to multiple sentences. She has too many factors going for her: a good learning ethos, relatively small classes, alert and informed parents, and students coming from homes where a developed sense of tactful reasoning and community spirit exists.

Alas, in other schools teachers frequently work with large classes of children from difficult—often belligerent—homes. Inevitably, and rightly, teachers make many allowances in learning and deportment, in tardiness and truancy. Many of these students live in an out-of-school-world where action and force show strength. Reasoning? Well, that's often considered bordering on wimpy.

It's not a "once upon a time" scene so let's quit inferring teacher inadequacy or giving them a guilt trip when their correction sanctions do not align with the hothouse perfection portrayed in some classroom management courses.

Instead, let's forthrightly recognize that teachers in some consolidated districts, mill towns, and inner cities often find it humanly impossible to give the personalized attention, which, as professionals, they know is the students' due. In selecting deterrents, these hardship-post educators must settle for the possible rather than the ideal, strive for fairness and moderation. These are honorable goals. Writing sentences can be a moderate and fair—although a miserably dull—reminder that society values order above most other virtues. And rightly, for in chaos both fairness and moderation also disappear.

"I Won't"—200 Times

Clearly tell your Merry Andrew that you consider 200 versions of "I will not . . ." a bore and time-waster. But his conduct has brought the issue to a head. He has forced you to choose and you have chosen the lesser of two evils. Writing sentences, he wastes only his own time. Talking or horsing around, he wastes others' time and the taxpayers' money, and has been negating the fundamental purpose of school.

TATTLING

Tattling is often done to hurt: the child who tells of another's indiscretion wants to gloat while the second student suffers lowered esteem or punishment or both. Prevalent in second grade, tattling tends to disappear in the middle years and then reappear in the upper grades. A spiel to your class about a *sincere* desire to help the teacher and other students can do much to clarify the atmosphere.

Several talented teachers offered the following steps to curb this annoying, petty nuisance.

Inane Information—Lots of It!

List ten or twelve tattles you have received. Take a few minutes and read them all aloud. Just hearing the tattles in aggregate usually effects a permanent cure for the entire class. Another classmate's tattle touches on no emotional sensitive spot in the listener, so he sees tattles as the foolishness they are.

Tattle Tail

Obtain or make a yarn tail. String on it little tags labeled Tattle Tail. Hang this tail on a bulletin board. If a child makes a nuisance report, direct his attention to the display.

No Ear Trumpets Available

As the tattler starts his report, put your fingers to your ears, smile, and shake your head.

Classify and Reclassify Misdemeanors

Explain to your young, confiding friend there are worse misdeeds in this world than her classmate's actions. Then with a gentle voice tell her one of them is being a tattler.

SWEARING

Swearing is a poverty of expression, a paucity of thought. Society draws numerous lines, and makes many erasures in the boundaries of vocabulary which is considered acceptable, respectable, in good taste. Many adults are no longer sure of what's in and what's out. How can a child be? Foremost, he needs a rule of thumb, a guidance gauge applicable to all occasions.

The only real, permanent gauge is well-developed sound judgment of his own. You might tell students that one mark of a sharp person is his ability to select the right words for the setting. Different circumstances mean different ways of talking. Try quoting a bit of Shakespeare to illustrate how ridiculous inappropriate phrases can sound for a given scene in today's world. Examples:

"I prithee, take thy fingers from my throat." (*Hamlet*)

"Draw forth thy weapons, we are beset with thieves." (*Taming of the Shrew*)

"Brave followers, yonder stands the thorny wood." (*King Henry VI*)

Would your favorite television detective character or a newscaster use these terms? Likewise, swearing can sound just as ludicrous in the classroom or on school grounds.

Perhaps you'll want to add that an important reason for attending school is to learn new vocabulary. Most terms he can use anywhere, a few words he'll need only for school or work. Safe ground: a metropolitan daily newspaper is a fine guide to acceptable usage. It includes slang but excludes the extreme. When in doubt, a child can ask himself, "Would I see these words in my hometown paper?"

Children, regardless of cultural background, have strong feelings of loyalty to family, friends, neighbors. If a community permits greater leniency in language standards than your own, try to elude the trap of self-righteousness, even in your thinking. Your advice will be more readily accepted if you haven't set up an unspoken critical division between the students' school and home worlds.

There is "home" talk, "street" talk, and "school" talk. In training kids to differentiate vocabulary intelligently in various circumstances, we'll be helping them accept Shakespeare and modern writers, playwrights, and novelists with greater aplomb.

Current literature notwithstanding, one large group of highly respected teachers adopted the following basic rule for their school. They would individually accept and expect the same language standards in their classrooms that they would accept and expect in their private homes. Of course there would be differences from teacher to teacher but it would be up to the child to adjust. This decision was taken after they collectively considered the aspects of intent to insult, the students' background, current plays and literature, and their own moral convictions.

One final bit of advice. All of us learn language by parroting others, and swearing is as contagious as slang. If students are not pressured to stop swearing, other children who formerly didn't swear will start.

Here are several contributions by teachers who are savvy about today's world.

A Facade of Bravado

Have the child write a definition of each word used. More often than not you'll learn he doesn't know the real meaning. The written page makes an excellent basis for initiating a talk with him.

Cussin' and Fussin'

Talk with the offending student about the reasons people swear: frustration, indignation, anger, showing off, or appearance of being tough. All negatives. Why is he feeling so negative? Assign the swearer a task of looking up ten replacement words in a thesaurus. Make a list and keep it at his desk.

Dragon Teeth on Paper

Ask a swearing child to compose a paragraph on why and when he finds cursing necessary. The essay makes an excellent basis for initiating a talk with him.

Cuss Box

If a student feels an urge to swear, he's to write the word and slip it into a cuss box. Children offered this idea.

Could Be Vapid, Could Be Valid

Suggest to your tempted friends that instead of swearing, they are to invent one, two, or three personal expletives and use these to vent exasperation.

HONESTY VS. LYING

Children rarely lie in the precise adult sense of the word. We all enjoy the sparkle of their imagination and the lucidity, candor, of their preferences. When questioned, the lads and lassies in our classrooms merely tell the story as they see it. Therein lies the problem.

An untoward event occurs and you require a fleshing out of information in order to act intelligently. Ask three eyewitnesses to tell their versions. As you question students, try to phrase your inquiries in a fashion that avoids cornering an individual or backing him against a wall. Fit the information together, if you can. Then act.

In Calhoun County, We Took a Liar and . . .

You expect conflicting reports on an incident. During the preliminary interviewing, try to keep the students apart: (1) Talk to each child separately. (2) Have them meet as a group. (3) Ask the children you trust most to speak first and repeat their stories. (4) Finally, ask the person whose word you doubt, "What is your comment?" If there's a discrepancy between his and the other two accounts, dismiss the others and talk to him privately.

. . . And a Sepulchral Voice Said

Several students offer dumb excuses, lies, for incomplete homework, being late, what have you. Without using the words lie or liar tell them that with their imaginations you expected better. In fact, the penalty will be to write a 300-word story beginning with, "There I was in the cafeteria and on the menu wall I saw a vision . . ." Or, "I was on the hall stairs when I heard chains rattling . . ." You'll have made your point, they'll have fun writing the stories, and yet, the sanction is real extra work.

Do You Think I Believe You?

You don't. Plainly tell liars, "You haven't told me the truth. We'll talk about this after school." Unemotional candor on your part, honest respect for their feelings and need for privacy, often bring far better results.

Call the Shots As You See Them

If you are *absolutely* sure a student is lying—and this is a patterned behavior—say in front of the entire class, "You are lying to me, and though I now respect you, if you continue to lie, I will lose most of my respect for you.

NAME-CALLING

Most often rampant name-calling is dissolved quickly by counseling the target child. Naturally you'll be sympathetic with his plight; if you can cite a similar episode where the scapegoat won in the long run, tell him. Meanwhile, advise him not to react, or at least try not to show his reactions. This way he'll take the punch out of the heckling.

Ask the suffering child to inform his tormentors, "You are making me angry enough to hit you," but emphasize he is not to whap the bullies. Instead, ask him to see you. Since they're pitting their combined strength against him, it is manly for him to gather more reinforcement for his side. When you have the opportunity to speak privately with the tormentors, express glowing comments and compliments about the scapegoat.

Here is another way of handling scapegoating. Suddenly, one day, you become aware that the class is making a scapegoat of one student. A subtle counterattack can bring the swiftest solution. Say not a word to the ringleaders; rather make an opening in class to quote a coach's or the assistant principal's praise of the scapegoat. Repeat the compliments as often as necessary, but make sure the group realizes that some well-liked authority respects the target child. The bullying and blaming dissolve, usually.

Remember the Day They Enrolled?

Guide your children in planning for the arrival of two infamous characters, two fictitious newcomers, to your class. Endow them with vivid personalities and christen them with descriptive names. Set an enrollment date. That day you can introduce large papier-mâché models and assign them seats. These pawns provide opportunities for projective techniques; they make good scapegoats and serve as a safety valve. As for their mythical behavior problems—you and the students can have a field day discussing and correcting them.

NOTEWRITING

Notewriting brings its greatest detrimental influence to the writer himself, for it diverts thinking from a task at hand and concerns itself with trivia, even from the child's viewpoint. Wiser teachers adroitly discourage notewriting rather than punish it.

English in Practical Application

Intercept a note. Grade it for punctuation, spelling, capitalization. Use the grade as the writer's language arts mark for the day. An additional written comment about direct objects, verb agreement, subjunctive, can be marvelously tongue-in-cheek.

The Third Person

Intercept a note. Orally ask the questions in it. For instance, Susie has written to Jennie, "Will you meet me after school?"

Ask Jennie, "Will you meet Susie after school?" If she says "yes," then tell Susie, "The answer is 'yes.' " At this point you'll have the class with you. Your next remark can well be a brief comment on deciding social matters at recess.

Latest Press Release

Intercept a note. Read it. If it doesn't embarrass the writer, post it on the bulletin board.

A Correction, My Good Fellow

When a student is notewriting rather than notetaking, glance over his paper and say softly, but abruptly, "I disagree." Follow this opener with an irrelevant comment, such as, "King George III was not so dumb; why he could write his name and spell it correctly without help from anyone."

Underground Communication

Intercept a note. Start reading it aloud with the student's salutation and perhaps the first sentence, then switch to a jingle, something like:

> Ah, yes, I wrote the "Purple Cow"–
> I'm sorry now I wrote it.
> But I can tell you, anyhow,
> I'll kill you if you quote it!
> —Gelett Burgess

I can assure you the class will gasp as you start reading the first sentence, and then break into appreciative laughter after you've switched.

Stamp CENSORED!

If a note's contents are unsavory, casually remark, "Perhaps next time, I'll read not only the salutation and a jingle, but our local author's work as well." Class will gasp even though they haven't the foggiest idea of the note's contents.

CONCLUSION

Mankind has many ways of communicating, but teachers are often convinced students have mastered only one, talking. A curious corollary, but worth noting, is the fact that teachers tend to be the most talkative of adults. So, if you're an environmentalist, you know where you would recommend tackling the problem.

To gather all your students into a fused, lustrous class so they may radiantly take on your next lesson, you must have their attention—at least from time to time. Adults respond readily to a variety of charming, clever comments; children, however, also welcome a prearranged sound or action signal. They're comfortable with a touch of ceremony, a bit of tradition unique to Room 103.

Pesky problems such as tattling, swearing, lying, can be alleviated or dissolved through simple remedial steps. Correcting rudeness is handled in this text under the heading of courtesy. (See Chapter 5.)

The frequency of chattering, clowning, or messing around thrusts new importance on erasing them. Usually each incident is not that serious, but in the aggregate they seriously eat into a learning day. And the impact is greater than the sum of the components, for the disruptions and your actions in settling them directly contribute to the room's climate—the ripple effect as we like to say. And a dozen or two little incidents can be as wearing as a major crisis. If the stress continues too long, we call it teacher burnout.

When insisting a child's actions and speech stay focused on-goal, you won't necessarily muffle or damage his individuality. You'll enhance it if you do your job well. A person can be a conformist and still be very much an individual, providing he retains his spunkiness and conforms from conviction, never from fear. As easily as stepping into and out of a pair of shoes, a truly strong individual can step into and out of conformity with the customs of the group and the fashion of the hour. By the same token, an eccentric may inded be a real independent—

or he may be a fraud, incapable of authentic individual thinking and action.

Most of us agree that the spirited child's spunk is precious and must be preserved, and only the rambunctiousness and perverseness should be buffed away.

Concerning misdeeds, our aim is to reach the child in the language of reason, of cause and effect; but we're dealing with an individual who best understands the language of action, for he lives in an action world. Any diplomat worthy of his profession would converse, at least in part, in the language which his guest prefers. So, in dealing with students, a discerning but brief talk combined with a simple action penalty will bring better results than either a talk or action alone.

Since talking off cue is the number one trouble area for students, here are several constructive exercises, which may be written or taped, to use with children who keep on chattering to their own detriment and in spite of repeated warnings.

1. Ask her to imagine she's a jet pilot. Have her describe what might happen if she kept on talking while the control tower was issuing instructions on procedures.

2. Ask her to imagine she's a TV news reporter. Have her describe an interview where she did all the talking. How much information would she obtain? How newsworthy would the segment be? Would the channel run it?

3. Ask him to learn, and file a report with you, about the penalties meted out to professional athletes when they get cheeky.

4. Ask him to imagine he's a firefighter. What would he think of the intelligence of people in a burning building who kept on chattering and ignoring his instructions to climb down the hydraulic ladder?

Four

TEACHING INDIVIDUAL AND GROUP SELF-GOVERNMENT

There can be order without freedom, but there can be no freedom without order.
—John Gardner

Chaos is a crimped freedom. In teaching individual and group self-government, we must show children how true law brings freedom in exchange for obedience. True law evokes, not curbs, a higher form of freedom, since relying on a body of sound laws opens the way for more expansive thinking and action. Traditional folklore repeatedly imparts that school constricts individual rights. Admittedly true today, this was far more often true in the past. However, we may dispel these inward, limited expectations of school, this narrow definition of order, only by proving differently to our students. We are opening the way for their acceptance later in social clubs, peer associations, unions, and government.

In this chapter we will present some techniques for helping each child learn more about self-control and for establishing effective, fair methods of class control. Next, we'll consider making and changing group rules. Sowing the seeds of social change by trial and error is rarely a tidy process, but a willingness to try reasonable change encourages a feeling of vitality and freedom which promotes greater serenity and stability in the long run.

Elections are a cornerstone in our concepts of democratic process, but as we all know, many elections are far from democratic. Real issues remain camouflaged. Often voters choose inferior candidates over better qualified ones. The reasons? Emotional or charismatic appeal. Nonetheless, virtually no American advocates discarding the process of elections. Shortcomings indicate that the electorate needs information and encouragement to think and reason more lucidly and farsightedly.

The classroom is a microcosm of broader society. Though a few classrooms are suggestive of 476 A.D., the vast majority of American students can benefit greatly from training that eases them into a better understanding of democratic responsibilities and rights. Classroom standards represent the law in the student's world.

Today's older students fully understand their right to be heard, but few seem equally aware of a duty to know what they're talking about before they speak out. What an opportunity we have with younger children! How precious are these moments for teaching them to look beneath surface charms and persuasions, for teaching them to hold their thinking above mass hypnosis and media-inspired trends, for developing their awareness of subliminal influences on decisions. If we can convince them that the machinery of a well-run election guarantees nothing, but that voter thought processes are all-important, we'll have done much.

Next in this chapter we'll take up several ways of defining and distributing student leader duties. Patently clear responsibilities promote sensitive, yet well-directed leadership. Although some kids show a demonstrated talent for leading, many more have natural aptitude lying dormant, just below the surface.

Leadership requires more than a flair for it; the largest elements are good training and the desire for assuming duties. Student leadership training can be most stimulating to the general learning ethos; it's a graphic lesson to youngsters that school benefits can come, notch by notch, now; the glories and awards for "working hard in school" are not all assigned to the sweet by and by.

Some good ideas on developing teams within the class are also included in this chapter. Channeling a portion of the students' spirited energies into worthwhile team goals directs some competitiveness away from classic teacher-baiting challenges.

INDIVIDUAL SELF-CONTROL

A self-disciplined or self-controlled classroom is simply a room full of self-controlled individuals. More than learning to govern oneself, each child must learn to accurately appraise his own conduct, and understand how important his own conduct is, before he can be a real asset to the class.

As I interviewed many teachers I questioned them about individual self-control. More and more I realized how each teacher's attitude permeated her room. May I offer for your consideration some of their techniques for helping students get a wider, more complete picture of intelligent conduct—for helping a child who may be stumbling?

Turn with me, please, to the fact that children live in the now. Yesterday hardly existed. Tomorrow is forever. Here are several ways of teaching them that tomorrow starts with today.

According to the Public Record

A good citizen chart! Hang a large pocket chart on a wall. Print each child's name on a colored card and insert it in a niche. When a child misbehaves, the teacher asks him to remove his card. IMPORTANT: The student himself must do the removing, not the teacher. He then hands it to her. She dates it on the back and tucks it into her desk drawer. On Friday every child whose name card is still on display may get it and paste a star after his name. This social event is a highlight of the week, much treasured by the students. Monday brings a fresh start. Preferably, each student whose card is down, replaces it in the chart himself. Since this strategy is encouraging and refining, it is most effective where a reasonable climate is an established condition.

Custom Tailored for the Best Fit

Ask your rowdy dowdy to stay for an after-school visit. As you talk, work. Rule a check sheet outline on oaktag or shirt cardboard. (See the sample in Figure 4-1.) Making each copy an original heightens a child's sense of uniqueness and importance (more than a ditto would). Ask for his suggestions on improvement points. Start with items he feels deserve highest priority and on which *he* feels he is most apt to be successful. Then, for a week, he's to keep the card at his desk and maintain a record. Over the weekend send the card home for a parental signature. Repeat these cards for about four weeks. Generally speaking, avoid having more than six students on this project at any given time.

Figure 4-1

Success ✓ Chart for Peter Improvement ✓– Failure o	M	T	W	Th	F
Peter tries to: Be ready for work when bell rings	o	o	o	o	
Stay in his seat	o	✓	✓–	✓–	
Not to interrupt others	o	o	o	✓	
Use library time well	o	✓	✓	✓	
Not to run or skip in halls	✓	✓–	✓	o	

More Than Pillar to Post

Self-control—it's all well and good to speak of it, but why should a student develop this trait? From her viewpoint? Some teachers let each student sit down, usually in the autumn, and decide on *personal* goals for *this year*. Alone, the act of focusing helps to prune the vague and grandiose and leaves a realistic residue.

Who's Counting Raised Hands? Everyone!

Draw a clever cartoon of a student raising his hand and add the numbers one to twenty-five in boxes. Distribute one ditto to each class member. Every time during the day the student remembers to raise her hand, she is to check off a number.

Knights Aimed for the "Targe"

The teacher and students set a daily conduct responsibility target after discussing which ambitions are feasible and which are too vague. The children write a statement naming the target, time limit, and an evaluation of their target score. (See the sample in Figure 4-2.)

Figure 4-2

My target today is:

(Listen to lesson directions carefully)

I will hit my target by:

(2:00 when our last lesson has started)

I have a good target score because I:

(Not once had to ask my seatmate what's going on)

Incidentally, the class might enjoy learning that the word target comes from the French word *targe*. When jousting, knights aimed for the opponent's left shoulder, thus armor makers started adding an extra plate or thickness there which even in English is called a targe.

Duties of a Self-Manager

Each class member completes a form like the one shown in Figure 4-3, which is dittoed and distributed at regular intervals. A great cumulative record for student folders! When you develop your form, make another set of the figures, somewhat bigger. By using an opaque projector, you can enlarge these figures on a chalkboard or bulletin board; students enjoy tracing the bigger scale figure outlines in colored chalk. The assignment makes a nice treat.

Figure 4-3

Date_____	Name_____		
I manage my own behavior:	Sometimes	Getting Better	Almost Always
1. I can get myself in and out.	😐	🙂	☀🙂
2. I use good listening skills.	😐	🙂	☀🙂
3. I am able to get ready for work.	😐	🙂	☀🙂

Figure 4-3 (Cont'd)

I manage my own behavior:	Sometimes	Getting Better	Almost Always
4. I follow directions.	😐	🙂	😊
5. I carefully complete my lessons on time.	😐	🙂	😊
6. I am able to wait patiently.	😐	🙂	😊
7. I can work alone.	😐	🙂	😊
8. I can work with others.	😐	🙂	😊
9. I can use my free time wisely.	😐	🙂	😊
10. I take care of school materials and return them to the proper place on time.	😐	🙂	😊
11. I take care of my own property.	😐	🙂	😊

Figure 4-3 (Cont'd)

I manage my own behavior:		Sometimes	Getting Better	Almost Always
	12. I respect the property of others.	😐	🙂	😄
	13. I follow good safety rules.	😐	🙂	😄
	14. I am thoughtful and respectful to others.	😐	🙂	😄
	15. I can get myself to and from school without problems.	😐	🙂	😄
	16. I return things that I find to the proper owner, teacher, or office.	😐	🙂	😄
	17. I show good sportsmanship.	😐	🙂	😄
	18. I make myself available to help others when I finish my work.	😐	🙂	😄
	19. I am helpful to the teacher.	😐	🙂	😄

Signed, Countersigned, and Sealed
With the King's Wax

A room meeting covering day-to-day behavior standards is a splendid introduction to using this record device. (See Figure 4-4.) Done on a weekly basis, it makes a good record for the quarterly grade. A straight "Above Average" student would receive some sort of public recognition—possibly a written comment, "Well done, Charley," and the signature of the assistant principal?

Figure 4-4

Name _____ Room _____ Date _____		
Above Average	**Average**	**Below Average**
Self-Respect		
Courtesy		
Thoughtfulness		
Dependability		

Student is to score himself on the above points and then sign.

Student signature _____

Above Average	**Average**	**Below Average**
Self-Respect		
Courtesy		
Thoughtfulness		
Dependability		

Teacher is to score student and then initial _____

Silver Seal Market Cornered by Room 103

This award can be typed on a primary typewriter (extra large type) and then decorated with a silver notary seal and red ribbon. (See the sample in Figure 4-5.) The security behind it is three weeks' good behavior.

Figure 4-5

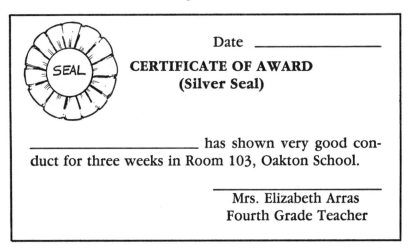

Date _____

CERTIFICATE OF AWARD
(Silver Seal)

_____ has shown very good conduct for three weeks in Room 103, Oakton School.

_____
Mrs. Elizabeth Arras
Fourth Grade Teacher

This teacher also divides her room into four or five teams, and uses a plus and minus point system covering many aspects of conduct. A silver certificate earns five extra points for a team. A gold certificate brings fifteen.

Cornering the Gold Seal Market

It takes three silver seal certificates to move into the gold seal market. The design is the same as in Figure 4-5 above, but the message reads: "_____ has shown exceptional behavior in the classroom. Your child is a good citizen of Oakton School and Room 103." Obviously, use a gold seal and red ribbon.

TAKE THEM TO THEIR LEADER

A first task for any supervisor—whether he's running a steel plant or leading a Cub Pack—is to let people know what is expected of them. Effectively and explicitly, he must establish the priorities and scope of their responsibilities. One unusually courteous middle school teacher distributes a bulletin (see Figure 4-6) to his classes at the beginning of the school year.

Figure 4-6

Sample bulletin   **Information needed for Mr. Gillie's Math Class**

CLASSROOM PROCEDURE
Try to acquire these traits and habits:
1. Raise your hand when you have something to say.
2. Be in your proper seat and ready to work when the bell rings.
3. Discard paper and other rubbish only at the beginning and the end of the period—the first and the last five minutes.
4. Get a note if you are tardy. Remember, three unexcused tardinesses constitute a U for a citizenship grade.
5. Get permission before leaving your seat or the room. Going to the pencil sharpener is the only exception for leaving your seat. Also remember, you must always sign out before you leave the room—even with permission.
6. Quietly follow the teacher during a fire drill. The students in the last row should close the windows.

Figure 4-6 (Cont'd)

Try to avoid these antics:
1. Speaking without being called upon to do so.
2. Chewing gum or eating candy.
3. Writing, marking, scraping on, or generally mutilating desks or chairs.
4. Writing and passing notes.
5. Talking to your neighbor when you should be working.
6. Being tardy.
7. Being at the pencil sharpener with another person.
8. Talking or horsing around during a fire drill.

NECESSARY EQUIPMENT
1. Unlined 8½ ″ × 11 ″ typing paper (regular bond).
2. Pencils—always sharpened and preferably No. 2 (no drawing pencils or felt-tipped pens, please).
3. A 12 ″ ruler. It should also have one edge with millimeters and centimeters on it.
4. Protractor, compass, book cover.

TESTS
1. *Importance:* The tests results will constitute the major part of your quarterly grade. *They are extremely important.*
2. *Tests are announced:* All tests will be announced in class several days in advance.
3. *Material covered:* Tests will usually cover several parts of a chapter or sometimes even a complete chapter.
4. *Retesting:* The tests will usually be given only once. Only in unusual circumstances will a test be given a second time.
5. *Absent from test:* Students absent from a test have the self-responsibility of making arrangements to take the test within two weeks.
6. *Number of tests:* Customarily, there is a test given about every two weeks. Therefore, there are from

Figure 4-6 (Cont'd)

four to five tests in one quarter, a nine-week period.

7. *Letter grades:* Numerical grades can be converted to letter grades with the key below—

A = 95–100	D = 70–74
B = 85–94	F = Below 70
C = 75–84	

HOMEWORK

1. *Day of homework:* There will be an assignment in mathematics on Monday in the 7th grade and Tuesday and Thursday in the 8th grade.
2. *Length of homework:* During the first semester it should take about 30 minutes and during the second semester, about 45–60 minutes.
3. *Day assignment due:* Homework will be discussed, checked, and collected the day following. These papers will be filed in a folder given to each student.
4. *Grade:* There will be a cumulative grade given for homework each quarter. The grade will count as one test grade.
5. *Delinquent assignments:* Failure to do these weekly or biweekly assignments will place a student in serious trouble. Only one day is allowed if the student was not absent.
6. *Excuse for not doing assignment:* Usually there is no excuse. The only exception is a person who was absent. In this case, this person has the self-responsibility to get the assignment and to turn it in within a week.
7. *Heading the homework paper:* Follow this example—

```
                          Joe Doe
                          Dec. 9, 19XX
                          pp. 39 ex. 1–8
        Math
```

Figure 4-6 (Cont'd)

DISMISSALS

1. When the bell rings, the class is *never* automatically dismissed. The teacher must verbally dismiss the class.
2. Each day of the week, the class will leave the room differently. But, any day of the week will be the same during all the weeks.
3. *Monday:* The first row will leave first, then it will be followed by the second, third, fourth, and the fifth will be last.
4. *Tuesday:* The second row will leave first. Then it will be followed by the third, fourth, fifth, and the first row will be last.
5. *Wednesday:* This same procedure will continue with the third row leaving first, etc., through the rest of the week. On Monday, this procedure will start over again.

SOME POSITIVE SUGGESTIONS

1. Participate in classroom discussion daily.
2. Ask questions when you fail to understand a concept.
3. Make an appointment with the teacher for a before- or after-school session if your misunderstanding persists. Please do this soon or immediately after you have trouble because I will not tolerate a class full of people after school the night before a test.
4. Be punctual when coming to class.
5. Hand in your homework promptly and make sure:
   a. It is neat.
   b. Each problem has been properly numbered.
   c. The paper is correctly headed.
   d. It is checked and recorded.

If you take note of this entire bulletin and follow these suggestions, you will find yourself thoroughly enjoying and learning mathematics this year. Finally, and hopefully, you will be doing well, too.

Ben Gillie

MAKING AND CHANGING GROUP RULES

Probably the most fundamental of all disciplines is that of sharing; it's a major key in all communication. Understanding, empathy, self-discipline—all these traits are required. Sharing the experience of making and changing group rules deepens and enlarges the students' sense of community, "our room." Before rules are adopted, it's wise to have a thorough discussion, which should include questions and comments about suitable sanctions for each rule adopted.

Later on, great day! You may find a rule superfluous because rarely is it applicable . . . or because the school has issued a new building regulation, e.g., no toys at school. This presents an opportunity for leading the class through the process of deleting and substituting. Learning the process of gradual change —passing laws and then repealing them—is in itself excellent training. Often it's a needed experience for the students.

Again, I collected most of my material on this topic during interviews with outstanding teachers in their natural habitat. If the classroom had a good climate, I included the suggestions even though some seemed a trifle bland.

Checking Chitter Chatter

Group self-government can begin at a very young age. Try the student-chairman system to monitor whispering and roaming in the room. The term of office is one week and an imperial privilege of this office is naming one's successor.

Setting the Sails

Use the first five or six days of school to establish definite patterns and procedures. (Children can enjoy this period very much because, with their intense interest in each other, they welcome learning how to get along with the class.) The following facets are basic guidelines that need to be tailored to fit the scene:

1. Under teacher direction (light-handed rather than heavy-handed), the students make class rules, five to eight of them.
2. Students are assigned seats, which are changed five or six times during the year. Later changes should consider student preferences, if possible.
3. Students choose workmates and line partners, at least to start.
4. Learning is the first goal of the classroom. Anything that interferes with this will be questioned.
5. *Respect* of others is all-important. Class members don't have to like everyone, but they must extend respect. Emotionally mature people, of any age, like people—of any age.

During the first week of conduct training, you may intersperse general orientation with school work-related movies, stories, records, and news discussions. Since good teachers always feature a review of last year's work to freshen memories, introducing new or important academic units is best delayed. A properly chosen movie preceded with a solid introduction and followed by an exchange of ideas can be, simultaneously, good instruction and a conduct-training device.

One Winner and Two Attendants

Load your instant camera and take a picture of the "Most Improved Child of the Week." Then place it in a frame with an appropriate title. Another twist: Let the child you select as most improved choose two classmates whom he thinks made good runners-up to this honor and take a picture of all three.

This Week's Letter Goes to . . .

Here's a fresh twist on sending letters home complimenting students on exceptionally good conduct. One teacher pinpoints mundane, usually overlooked acts of cooperation, courtesy, or honesty. Then, she makes sure that a few of her one-foot-in-trouble children are among the first to be recognized when they contribute positively to group harmony. Most times it has an ameliorating effect on the attitude of students whose behavior needs improvement. And their parents are usually immeasurably grateful.

This Bill Was Sponsored by . . .

Class develops six or eight vital rules with the teacher or student writing these suggestions on chalkboard. The first person who makes the suggestion is named its author. The teacher, without directly mentioning the fact, is wise to change the wording of suggestions from "Thou shall nots" into positive directions as she records on the board. Here are some examples:

ROOM 103

Be in seat and ready for work when last bell rings.
—Johnny Wood

Gum chewing at recess and lunch time only.
—Chiu Wong

Soft voices in room, ordinary talking at recess and lunch.
—Peter Johnson

Take turns and be fair to other students.
—Brad Carlin

Turn in homework on front table before school starts.
—Nancy Martin

Sharpen pencils between first and second bells.
—Patti Anderson

Keep extra belongings in lockers, not at desks.
—José Sanchez

Get permission to leave assigned seat.
—Sylvester Greene

Rewards	**Punishments**
Extra recess or gym	Not included in class discussion
Join another class for movie	Apologize
Tell a joke to the class	Sit at special table
Extra computer time	Do clean-up chores

Talk It Over—Before the Fact

Often a teacher sees an incipient negative condition. Rather than merely hoping it will fade away, tackling it with an assertive approach makes good sense. Read library book stories to the class on problems similar to the potential danger, such as fighting, shyness, Schlapp Hans work. After reading the example aloud, discuss salient points. When the discussion reaches a lively tempo, shift emphasis from the general to how it pertains to your neighborhood.

An Ounce of Prevention

At the beginnning of a class period (or day) make this announcement: The student council representative will take a group grade to the office directly after class—or at specified times during the day. This report will have dual marks, one reflecting conduct, and the other reflecting quality of work/ diligence. If needed, names of troublemakers will be added so the class won't suffer from the antics of a few. The swiftness of accountability has a magical touch. Naturally, you'll need office cooperation, but the strategy is pleasantly efficient in promoting a healthy, normal climate. It's great for taming a class with a prior wild and woolly reputation and invaluable for helping a substitute or novice teacher.

According to the Rules

Infraction and penalty, both are known quantities. Each time your group decides through discussion on a necessary rule, have them consider a basic fixed penalty for infractions.

Our Room Has a Balanced Budget

Weekly dues of 10 cents per class member shortly develop into a workable sum. These monies can be used for a room magazine, a gift to the school library, parties, a reserve pencil pool, a small gift for a long-term housebound classmate, a sympathy card. Most often, class officers handle the funds and expenditure decisions come as a group consensus.

Every Fiefdom Has Different Laws

Two-week-term officers are elected by secret ballot or show of hands. Since they are student-elected, don't remove anyone except for malfeasance of duties. Use a pocket insert chart with name cards. Officers and their duties:

Chairman
Waits for order in morning
Initiates pledge
Leads song

Supply Officers (2)
Distribute fresh paper
Care for equipment

Libraries (2)
Arrange book displays
Maintain order

Custodians (2)
Empty pencil sharpener
Draw draperies for films
Switch lights
Clean art project messes

Master of Ceremonies
Leads current events discussions
Handles details of elections

Traffic Officers (2)
Lead lines
Hold outside doors

Mailmen (2)
Return papers
Deliver out-of-room messages

Chalkboard Keepers (2)
Clean boards
Clean erasers
Hand out chalk (in some cases)

The Day Teacher Is Absent

So often a teacher has nice control because the children like her and feel a loyalty. One day a substitute appears. Of course, she'll handle routines a trifle differently, and then too, the youngsters have a degree of buoyancy and bottled impishness ready to bubble over. When you leave the lesson plans schedule, openly place it on your desk where children will see it. Add a special note for the agenda: "If the class cooperates nicely, please give them an extra work period on our current papier-mâché project (or whatever)." The word will spread, and the class will have a much more solid day of learning.

This Time, Write the Rules

A few imps haven't absorbed the meaning of the class-created rules even though the other students are adhering to them quite well. Take them aside and briefly review firefighter rules and why, bicycle traffic rules and why, school rules and why, Room 103 rules and why. Have the imps copy room rules from six to twelve times.

Twelve Good People, Tried and True

You might introduce this strategy by mentioning a bit of English history and common law, and by explaining how our present jury system evolved, from the original Anglo-Saxon tribal laws and traditions under which a culprit's fate was decided by his peers. When a rowdy dowdy repeatedly disrupts matters by ignoring group-established rules, the class can assume a jury role to offer a suitable resolution for the constant infractions. You, as judge—not tribal chieftain—reserve the right to modify their decisions. You might add yours is an earned right based on wider experience in school affairs and by virtue of your school board contract.

SELECTING STUDENTS FOR OFFICERS

Occasionally one clique wins any and all elections. Sometimes they are "natural" leaders, other times they are the charismatic personalities, the town social set offspring, or simply a smoothly aggressive junta. Once in office they acquire experience and enhance a reputation which yields even more self-confidence to, wittingly or unwittingly, pluck the next leadership role.

Several imperative reasons exist for increasing the spectrum of eligible talent. Leadership is not merely a natural trait, it is also a trained one. The kid who almost wins is usually a trifle short-suited in one personality facet. She could gain much from an office term, especially if it comes coupled with subtle guidance from you or a cooperative classmate who previously held the post. An office is a powerful influence. It can stretch anyone into using dormant abilities. An additional note: a school guidance counselor might enjoy helping the almost-winners by explaining a bit about group dynamics and campaign techniques for the future.

Letting others do us a simple favor is an often-overlooked strategy for kids and adults. When we do another a good turn, it makes *us* feel stronger; however, asking another to do a favor for us enhances *his* feeling of strength, self-worth, good will. If not overdone, it works like gangbusters!

Sociometric plotting is a good device for learning who is the most popular—to assess the unwritten pecking order—but it would be foolish for any teacher to go overboard by following only this strategy. The goddess popularity doesn't distribute her favors on a fair, democratic, or even a thinking basis. She is also fickle. As we know, sometimes personal popularity is won on fleeting or superficial qualities, good looks, or an unrelated prowess. Students get a healthier education when they witness character qualities which make for long-term success being identified and rewarded.

Respect for students' individuality doesn't require teachers to abandon all their influence. Nothing rules out blending adult and student opinions; indeed, heavy precedent rules it in. Most government and business leaders use their earned right to influence political candidate appointments—not by arbitrary edict, but by friendly persuasion and an unwritten code of approval nods. In the last analysis, schools are charged with developing active, enlightened, educated citizens, not a generation of charming salesmen and passive customers.

Figure 4-7 shows the spectrum of activities in which students, as school citizens, can participate.

Figure 4-7

SCHOOL CITIZEN PARTICIPATION

Holding office Being a candidate for office Candidate campaign manager Attending a strategy meeting Hanging posters, distributing buttons	Thick-of-contest activities
Attending rallies and meetings Getting permission to visit other rooms Making posters, buttons, fliers Making other time/money contributions	Transitional activities
Wearing a button or sticker Trying to influence another's vote Starting a political discussion Voting	Spectator activities
Reading the posters	Apathetic

WEIGHTED POINT SYSTEM FOR HOLDING OFFICE

This arrangement governs the total time any single student spends on extra activities; it overcomes in-group constriction and simultaneously avoids the pitfalls of excessive teacher interference. Setting up this system is a natural chore for the student council and their faculty advisor at the middle school level.

Points are assigned to each elected office according to time demands and prestige. No student is permitted more than a specified point total per year and points are cumulative from year to year. Example: Nine points, and the student must retire with honors.

Five-point Posts

Student Council Officer	8th Grade President or Secretary
Girls/Boys Club Officer	7th Grade President or Secretary

Three-point Posts

Student Council Member   6th Grade President or Secretary

Two-point Posts

Computer Club Officer   Patrol Boy Captain

Stamp Club Officer   School Representative (to anywhere)

One-point Posts

Room Officer   Special Drive Chairman

This is a simplified version: the program is even more effective when there are thoughtful gradations. Another point, a
child is ineligible for an office candidacy which would put him
over the legal limit. Thus he and his friends must think and plan
ahead. "Now, let's see. Our buddy, Charley, has been patrol
boy captain and a room officer. If he runs for computer club
president, he'll be ineligible for 8th grade class president. Which
job would he like best? Where would he do the better job?"

Halfway-to-Australia Ballot

Elicit candidate nominations and write them on the board.
Then each child buries his head in his left arm on his desk. The
teacher stands at the board and calls each nominee's name. Children vote by raising their right arms. If they peek or raise left
arms, they spoil their ballots.

Australian Ballot

Ditto and cut ballots. Have children drop votes in boxes in
the rear corners of the room but place a judge's table in front
center. Choose a judge, a ballot opener, and a tally keeper.
You'll need to teach younger students how to keep a stick tally.
Each step of the election is an opportunity for a *succinct* explanation of a similar step in government. You know your group
best, but it could be fun to also choose two kids to be poll
watchers—to keep any unscrupulous Room 103 politician from
stuffing the ballot box.

Selection, Not Election

Occasionally, a few win every time, thus clipping leadership development of others, some of whom have real potential.

To counteract the unthinking tyranny of the clique, put six, eight, or ten names in a hat and let a student draw. Thus you control the situation insofar as you know a reliable child will represent the room, broaden the base beyond the usual winners, and no child knows for sure whether he was in the running.

DUTIES OF STUDENT LEADERS

Most jobs for younger students rather define their own limits, e.g., eraser clapper, chairman of broken crayons. The posts older children earn are defined by rules and school tradition. The only major job which often has an aura of vagueness is that of line leader. I recommend that you sit down and write a point-by-point duty description. Since this is so individual, I have included only one example given me during the interviews.

Rod of the Empire

Select a boy and a girl for line leaders. They are actually class leaders for the week. If they do especially well, the term of office may be extended one week.

Leaders walk at head of the line going to gym, auditorium, playground, another class, and at dismissal. Leaders halt the line if there is talking. They either wait for quiet, or approach offenders and direct them to last place in line. The teacher walks at the middle or tail of line.

After gym or playtime one leader chooses, by rows or individuals, those who are ready for drinks. The other leader holds the fountain faucet. At dismissal the leaders check for cleared desks and for gym shoes in hand to be placed in lockers. They distribute fliers and notes bound for home.

During indoor playtime leaders take the nomination and conduct voting for game choice and then direct the game. They keep reasonable order.

Leaders choose their successors, not best friends but classmates apt to handle the job well.

TEAMS WITHIN THE CLASS

Ball teams! Spelling bees! Swimming teams! Teams are fun! Team grouping brings an evolutionary step into the classroom; it's an intermediate level toward helping students acquire individual self-control. It prepares the class for a required behavior modification, alerting them to the continuing shift called growing up. The pivotal agent in this strategy is the student monitor or captain . . . "brethren of a common lot."

So many earnest graduates leave teachers' college convinced of the importance of respecting the inherent rights of students. Great tact and love are in the novices' hearts as they plan to establish truly democratic classrooms; visions of stimulated little scholars enjoying lyric poetry dance through their aspirations. Suddenly . . . they're torpedoed broadside. They have a pack of youngsters and a condition which undoubtedly the Greeks had a word for—but the word was not *demokratis.*

Often much of the immediate trouble can be traced to the omission of a transitional stage. The earlier training of the class, which may even have been excellent in its type, was benevolent authoritarianism. If most of the staff in a school subscribes to this approach, obviously students will arrive thus groomed. And equally apparent, this must be the starting point for change, a gradual change, a step by step replacing of one type of control for another. One trains a child to swim in shallow water first.

Team arrangements make for a goal-oriented transitional stage which is almost vital in reaching for more student self-responsibility and self-direction. For example, children who transfer from church-run schools to permissive suburban schools frequently get into hot water, not because they've suddenly become defiant or mischievous, but because too much freedom has been thrust on them abruptly. Democratic methods in controlling students are like a plant which grows slowly and sturdily through years of nurturing, training. It doesn't sprout—like bamboo—overnight, nor usually will it break in high winds.

Almost everyone teaching in unenlightened areas tells of

feeling among the student body a resistance to the whole formal institution called school, a resistance rarely found in the same degree in skilled blue collar and professional neighborhoods. A small portion of this undertow can be chalked up to resentment of authority for no other reason than it is authority.

Often parents, or the one parent charged with the child's well-being, in depressed regions place less value on formal education. For many, the goal of survival has priority over school open houses. Frequently, their own schooling was a sorry mess and while they obey the law and insist the child attend school, tapping on their own experiences, they feel for the kid. Of interest, most of these parents when talking to school personnel will verbally express an appropriate attitude, society's stance, on the good the schools are doing. But scratch the surface and . . . antagonism leaks out.

Teachers in some neighborhoods may lean to authoritarianism because of retarded emotional and behavioral development among a large percentage of students, a deficient sense of community between home and school, a pervasive district philosophy, or large classes. Even inadequate or vandalized supplies contribute to the condition promoting authoritarianism.

The snowballed result is a far more competitive feeling between staff and students for control, for power. It's this exhausting tension, these cross-purposes of intent, and not the actual teaching, which makes teacher burnout widespread. Long before you and I ever thought of teaching, sociologists, ministers, legislators, university sages, and educational leaders were working on this and attendant problems. They will continue their tasks long after we're gone. One short-range device which alleviates and doesn't interfere with long-range efforts and effects is to channel student energy into teams competing with each other. Do keep changing teams and team membership on a monthly or six-week basis.

Respect is the most powerful weapon you have to dissolve students' residual antagonism toward school. Respect is power. Pointedly showing esteem for the youngsters' individuality, talent, future, makes genuine inroads on winning them. Please be slow in *expecting* respect; it's a duty the children have been told about, more than once. Your duty to respect them? As individuals? Probably no one has mentioned much about that. Teachers are constantly being admonished to be caring, loving, but most teachers and parents love them in a manner which the French say is "loving from high to low"; genuine respect meets others eye to eye, and it's felt intuitively.

Invitations Are Very Limited

Monthly, students compete for a best-conduct prize. Divide the room into, say, four groups of six or seven students in a unit. If the class is larger, have more groups but not larger ones. Classmates choose group membership, and each unit has a secretary who keeps an accurate record of plus and minus points. Good actions bring one to three points. Negative actions subtract one to three points. The winning team gets a twenty-minute party which is usually held during art period. They may invite others, or they may decide to celebrate aloof in royal splendor. The refreshments? A glass of punch or a little candy, no more.

Lingo Bingo

This game is included here because of its potential for building team spirit. Younger children ask for it again and again, even though team playing is not their long suit. After the class has learned this game as individuals, have them form teams . . . and the real fun begins! If a few students won't join in whole-heartedly, don't comment. Let the other children coax them. They will.

Directions: Explain the rules and choose the first leader. The rules are: (1) Each person writes a word on a piece of paper. (2) Leader chalks a letter on the board. (3) Each player crosses out the letter as often as it appears in his word. (4) Leader puts another letter on the board. (5) The first player to complete his word calls "Lingo Bingo." (6) Leader asks for the word. (7) Player pronounces his word and spells it slowly. As he spells, leader crosses out letter on the board. (8) If the word is spelled correctly and all letters are on the board, the winner gets to be leader. If player is short on either point, he remains seated.

CONCLUSION

Genuine law is not constrictive; it is liberating. Fuller, sound concepts of overall justice and law can bring to teachers and students alike much greater freedom in all their constructive pursuits.

A sense of law in the hearts and minds of individuals is the only reliable means of self-government, individual or group. Modern law is not found in statute books; it is merely recorded there. So also, the rules governing school buildings and classrooms are not found in the principal's office or on a bulletin board; they are simply posted there.

There's nothing wrong with authority. Tribal law, a primitive, personalized rule over chaos, is by nature normally quite authoritarian. A benevolent authoritarian approach is often the first step in gaining control in a classroom. So far, no harm done. Platitudes about democracy aside, many teachers like the accompanying security and structure; they don't mind working under authoritarian supervision. There's an honest consistency in their philosophy that deserves respect, even if we disagree with it.

A real wrong surfaces when a teacher decides she understands democratic processes, but her students are so low caste that they are incapable of learning or appreciating the value of self-government and it's a waste of time trying to teach them. This dual concept of native worth reduces her effectiveness and aggravates her feelings of futility. Perhaps the kindest thing she can do is to locate a teaching post where she believes she is among equals.

The flip side of this coin is a teacher, usually of blue-collar heritage, who is teaching in a wealthy suburb and holds a prejudice. She believes the fathers are too busy chasing success and prestige and the mothers are sloshing their way from one cocktail party to the next, both too self-indulgent to have retained intelligent concern and solid values for their offspring. This second teacher should also find another location where she feels her talents and training are appreciated.

As we work with kids on individual self-control, we start by helping them with classroom conduct and then extend our concern to helping them take responsibility for supplies, books, homework. Concurrently, we initiate rules with sanctions for breaking them. As the group develops as an entity, leaders emerge. This chapter has discussed various ways of guiding their paths, enlarging their numbers, and expanding student concepts of who makes a good leader. A weighted point system for holding office takes planning, but it is an effective strategy.

It's hardly new to say that teamwork contributes to students' welfare, but several benefits are often overlooked. Teamwork and setting up teams is a splendid training step in converting an entirely teacher-run classroom to a scene where students operate far more on self-directed motivation. Usually, it's a wise intermediate level. And in those poorer neighborhoods where there's a strong power conflict between faculty and students, establishing teams shifts part of the competitiveness away from the teacher herself, thus leaving her fresher, more enthusiastic to attempt imaginative teaching.

Five

INCREASING STUDENTS' DESIRE TO ATTEND SCHOOL

How does the ordinary student feel about the classroom, really? Certainly, for younger children it is a home away from home. Educators might consider it a haven. Others would consider it a base of operations.

The classroom as a haven? Yes, a refuge from the limitations which ignorance and the ignorant place on many individuals. It should be a sanctuary from the character-shriveling influence of frightening authoritarianism on one hand and aimless apathy on the other—the place to dissipate the illusion that life has a magic carpet ride to success. Life offers something far better than downhill roads to the top.

A base of operations? Tomorrow is built on today, so the qualities of curiosity and imagination must be coupled with systematic training in productive work approaches. Work can be most enjoyable. Students need help in the intelligent use of their time; time must be a servant, not a master, of actions.

97

Happily, the classroom can be a combination of all three: a home away from home, a haven, a base of operations.

In this chapter we'll consider ways of making the classroom more inviting, productive, and accepting. Since courtesy is pivotal in establishing harmony, we'll start with this aspect and lead into techniques for emphasizing each student's individuality, importance, and inherent worth.

This chapter offers a few strategies for handling children with problems, including shyness. A final section pinpoints devices that practicing teachers are using to add charming surprises to the daily routine.

COURTESY

As we know, polished manners result from a delicate sensitivity to other's feelings, combined with daily practice. Everyone enjoys being with children who express the gentle virtues, though some adults are astonished these days when they encounter polite students. So, if you think your class is "rude and scant of courtesy," yours is not an isolated case. However, once the tone and a few courtesy goals are set, the children teach each other remarkably well.

And the teacher does set a tone by extending to one and all courtesy fit for kings, earned or unearned. Let's not wait for disrespectful kids to respect us first, because Hades will freeze over and melt before this happens. Ordinarily, if children had known and been taught respect earlier, they wouldn't be rude or problem students; you know that. As you take the initiative and show marked respect, you will better control the climate and eventually, you'll reap results.

At times of extreme provocation you can direct embarrassment away from yourself by asking, "Is that *your* best thinking and talking?" Or, "Is that the best *you* can do?" The following can be tricky, but in some neighborhoods you an appeal to the respect due the office of teacher.

In schools where excellence permeated a vibrant air, I questioned teachers about teaching courtesy. Here are some of their suggestions.

Credit Card, Courtesy of . . .

No! But a *Courtesy Credit Card*—yes! Print COURTESY cards with a surprise privilege on the reverse side. An especially considerate child may take a card, the top card. No peeking in the stack. Example of rewards: First choice in music free sing . . . An extra drink of water at an undesignated time . . . Extra time in the resource or computer center.

Politeness Day

Once a month have a room Politeness Day. Each student makes and decorates a construction paper button which reads, "I'M POLITE." This day, any rude act or comment in the classroom invites corrective actions. An offending student is asked to remove his badge, and any class member who sees the rudeness has the authority to make the request.

In halls and other rooms, rudeness is merely noted and reported when the group returns. At 3:15 all who are still wearing buttons get extra points on their citizenship grade. Of course, suggest winners take their badges home and share them with their families.

Courtesy Contest

Make a class list on graph paper. Outstanding acts of courtesy score points. Students fill in squares themselves. *Caution:* Monitor this carefully because it's easy for the tempted to chisel!

WANTED by the Sheriff of Courtesy County

Take a supply of beige ripple bond paper because it somewhat resembles parchment and burn the edges. Each student is to paste a photo (or draw a picture) of himself in the middle. Caption the sheet WANTED. Beneath the picture each student is to write, "For a friend because . . ." and add words that describe qualities making for friends and good manners.

Trimming the Yuletide Tree

Label a bulletin board "Christmas Cheer and Courtesy" and display a large paper Christmas tree. Have the group create a bountiful supply of small paper ornaments and place them in an ornament box. When a student observes a classmate being extra polite or doing a good deed, he is to write the name on an ornament and add it to the tree. (Or, how about a pumpkin patch? Leaves on a branch? Easter eggs in a basket? Spring flowers in a window box?)

Secret Pal Books

One week have the students make little five-page booklets with a cover decorated in felt pen, crayon, or chalk. Then the following Monday morning have each child draw a name and write down one nice thing that person does each day. On Friday everyone swaps booklets.

Of Course the Ruffian Understands

Have an insolent child write on good manners as an asset. This essay *shouldn't be a confessional*; rather it should be impersonal and constructive. Perhaps have him list five courteous acts and the good ensuing to students who hold themselves to this standard. Require him to read it to the class.

ROLL CALL

Embellishing roll call, making it more personal, is a natural avenue for indicating your sincere interest in students as individuals. Once more, you can be fair in the amount of time devoted to each child and consistent from day to day. The children beam when you ask them about their likes and dislikes.

More Than a Name in the Red Book

Call roll. Each child answers with "present" and today's additional fact. One day ask for middle name; another time, favorite hobby, a pet's name, a favorite dinner. This last one strikes an especially responsive chord.

A variation: List about eight TV programs popular with the age group. Call roll. Ask each child to answer "present" and name her favorite show on the list. Have a student keep tally. Announce results. Children enjoy this, and it's a splendid step in building an "our room" feeling.

Combining Attendance With . . .

One first grade teacher combines taking attendance with the selecting of chocolate or white milk. Each student's name is on a large board with a peg beside it. When each child comes into the room, he selects a color coded card and hangs it on a peg next to his name.

Picture, Picture on the Wall

Place each child's picture over his locker or coat hook. They all like the distinction and now younger ones can't miss placing coats and hats in the right spot. If you take the pictures, pose several children on one exposure, cut and mount separately.

That's Me—Over There

Have each child draw a self-portrait, perhaps using a mirror. Then add each child's name and birthday on the completed drawings. Hang pictures low—under the chalkboard ledge, for example. Assign a child to take roll by turning over the pictures of absent children.

RESPECT FOR THE INDIVIDUAL

After reflecting on the idea, you'll probably agree that it's hard to dislike or resent anyone who we know respects us greatly. Someone less fortunate or inferior is easy to like; weakness often makes others seem lovable, but loving someone we consider our superior is harder. By the same token, it's easy to respect our superiors but more challenging to respect those under us. Respect those whom we are asked to teach and criticize? Indeed, we must. If we want the healthiest relationship, they must *know* we respect them.

That's All She Wrote

When sending a note home, please read the contents to the student or invite him to read it. This dissolves his fear of an unknown message. Surely, it's respectful of his feelings and a courtesy.

Private Property—No Trespassing

Your example establishes a tone of respecting other's privacy. Under most circumstances, ask your student, "May I look into your desk?"

At Your Convenience

Reasonable doubt hovers over a child's guilt about an incident—still, you must question him. Try asking him, "When would you like to discuss this matter?" Normally, his response will be most appropriate. (It's the same thing when the principal contacts a teacher with a note, "May I see you at your earliest convenience?")

My Lens Takes a Better Picture

If an untoward act of a normally reasonable student requires reproof, do let him know your concept of him is better than he thinks. Example: "I really thought you were a man here . . . the only character who kept his cool." Or, "Of all the kids around, I really didn't expect this of you."

Buck Up, Buddy!

Patting a child on the back is a friendship token. As you do, add a few warm words. Please be careful on two counts. One, patting a head top is patronizing. Two, consider in some cases even a shoulder pat could be misinterpreted.

EQUALITY AMONG INDIVIDUALS

Each person has a distinct personality; we often discuss that. But each group has a distinct personality, too. In recent years strong emphasis has been placed on racial equality, and slowly we are awakening to our obligations to minorities. However, other aspects of equality are important, too. We must guard against allowing IQ—and related test—scores to promote an intelligentsia aristocracy and an intellectual peonage. Working on fairness in school relationships, we must work on correcting the tilt anywhere it's found. Our interest should go beyond civil and intellectual rights to include personal, property, cultural, and social rights.

My Teacher Includes Everyone

Each day extend an individual welcome to each child including a personalized comment. At first you may need a check sheet to ensure you've missed no one.

A "Me" Collage

At the year's start, have every child make a *ME* collage and then decorate the room. Elicit general items to include and make a chalkboard list. This is also a good vehicle for teaching the class your art supply distribution and collection methods.

Everyone's Name Is Important to Everyone

If any student were teacher, he'd know every enrollee's name. During the first school week assign the task of learning every classmate's name, first and last. A bingo card approach is one method. (If this project is broken into short segments, it can easily be combined with lessons in an acceptable whispering decibel level.)

Chain of Names

Seat the class in a circle. The first student introduces herself by saying, "My name is Rita." The student to her right says,

"My name is Willie, and this is Rita." The third student says, "My name is Alfredo, this is Willie, and this is Rita." If the kids are quite young or timid, you may want to give each child a card with his name on it; thus, when a student halfway around the circle gets stuck, the student whose name has been forgotten can give him a cue card reminder.

Know Your Classmates

Direct your students to collect signatures of classmates who fit the description listed, with the admonition that no one is to sign another's paper more than twice. Here are some sample descriptions.

———————————————— 1. Left-handed person

———————————————— 2. Person with a dog

———————————————— 3. Person with a puppy

———————————————— 4. A Boy Scout

———————————————— 5. A Girl Scout

———————————————— 6. Person with freckles

Good Luck Comes in Many Tongues

Whatever cultural or ethnic influences are in your students' backgrounds, learn apt phrases of the language to write on the bottom of everyone's papers. For example, if you use the French *Bonne Chance*, include everyone not just students of French descent.

One Class of Citizens

Equality of opportunity? Here it is in action. Arrange math groups according to individual attainment but eliminate pigeon-holing by allowing for genuine flexibility. Insist that each student sit with her assigned group for the presentation. Then permit her to sit with other math groups as she chooses. She won't get all that's offered, but she will learn something. Generally, children choose rather well: those most ready for promotion to a more advanced section are the most grateful.

Birthday Celebrations

When a teacher takes a definite stand on keeping birthday parties and school separate, it circumvents many hidden hurts among children. Parents are notified that each birthday child is honored by a song, poem, birthday wishes, and a birthday badge. That's all. No cookies or treats are brought to school. Private parties are to be kept private: no invitations are to be distributed at school, and no gifts or favors are to be brought to school after home parties.

Save the Extra Shekels

Halloween costumes need not be more expense for parents and an unspoken line of financial stratification for students. Sending a note home expressing a classroom/school viewpoint sets the tone for wise economy. Figure 5-1 illustrates a sample note.

Figure 5-1

Oakton School

Dear Parents,

On Thursday, October 31st, children may wear Halloween costumes to school. Please do not feel obliged to buy a costume especially for this day. A piece of old sheet makes a ghost, an Arab robe and headgear, a Roman toga, or it's fun to celebrate in long skirts, old blouses, hats, pants, belts, jewelry, or cowboy suits.

Your child is to wear his costume to school. For your child's protection and comfort, NO MASKS WILL BE WORN IN SCHOOL OR TO AND FROM SCHOOL. Harmless makeup is fine, and more fun, too.

Thank you for your cooperation—and Happy Halloween!

It's the Individual Difference, You Know

Giving an Interest Inventory (see Figure 5-2) monthly shows a child her uniqueness; it carries an added bonus of also stimulating the child to pinpoint her interests.

Figure 5-2

Date_____   Name_____

INTEREST INVENTORY

1. At school, what I like to do best is _____
   _____

2. At home, what I like to do best is _____
   _____

3. What I like least at school is _____
   _____

4. What I like least at home is _____
   _____

5. I would like to study more about _____
   _____

6. I don't want to study any more about _____
   _____

7. When I grow up I'd like to be _____
   _____

8. The most interesting things I remember doing in school were _____
   _____

9. The happiest day I remember was _____
   _____

Figure 5-2 (Cont'd)

10. The things I try to save are _____

    _____

11. My favorite sports or games are _____

    _____

12. I know I need more help to _____

    _____

13. The kinds of books I like to read best are _____

    _____

14. If I could travel anywhere in the world, I would like to go

    to _____

    _____

15. In my spare time I like to _____

    _____

CHILDREN WITH PROBLEMS

Here are a few ideas on making life more livable for a troubled child and his teacher. As we know, often it's difficult not to be provoked or to wish the child and his family would move 1,000 miles—no, make that 2,000 miles—away. Expert counseling is the answer, but it isn't always available when needed; and sometimes it's just humanly impossible for the teacher to take the necessary time, even if she has splendid counseling qualifications. This section is not intended to impinge on specialists. However, troubled children often respond well to a series of small, patient, informal touches and strategies.

As Your Friend and Teacher, I Care

Early, assure everyone he *can* pass. You do care and because you care, you'll insist that each student do the required work. Eliminate any and all general threats of flunking.

Troublemaking Tommy

The first thing every morning, greet him with a compliment about something he has done right, no matter how small. It's a pattern of appreciation you're establishing.

This Is Your Captain, and We Will Arrive . . .

A teacher knows the year's educational route and pilots the course. It's easy to assume students have a clear understanding, but do they? Teachers who carefully explain features of this year's program, who roughly outline a map of projected activity and anticipated accomplishments for the children, report a definite reduction in student anxiety. If this overview is established in September, it alleviates uncertainty and its Siamese twin, negativity.

Leave Your Worries Behind

You see a scowling child coming through the door. Help her into the swing of school by immediately giving her a special responsibility, such as moving books, passing papers, posting a bulletin.

One Doghouse Is Enough

A student is well aware of his temporary outcast status when he's been sent back from gym or library. Don't scold. Without effusiveness, be a friend first. As an equal, talk on any subject he wants to talk about.

Breaking Bread Together

A hard-to-reach child is a natural for this invitation. Ask him to lunch with you in the classroom, once a week for several weeks. While conversing, work on developing friendship. Don't attempt an attitude change or to convert him to your ideas of the good life.

My Problem Is . . .

Use a filing card container for children's notes. If they would like more friends, have a demanding younger sibling, or whatever, ask them to drop in a note. It may be unsigned. Later, the group can discuss these dilemmas and offer solutions. A twenty-minute period weekly covers it nicely. (This is a good vehicle for refining good discussion rules.)

A Special Pal

This strategy has been used with hard-core behavior cases. The social worker and teacher decide jointly on an extra pupil–teacher friendship assignment for each staff member. No teacher is assigned one of her own students, nor given more than one problem child as a prospective "buddy." In each instance the social worker helps the assigned teacher decide on a flexible pattern of special activity.

SHYNESS

Charming as it may seem, shyness stems from egocentric fear. Obviously, a long-term improvement program for dissolving shyness includes overcoming fear, building self-confidence, and developing skills, while immediate steps involve encouraging the child to forget himself and think about others. Some of the following suggestions are excellent for teaching reticent children to be more outgoing.

Let Your Puppet Do the Talking

Give the child a puppet and take one yourself. Start a conversation between the puppets. Always insist that the youngster ask the questions. Then let the child's puppet continue to ask questions while you give answers without using a puppet. When the child seems comfortable with his puppet, encourage him to talk with a few classmates, using his puppet.

Warm As a Puppy's Welcome

A new student enrolls in the class. Select two friendly welcomers. If possible, pick children who were new last year and, if choice permits, select one who arrived shy and another who always seemed self-assured. Have a meeting. Explain: The newest arrival probably feels like odd-man-out and needs definite friendship acts. Ask the once-shy helper to remember how she felt during the first days at this school. She is to help from that standpoint. Ask the more poised student to remember what she did to make an easy adjustment.

Partners Day

This is a red letter day because each student gets to choose a partner for various activities. Privately suggest to your shy child, "Select a classmate you most want to be like." Almost invariably the shy one will choose a very outgoing youngster.

Fresh Thoughts Dressed in Warm Words

Daily, call shy Sally to your desk and briefly converse. Talk can be of many things. Continue these rendezvous for several weeks before you attempt an evaluation

Speak Out, Little One

Stretch a shy child by exposing him to new demands. Send him on errands to the office or other rooms. Give him oral, not written messages. Inform a close teacher friend of your motives, and ask her to lengthen her conversations with him.

Scuttling the Shyness Shakes!

Too shy to read? Tutor the student separately and ask her to whisper the reading words. Tell her you'll work together daily. Each day you expect her to whisper a little louder and clearer. Then set a goal of two weeks for her to surprise her reading group. Count off the days for her—seven more, six more, five more, and so on.

MAKING SCHOOL MORE
DELIGHTFUL

A senior/junior-partner concept of the teacher–student relationship is in step with present day American life. There's never a question but that the senior partner is boss, but every junior partner is recognized as having full potential and is expected to grow in personality, responsibility, and capability.

All of us need to feel we fit, that we are wanted. And we love to be where the action is. Our first step is to locate the right post, one where our talents are acknowledged and appreciated. Obviously, this move is vital in setting an enthusiastic tone: more than our well-being is at stake. Bruised egos, hurt feelings, fear, or frustration in a teacher take a pervasive toll in her effectiveness to help children enjoy school life.

Include, include, include. Attraction is based on being included. If you would attract children to enjoying the school community, include them not only overtly in daily actions but also silently in your daily thinking. They feel the vibes.

If you'd attract children to the joy of learning, include yourself in a learning role. This doesn't mean simply more university classes and seminars, conferences and lectures. It means honing one's intellectual and cultural curiosity, across the board. Wide reading. Travel. New sports. Strange foods. Astounding, but true, some relatively young teachers today with two masters'-degrees-plus have never been to Washington, D.C., or taken a trip to Europe. Others have never tried a video game or worked on a political campaign. Unbelievable!

Some charming teachers offered these strategies for adding zest—and in some cases, outright exhilaration—to the school day.

Mismatched Sock Day

Special Room 103 days do add to an *esprit de corps*. Let the group decide on a theme such as everyone wearing the same color, a collection of favorite buttons, rope belts, two hats, mismatched mittens or socks.

Curiosity Did What?

Let's hope it also stimulates kids. Have your students, early in the year, list things they would like to learn by June. The focus can also be narrowed to "this fall," "by Christmas," "this semester."

An Affairs-of-State Decision

Each state and most cities have a symbolic flower, tree, bird, and so on; Room 103 may decide to select symbolic emblems. This emblem choosing adds to a group feeling and selecting them makes a good theme for a room meeting or for teaching voting. Obviously, after the choices have been made they should be followed up with student graphics of some sort.

Cupid's Arrow Goes Straight to . . .

Adhesive paper hearts make a nice surprise on Valentine's Day. As each child walks into the room, ask him or her where you should stick the heart: some want it on the cheek, others on a shirt. Youngsters of all ages love the idea. And then there are Halloween, Christmas, and Easter stickers.

Harry and Whiskers

Puppets are great for impersonalizing and dramatizing school and class rules. No one need tell you how they appeal to kids' imaginations and playfulness. Have the puppets talk into your ear, and you relay the information.

Example: Harry and Whiskers have lived in Room 103 for so long they know all the rules. In summer they are confined in a box under the counter. In September after the children arrive they live on the counter top. They are overjoyed because it's great fun watching the class.

Harry is very shy, so he whispers into teacher's ear. He asks her dozens of questions, too. He keeps wanting to know why many rules exist. Whiskers has a physical weakness: noise hurts his ears.

My Cup Runneth Over

Fine tuning a reasonable climate into an excellent one and guiding students toward realizing that each class member is constantly, positively or negatively, contributing to the group is propelled with a graphic example. Take a large goblet or a stemmed, transparent flower vase and drop in a couple of marbles or poker chips. Explain to the children that from time to time, when everyone has been working diligently or has actively contributed to a lesson discussion, you'll drop in a few more. When it will hold no more, the group will have earned a party, an outing, an extra recess.

. . . And Lyrics by Room 103

Have fifth or sixth graders choose a familiar tune and write new lyrics. Before anyone starts writing, elicit a potpourri of ideas from the class on possible thoughts to be conveyed by the new words, writing these ideas on the chalkboard.

"For Whom the Bell Tolls"

Ringing a small bell in the classroom is an idea whose time has returned. In the morning it's a signal for everyone to start working. Use the ball to shift from one activity to another all day. Ring it sparingly for special announcements, but avoid using it to quiet the class. Relying on your cues, why not let a different child do the actual ringing each day?

Shades of Liza Doolittle

A Flower Day can add a nice note of mystery. The children send carnations to each other, unsigned. The teacher collects the funds and marks down the recipient's name. Most teachers would be alert to see that each child received at least one posey. A good fund raiser: Flower price: 25 cents; 10 cents cost and 15 cents to the United Fund (or Red Cross, if you prefer).

Freeze

This is a perennial favorite because the children consider it great fun. When you need the group's attention, call out, "Freeze." Everyone stops as if hit by invisible rays. Speak your piece and then command, "Unfreeze," to get the action going again.

Minutemen to the Rescue

Retell the stories of the original Minutemen. Today's minutemen are room helpers, ready on a moment's notice to carry out tasks and errands. Youngsters return huffing and puffing but proud as punch.

Every Ship Has a Log

Have your students keep a journal. Immediately before each day's dismissal, they are to enter one thing they have learned. Obviously, they enjoy this mounting evidence of their accomplishments.

A Can of Bookworms

Each student starts with a worm's head made from construction paper and, naturally, the worm grows a segment for each book the child reads. Obtain a large cafeteria can and have students decorate it. Kids get a great charge from having their worms grow to the point of dangling over the top of the can.

Two-Way Traffic on a Two-Way Street

Students turn in their work daily; return at least one set of graded papers each day. Show them, don't merely tell them how they are progressing. Simultaneously, you'll be demonstrating that you're prompt in keeping your part of a bargain. Then, if you like, re-collect papers and save them for individual folders.

Happy As a Clam at High Tide

Schedule two daily free periods. Elicit twenty or twenty-five class ideas for possible activities. Discuss briefly why some suggestions are viable and others are not. Then ditto and distribute a list. Schedule about ten minutes in the morning and twenty in the afternoon. Morning session occurs after assigned tasks have been completed; however, before lunch children work alone. Block a definite afternoon period, say 2:00 to 2:20. During this period a child, as he prefers, may work alone or with a partner.

Favorite Subject? Creativity

In this era of back-to-basics, clear this suggestion with your principal first or you will be creating havoc for yourself.

While the students are fresh, morning or afternoon, have a creativity period. Each day, that is. The period should last about thirty to forty minutes, but be flexible here and play it by ear. You'll sense when activities become aimless or listless.

Smooth operating requires having paints, papers, games, records, books, magazines, filmstrips out and in readiness. At first you may have to circulate among students suggesting activities. Children need natural, gradual training on using various devices and in learning to respond to imaginative impulses or discovery leads. Give the project a trial of several weeks before trying to evaluate it. It's a nice alternate for the portion of the class remaining when some go to the computer room, for it is basically exploration oriented.

Blackjack

No coaxing here and it does reinforce addition facts: teach children the card game called blackjack.

Recap the Year in Slides

Take pictures during the year on special events and holidays. Then have a thirty-minute showing the last day of school

—which we know is shot anyway. About twenty to twenty-five slides with pertinent comments make a good program. If you teach at the primary level, why not pass along these slides to middle- and upper-level teachers? In a few years your class will clap its hands in glee when they see the slides again.

Diagnostic, No; Effective, Yes

Let the children choose their initial reading texts in the fall. Surprisingly, between 60 and 75 percent of your class will select the level at which they should be working. Others readily accept your suggested changes.

Example: First, give the class a spiel about using good judgment and not trying to impress anyone. Then, place many readers on a table. If you have a fourth grade, put out easy and difficult third, fourth, and fifth grade texts. Send one row of students to the table at a time.

Land, Sea, or Air

Name reading groups after animals or birds, but with a new flair. Let children go to reading group imitating their animal. Ducks waddle. Lions and tigers stalk. Bunnies hop. Sea gulls flap their wings. Crocodiles snap their jaws but make no noise. Turtles bobble their heads. Don't be afraid of starting a commotion. It won't, especially if there is reasonable control in the basic climate. And the kids love it.

Chattering Teeth or Chattering Children

On a cold day have a warm heart. Let students eat and play in the room in extreme weather. One rule: If children elect to eat in the room, they may leave only for washroom or to get a drink. No frolicking in halls. And no one gets to change his mind and go out.

CONCLUSION

Home is where the heart is and the heart yearns to be where it feels it belongs. Warmth, protection, and a sure foundation stone are essential elements in both a home and a classroom.

Embellishing roll call is a natural way of highlighting the students' feeling of uniqueness and belonging to a group Good manners are, of course, mandatory for a wholesome climate. Emphasizing each student's individuality, worthiness, and importance to the group can be effectively accomplished by persistent, consistent application of small tokens of esteem and inconspicuous strategies. Change doesn't come overnight; it's a matter of gradual growth in teacher and student. Finally, this chapter offered suggestions by practicing teachers on ways for making school more productively pleasant.

Six

SOLVING ATTENDANCE AND RELATED PROBLEMS

A red brick and stone fortress, the newer part completed in 1893, it squatted glowering in a factory neighborhood predominately Slavic. As we stood in the central hallway with its dark woodwork, naked pipes, and extremely high ceiling, we could see stairwells at either end. The teachers had their classes lined up on both sides of the stairs, waiting for the second dismissal bell. Perfect order. Perfect quiet. Perfect patience. The newly assigned principal looked at one end, and then at the other; then she shuddered, and mumbled, "You know, at times I don't think I can take one more day of their docility."

Indeed, wasn't she perceptive to feel the unnaturalness, when it existed, of thoroughly subdued, rather than self-controlled, children? And honest, for refusing to take pride in the "order"? Let's take heart and remember her remark the next time our children charge into the building as if they're playing a new game called "Storming the Bastille." Of course, that's unhealthy, too. When children have developed a natural self-control, there will still be a few wiggles, giggles, and dropped books, but the general tone is orderly.

In this chapter we'll consider the processes and problems related to students' arrival and departure, tardiness, lockers, halls and stairs, absence, and dismissals. Making and enforcing general rules covering these situations, coupled with prompt handling of deviants, are most valuable for increasing stability in the scene—until eventually some things "just aren't done in our school."

PUNCTUALITY

"Punctuality is the politeness of kings," and indeed, a hallmark of consideration. Since it's a habit, and a habit which involves thinking ahead a trifle, the underlying correction to tardiness is recognizing the importance of promptness and learning to allow leeway for the unexpected. This leeway helps anyone arrive *s'arranger* as the French would say (to have oneself organized, prepared).

Of course you know it's important to start the class as a unit each morning—on time. It keeps our thinking clearer if we remember, even when thoroughly exasperated with a tardy student, that insisting on promptness has its greatest value in helping a child learn group or community feeling and *his rightful place* as a responsible member.

In some homes every family member is on a different schedule, or none at all. Some children have little opportunity to observe that society considers time valuable. Thus, they need coaching—perhaps coaxing—into learning this fact of life. The growth will help them fit into the world as they'll find it—not as they would have it, not as we would have it, but as it is.

Whether shuffling down a rubbish-strewn alley or ambling through a meadow, almost every child is accompanied on his way to school by a sprite riding on his shoulder. The sprite's name? Curiosity. School bells seem very abstract when Curiosity whispers, "Is that a baby chipmunk under the broken branch? No, silly, it's a baby mouse. Let's see where he lives." And the next thing—our friend has collected another tardy slip.

Here are some suggestions which gifted and sympathetic teachers have offered to share.

Hurry Up? For What?

If tardiness is prevalent, try a two-pronged approach. Issue slips or checks, whatever the system is; and second, make the first fifteen minutes of school especially inviting, that is, daily read aloud from a fascinating children's story or have students choral read appealing poetry. Habitually tardy youngsters are not going to rush toward punctuality if they know they'll be assigned preschool math problems.

A Dillar, a Dollar, a Ten O'Clock Scholar

Tardiness is a chronic affliction of his life? Send a note home. Ask the lad to return it the next morning—signed. If it doesn't come back, send another note. If number two note doesn't come back immediately, phone the parents.

4 × T = 40

T stands for tardy slip, 4 stands for the number of days a particular student has received one, and the 40 represents a forty-minute make-up period before, during recess, or after school.

Countersigning the Record

Ditto a tardy form (see the sample in Figure 6-1) and let the class secretary maintain records in a small file box. *Caution:*

Figure 6-1

Date _____	TARDY
Date _____	
Date _____	
Minutes Late _____	
Reason _____	
Signed _____	
Student	

Don't attempt this process until you have reasonable control of the group.

An Offender States Her Case

The office discipline form makes no provision for student offender input. One teacher simply has the student write in a brief description of the error and recommend a penalty. (See Figure 6-2.) Almost always, the students suggest harsher punishments than the faculty would impose. At first, the teacher was alone in his adaptation; now other teachers are following the example.

Figure 6-2

```
VALHALLA CONSOLIDATED SCHOOL
          Discipline Notice
_____

Offense         Student:                  Room:
Date: 10/18       GEORGIA BROWN            103
_____

Notice     Time:           Referring Teacher:
Date: 10/18    9:00 A.M.      DAN STEFANILO
_____

Offense: LATE FOR CLASS 5 X's IN 2 WEEKS (D.S.)

I was late for class more times        (G.B.)
than Mr. Stefanilo allows. I suggest 3 hours
                                      after school.
Disposition:
_____



_____



_____


                              Administrator
```

MISSION: ESCORT

Kenny lived nearby but always arrived after 9:00, and often he claimed his mother was responsible. Soon his teacher started checking the playground at 8:50. If Kenny was not there, she phoned his home. If he had departed, she sent a dependable child to the corner to meet and hustle him. The second child was to go no farther than a corner she could watch from her classroom window, and consequently the second child was not off school grounds unsupervised. Obviously, such an arrangement should be cleared through the office.

Promptness in Other Times and Places

As constructive deterrents for a chronically tardy student, please consider these assignments.

1. Have her list interesting occupations that require an acute sense of timing or promptness. A few examples: a dynamite expert, jet pilot, astronaut, movie stunt person. Classmates may help; twenty-five occupations is a very long list.

2. Have him describe the importance that television shows place on precise timing. What would happen if the child's favorite star arrived twenty minutes after the show was on camera? Or, answered a cue ten minutes late?

3. Ask her to research time zones in an encyclopedia and then describe what life must have been like before they were established. Or, have her research Greenwich time and the twenty-four-hour measurement system.

4. Have him describe what might happen to a counterspy who arrived ten minutes late for a secret rendezvous.

5. Structure a hypothetical situation. An international pilot is careless about a few minutes here and a few minutes there. As a result he runs fifteen minutes short on fuel over the Atlantic Ocean and must ditch the airplane. Have the student look up ditching and tell you about it.

DAWDLING AT LOCKERS

Nuisance locker problems tend to disappear as students grow older, but while they're prevalent they add an element of boring waiting for the rest of the class. Brief remarks combined with one of the following actions shorten the dallying.

Locker Lockout

The group has learned the rules, but a few exceptions are still slamming doors, dawdling, or fighting. Deny them their lockers for a short time. Have them keep coats, mufflers, rubbers, mittens, and caps at their seats. Insist they not bother other students by allowing personal belongings to spread or scatter.

On Your Mark, Get Set, Go

One day keep locker dawdlers in at recess. Using a timer, let them practice coat-cap-boot routine.

Aye, Aye, Right Away

Tap a dawdler for line captain, front or rear. Still another slowpoke? Make him door holder. It does speed them up.

Please, Teacher, It's an Individual Difference

Think it over carefully. Sometimes the kindest way of coping with dawdling is to allow the slowpoke to go to his locker ahead of the class.

The Girls We Left Behind

After slowpokes have been warned several times, one day suddenly announce that they will not have recess; instead they are to report to Room 110. While there, they may color or read

a library book. In nice weather you only have to pull this once
. . . in nasty weather this could boomerang.

ABSENCES

Particularly among younger students you may find a few
who have vague "tummyaches" and other semiauthentic reasons for staying home frequently. Perhaps the home errs on the
side of protectiveness but rarely can you say anything, at least
directly.

We're well aware that excessive absence is most prevalent
among children who are not succeeding. Which came first, the
chicken or the egg? Lack of success brings on lack of interest
and lack of interest (or diligence) brings on lack of success. The
first priority for long-range correction is to fortify the child's
confidence, insist that he learn to do something well. One immediate step to counteract excessive doubtful absences is to
casually and sincerely remind him of his deprivation. Perhaps,
when the class is discussing yesterday's movie, add, "Oh, that's
right, Jeremiah, you missed it. I'm sorry you didn't get to see
it." This type of remark, made low key and consistently, usually helps.

Most schools have well-defined practices for handling absences, but here are a few room ideas teachers have offered for
your consideration.

At Least He's Got Something to Do

The class secretary maintains absence records in a file box.
Ditto some forms for him, and let him remind returning absen-
tees about bringing written excuses (see Figure 6-3). Having the
student countersign the absence slip has a salutary effect.

Absence Makes the Heart Grow Fonder

Tell wandering, class-cutting students that you missed
them and you want to know them better. They now have an invitation to your very exclusive Morning Club. Since it's only

Figure 6-3

Date _____   ABSENCE
Day absent _____
Reason _____
_____
Written excuse from home   Yes _____ No _____
Signed _____ Student

polite to be prompt for this social event, ask them to arrive when you do in the morning. Inasmuch as they missed an earlier feast of knowledge, let them nourish their minds by studying.

French Leave?

You suspect the absent student is truant. Call his home. If he's not there, ask the home not to mention your call. When he returns to class, ask him for an explanation. If he tells the truth, apply sanctions mildly. If he lies, take firmer action.

Swapping One Hour for Another, Plus

If a child cuts class within a week or so of an all-school event, keep him in the classroom—or deposit him on the office bench—on the special day. Explain to him that you're cutting into his time because he cut out—but he is paying the additional price of missing the festivity.

HALLS AND STAIRS

Halls reveal the atmosphere of a school, or so say many experts, with passing periods between classes providing especially significant clues. One thing—if, at a period's end, students burst out of a room like a lid coming off a steam kettle, they probably have been under tension in the classroom with little real learning taking place. If they amble and scuffle out, they are more apt to have had a productive class.

Most teachers are expected to monitor the door and greet arriving students. Though the few minutes between classes can be incredibly precious for picking up loose ends and miscellaneous details, teachers are, in the long run, wise to adhere to this regulation. First, it announces, nonverbally, the teacher's alertness; he is at the helm, controlled and organized. Second, he can observe the condition of students, and adjust to them if they're arriving tense. There are three different ways of handling a tense-on-arrival class. One, let them chirp and chatter momentarily. Two, talk to them yourself. That is, talk about topics not related to your subject or the day's work. Keep on talking until you sense a calmed-down climate. The third, and best, is making a humorous remark that gets them laughing. Laughter breaks tension, quickly and surely.

Here are a few suggestions teachers made when I questioned them about halls and stairs. In several cases you'll notice the manner and type of remark made by the teacher lifts an exhortation from a reprimand to a friendly reminder.

Preempt Their Stance

When you encounter a cluster of students horsing around in the hall, try, "I hate this school. I can't even walk down the lousy halls without some jokers bothering me." Briefly, ever so briefly, they're speechless. You've lifted favorite words. Then they'll usually start chattering and will cooperate with any additional comments or advice.

Cozy Cuddling

A boy-girl combo is too close for good taste. Speak to the boy: "If I take Janet's fingerprints, I don't want to get yours." They'll respond to this hint without embarrassment and without resentment.

Your Physical Welfare Is Important

Stop a running youngster. In mock seriousness ask him if his insurance is paid. Give him a flamboyant, tongue-in-cheek reason for your question. No longer are you stopping kids just because of building rules; rather, you have a growing concern about student health and physical welfare. In this case, the child has you so worried it might interfere with your sleep!

Down the Stairs at Eighteen Knots!

Knotted ropes make a great training aid for teaching primary and middle grade students how to form and keep straight lines, evenly paced and spaced. It is also useful for getting younger children across a street safely.

Example: You have 18 boys and 23 girls in the room. Take two lengths of rope, putting 18 knots in one, and 23 knots in the other. Each time students line up, have them use the rope as a spacer. During the first weeks of training have them walk from the classroom to the building front door, each child holding his knot.

Early on, start testing their progress. Use the rope to form lines and then leave it in the room. Next, have them form lines without using the rope, then test their sense of spacing by measuring with the rope.

A Note About Student Hall Guards

Until it becomes the mode for schools to install surveillance TV cameras, there will be two types of student hall guard systems, stationary and roving. The roving squad can be much smaller (for example, three or four students per period for a junior high enrollment of 800) than a stationary guard. Naturally, rovers are free to ferret pupils out of favorite building hideaways—which change quickly from week to week. One drawback, the roving squad is constantly being challenged by teachers who don't realize which students are on duty for a specific period. Most youngsters prefer carrying a badge or an impressively worded identifying card to wearing an arm band.

The stationary crew is larger (for example, eight or ten students each period for an enrollment of 800). Class-cutting students are more wary of stationary crews; it's harder not to get caught. Training the student who occupies the front door station *to stand up* as he cordially and courteously greets visitors impresses them greatly. As we think about this standing up, it's more than showing respect for elders; it's a move we all make in our own homes.

Student monitors in lunch rooms are rarely effective.

Usually, hall guards have earned the privilege of office through good citizenship. One balanced plan is to choose them on a yearly basis, but then switch their duty periods more frequently—at least at semester break. Everyone welcomes the change.

BATHROOM AND FOUNTAIN

Although the term "bathroom recess" started as a school euphemism, many children have adroitly revamped the session into an accurate phrase: they get into lavatories and play. One thing you'll notice is that if bathroom recess comes after outdoor play, the children often fiddle and diddle and it takes them fifteen minutes. Try taking the class to the lavatory five minutes prior to outdoor recess. Certainly, while the weather is nice, this order of events works well to speed matters along.

Here are several ways different teachers have learned to handle bathroom and drinking fountain requests.

Control on the Ledge

When no group bathroom break is scheduled, cards can effectively control traffic. Have one marked "B" and the other marked "G." Place these on a front chalkboard ledge. When a child leaves the classroom, he simply turns a card over. Never more than one boy and one girl are gone at a given time. When the cards are removed from the ledge, it means no one has lavatory/fountain privilege. These times include one hour after school has started, morning and afternoon, and during important tests or group discussions.

How Many Minutes? Let's Count

"May I go to the bathroom?" peeps a little voice. "May I get a drink of water?" Is the need real? Say pleasantly, "Yes, you may go, but you'll have to make up the time." Many inquirers then change their minds about the trip. Still, you haven't said "No." Always, there'll be a few students for whom you'll have to make the decision.

Boys Enter the Door Marked BOYS

This seems like nonsense to some students for at home everyone uses the same bathroom. So, if a youngster tries to peek into the girls' washroom, you must handle it, but treat it lightly. You might require him to write a paragraph on why his school needs a supply of boys' hair bows and ribbons. Thus, you're not making a federal case of an impish impulse, yet the girls feel you have "done something" about the unwelcome eyes.

Count Slowly for Your Friends

Assign one student to hold the drinking fountain handle for everyone. Have her count to three while each classmate sips. In hot weather increase the count to ten.

Two by Two

If the class doesn't have a group bathroom break, send students in pairs to the bathroom and for a long drink. A disobedient child loses this privilege for a period, say a week, two weeks, a month. Make an exception if you're taking the class somewhere, for example, to an assembly.

DISMISSAL

Time to go home! As early as 1919 some thoughtful educators were objecting to the "outmoded" practice of lining up children by classroom membership when they are leaving or entering the building. Certainly we can feel the humanity of their intentions, though in many schools we must realize the impracticality of the total freedom—chaos?—which their advice implies. In government we have the concepts of pure democracy and the pragmatics of politics, the art of the possible; in schools, along with concepts of pure and maximum individual development, we must have professional realism, the art of the possible, for a given set of circumstances.

Since procedural training in the mechanics of arrival and dismissal are most important in the lower and middle years, most of the suggestions included are pointed toward those age groups. However, the detailed information on dismissing a class row by row is applicable for any grade level at any time of day.

Casual clusters or a formal line? If a teacher sincerely objects to regimenting children, let's ask her to consider thoughtfully the overall picture and her alternatives. Students do need a continuity of ground rules from year to year. Thus, if her colleagues who believe in line-ups are in the majority, surely she can flexibly go along with the consensus of opinion. In such a case she certainly may explain to the children her personal feelings, but that she also is deferring to the faculty decision and will insist on adherence to the rules because it is fairer for everyone concerned. Other professionals follow this mode of not breaking ranks.

Here are some suggestions for handling the fluster and flutter which occurs in most classrooms near dismissal time. You'll notice there's nothing mysterious about them.

Didn't You Hear the Bell, Teacher?

Yap, yap, yap . . . Don't nag about that noise the last few minutes. Once or twice, ask the students to be quiet. Still chittering? Go to your desk and start marking papers. Show no concern over conditions, but when the bell rings, ignore it. Soon your charges will worry and inquire about leaving. Explain they will be quiet and orderly for three, four, or five minutes before you give permission to leave.

Keep It Under Your Hat

Ask children to insert important notes and notices under their caps, in their mittens, or better still, in their boots.

Stapler Security

Several papers are destined for home today? Fold them in half and staple them together. This way a child won't lose one paper, or perhaps drop it while crossing a street and run back to retrieve it.

Going-Home Groups in Little Circles

Cluster students according to the direction from school in which they live . . . bus children, railroad crossing children, and so on. Have children collect their coats and boots from lockers and sit in their respective clusters to don them.

Homework Assignment: Zippers and Boots

Send each home a letter (see Figure 6-4) about primary pupil's vital need to personally manage his outer clothing with an absolute minimum of assistance. Eagerly, most parents want to help, and if they cooperate here, it will in turn add about fifteen minutes a day to real school activities.

Along the Line-up Wall

When forming lines for dismissal, instead of repeatedly asking students to be quiet, consider giving them something on which they may focus attention. Along the wall where they stand and at child's eye level, place long cardboard strips which display unusual magazine or newspaper pictures. (Several upper class students might enjoy drawing signed cartoons for this project.) Rarely do students line up in the same order, so they'll find the pictures interesting for a week or two. *Caution:* Use paste and the kids won't fiddle with the display. If you tack up

Figure 6-4

Dear Parents,

Winter is fast approaching and you are probably getting out the boots and snow pants. This is a good time to have practice sessions at home before the first big snowfall.

A child needs patience and practice in learning to coordinate. Does your child need to know about zippers at the bottom cuff of the snow pants? Does he understand about pulling it over the heel of his shoe? Does he know how to pull his boots on over his regular school shoes?—how to fasten the boots?—how to take off his boots alone?—quickly?

There are still mittens, hats, caps, sweaters, and scarves unmarked. Please help us keep the children's outfits intact.

Thank you very much for your cooperation.

The Primary Teachers

the material, your carefully chosen pictures won't prove as stimulating to the imaginative as a fresh source of pins.

Footsteps From Behind

The sound may not be mysterious but students know surveillance is taut. During dismissal let a student captain do the leading. Obviously, this frees you to gather dawdlers and forgetters of treasured trinkets and needed books, and to close the door. The expedition to the front door should be broken into sections, and the cardinal rule for segment length is: How far can you, teacher, see? Instruct the line captain, "Lead the class to the end of the hall and wait." When you catch up, then say, "Lead the group down one flight of stairs and wait until you get the next signal."

Paradise Lost and Regained

Many comprehensively thoughtful teachers are very slow to deny recess because a child physically needs the exercise. Also, getting outside is a mental break, as important to the student as the lounge is to a faculty member. Occasionally, an unruly child has lost his recess. Ask the teacher with yard duty to require him to sit on the sidelines and watch . . . and then for the last few minutes, let him romp, too. Not only will play time be more precious to him, but a more relaxed, refreshed child will return to the classroom.

CONCLUSION

Smooth methods and harmonious mechanics for getting a class in and out of the classroom, the lavatory, and the building hold their greatest importance in releasing time and energy for more rewarding pursuits. School is surely more interesting when the mundane is minimal.

An individual's habit of chronic tardiness can be costly to him in later years, but it's also costly in time and an imposition on the classroom climate right now. Rarely is it caused by deep-seated rebellion. Imaginative ways for alleviating this tendency help, but most of all it takes persistent application of pressure by interested adults.

The next facet we considered was absence, especially excessive absence for nebulous reasons. In our attempts to moderate it, we must first examine underlying reasons, because this problem can be dissolved only at the source. Usually, it's intimately connected with a feeling of lack of success, either in school work or in personal relationships. A few children simply want to play Peter Pan; they resist growing up because home is less demanding.

Halls indicate the ethos of a school. Almost every experienced teacher and educator can accurately judge a building the moment he opens the front door. Courteous, efficient hall guards enhance a school's reputation, inside and outside the premises.

Dismissal procedures are not traditional (read *regimented*) or modern (read *casual*) only because of personal faculty preference. Usually the staff's professional decision considers the total environment of the school and neighborhood and adjusts accordingly. Parents in many areas respect a school code that requires students to file in and out of the building in orderly fashion on arrival and dismissal. And again, some superior schools can and should extend a more casual freedom in entering or leaving a building if the parents have prepared the children for handling the increased liberty.

Seven

USING STUDENT RECOGNITION FOR PROMOTING DISCIPLINE

Since we're all benign and discerning teachers—well, aren't we—we're acutely aware of each student's primary need to realize his native worth. His identity is distinct, expansive, and expanding. Necessarily, school work emphasizes a restricted value standard, and the best of achievement and aptitude tests are limited. None fully measures nonacademic intelligence, talents, and qualities, yet motives and desire, responsibility, persistence, stamina, flexibility, and self-confidence are prime ingredients in any life success story.

Once Albert Einstein advised in effect, "Be a man of quality and success will follow." Quality workmanship is always in demand, whether it is clear, concise, comprehensive thinking; master craftsmanship; or thoughtful and gracious customer service. Building with superior habits establishes the solid foundation which lends itself to supporting, and sturdily supporting, future projects, regardless of their nature.

In this chapter we'll consider helping students hone their life ambitions wisely. Encouraging ordinary students to reach out and up can often be accomplished by explaining the limitations of formal, standardized tests. Following this topic are a number of suggestions for giving student recognitions a fresh slant. Next are strategies especially apt for slow or discouraged children; some of these add zip to anyone's school life.

GENIUS SOMETIMES WEARS A MASK

Periodically, we meet a student who expresses unrealistically high life goals, or so it seems. Please, let's not be too sure of our appraisal. Our indulgent smile or damning with faint praise could chill the aspirations of a daydreaming mental giant. During these years we may be the only person he can talk to freely.

Let's not play God. No matter how much insight we believe we have, let's counsel him humbly and gently. First, have him examine his motives, honestly. If false pride, surface prestige, or hero worship has undue influence, help him reexamine his propellant so tactfully that he doesn't realize he's been corrected. Sound goals require a sound basis.

Second, help him nourish his dreams quietly. Caution him to keep his affairs in Egypt . . . especially while his aspirations are nebulous. Several good reasons dictate this move: his cronies and family, classmates and cranks, will spout advice, and many will be spouting from their own limited horizons. Even advisors who carry credentials can be mistaken. Let's remember that an experienced Ellis Island immigration inspector admitted Charles Steinmetz, now considered an electrical engineering genius, with great misgivings. More directly applicable, Charles Darwin and Winston Churchill were real headaches to their schoolmasters. Thomas Alva Edison's teachers sadly shook their heads and decided that this kid was a nerd, a real loser. And how about the law school dean who advised Earl Warren, later Chief Justice, to forget law? However, turning back to our aspiring young friend, as he moves forward some of his present companions will choose to linger behind, and his progress may provoke the hostility of envy. Strange, but true. If they're unaware of his higher goals, they'll be less tempted to torpedo his daily successes with snide remarks. As a youth Harry Truman used to quietly leave Independence and go over to Kansas City to read in the libraries and enjoy the art museums; wisely, he said little or nothing about these trips to his neighbors.

Naturally, directing our student's attention to pertinent trends and fresh information concerning his goals is kind.

But, most essential, we can help our student set up realistic, intermediate steps leading to his private ambitions—well-planned levels including several points at which he could stop entirely, or shift goals, and not lose his original investment of time and effort—or lose face. These ascending steps also stimulate indirect benefits.

1. A gradual change of mental and physical environment, expanded horizons. New opportunities do surface. Often a youngster discovers an occupation, previously unknown to him, which would have eluded his attention completely had he not embarked on his "impossible dream."

2. A cultivated, daily persistence, a building outlook that yields to a success spiral.

3. A tendency to appreciate his known capacity. Often this, in turn, unfreezes more talents.

4. Achievement in grappling with increasingly difficult problems.

Is this rather heady anticipation appropriate? Studies repeatedly show the advantages accruing to children with clearly defined goals; when undefined desire is changed into defined desire, it gains power in application. Many students daydream of stardom in a vacuous sort of way, but rare is the child who targets too high and seriously expects to reach it in one *grande jetée*. If you encounter one, look for a pushing parent. Then perhaps a little open-minded counseling is in order. Referring again to Professor Einstein, he was convinced each educated person should have two modes of earning a living, a trade and a profession. Confident competence in one doesn't conflict with the other.

THE YEARNING MIDDLEBROW

Any group will listen, but average and low average students warmly welcome a succinct but solid explanation of the limitations of IQ tests. Instinctively, and by professional training, teachers know that IQ tests are almost tunnel vision in the announced results. The class doesn't know this. But, they've been well aware from the first grade on—no matter how euphonious the names—of the ranking order of the bluejays, cardinals, and sea gulls.

A tactful but sincere discussion clears the air. You might explain how these tests are tilted for a verbal student. Individual scores can vary up to 30 points and more; certainly, no teacher would be remiss to cite a case of radically changed scores. Moreover, these tests don't provide an accurate reading on a clever imagination, on artistic or mechanical talents . . . not to mention other types of intelligence.

Current research on the multi-faceted nature of intelligence backs you to the hilt. Project Zero at Harvard University has identified seven types of intelligence: *linguistic*—writers, poets, orators; *logical*—mathematicians; *music*—composers; *bodily movement*—dancers, athletes; *spatial*—sculptors, surveyors; *interpersonal (understanding others)*—religious leaders, politicians; *intrapersonal (understanding oneself)*. Tests measuring these types of intelligence are in the developmental stage, and it will take several years to refine them.

This background information is face-saving for children whose gifts lie in other directions, and for a few, this news would bring their first glint of hope.

Intuitively, many students feel cursed with mediocrity; grading on the curve reinforces a warped horizon. A low average student often wearies in faithfully holding to duty; he feels nameless and faceless. Generally he behaves or is simply docile, so he reaps no individual attention there—yet the glory of outstanding grades is not his, and he knows they probably never will be. Like any human being anywhere, he craves to be distinctive.

This type of student usually responds well to the following technique. He happens to mention an interesting, obscure fact pertinent to the group's discussion—something you did not know. Pause. Then emphasize his contribution by very plainly announcing, "Class, listen to this. I just learned something from Tommy, and I want you to hear it, too. Tell us again, Tommy." If you keep your voice tone low-key rather than effusive, you'll run less risk of embarrassing him and simultaneously, the compliment will be more convincing. Believe me, Tommy will glow.

As classmates witness constant recognition of the not-so-clever Tommy's step-by-step gains, it puts life into flaccid hopes and loosens fetters of gnawing futility feelings the average child has about his chances of ever being really outstanding. School becomes more acceptable because it appears more genuinely, across-the-board, accepting. Top-notch scholarship and athletic agility are not synonyms for individual worth; we know this, but students need concrete reminders.

Now, and in the future, every child is capable of expressing his heritage of freedom to obey his enlightened conscience within the restraints of law-abiding reason. Mentioning law-abiding reason leads us into the subject of teacher-reasoning. Some of it is rather strange, isn't it. Or maybe it's semantics, but for instance, teachers speak of "giving grades." No teacher is issued a coffer of A's, B's, and C's, hers to distribute according to whim. Giving grades? Yet we know that students' grades have their real source in student learning participation and accomplishment, not in the teacher's beneficence. Thus a more precise wording or thinking, reflecting an earned reward, suggests a term such as "issuing" or "recording" grades. Focusing on the nuances here, we promote our grading skill to its healthiest perspective and clearest light. (Also see student report card protest in Chapter 2.)

RECOGNITIONS

Well-seasoned, traditional awards and positions of esteem which fit classroom tenor and tempo may include new accents. These are:

- *Tasks performed for the teacher.* Switch them around. Give the most difficult chores to average students so they may practice thinking on their feet. (Sometimes it's natural to tell the child that ordinarily you give this task only to an A student but . . . a new day has come.) Then use slow students for average tasks. Yes, this leaves bright students with the repetitious, but they usually enjoy school anyway.

- *Honor roll.* Print lists for the behavior and grade elite as always. Add another list for the up-and-coming crowd. Please don't title it Greatest Improvement; it's apt but so hackneyed. Put an imagination feather in your thinking cap and create a new acronym such as YAPPIES, Young and Promising Pupils . . . you finish it. (Chatterers or yappers can become YAPPIES.)

- *Responsibility in room.* Well-performed duties are acclaimed by letting a student name his successor to office.

- *Citizenship recognition.* Teams and a point system are typical approaches. In Chapter 3 you'll find award forms.

- *Student tutor.* Instead of asking the brightest students, try an average student. Asking him to help another when he finishes his lesson almost certainly will quicken his study pace.

Here is a collection of fresher ways to recognize hard work.

Many Hands Make Light Work

Tapping students for classroom duties is older than Horace Mann; the concept of having every single class member on a chore assignment at a given time is more recent. Is it wise? Well, that depends. Everyone is included, great! But rotating chores can also be all-inclusive. Student-performed tasks do take more time and can interfere with a flowing momentum. Keeping some jobs in reserve gives a teacher an interesting selection of spontaneous recognitions, a surprise element for the deserving.

At any rate, here's a partial listing of possible tasks:

- *Host monitor.* Greets visitors by rising and going to the door to welcome them. If the teacher so directs, he offers them a chair.

- *Errand monitor.* Carries all messages to office and to other classrooms.

- *Pencil monitor.* Collects stray pencils from the floor, sharpens pencils, and empties sharpener.

- *Workbook monitor.* Collects and returns workbooks.

- *Bird/animal/fish monitor.* Feeds the creatures and cleans the receptacles.

- *Milk and cracker monitor(s).* Distributes snack and collects cartons.

- *Science table/center monitor.* Arranges displays of new materials and equipment and keeps them tidy.

- *Library table/center monitor.* Keeps books orderly and arranges new displays.

- *Art supplies monitor.* Keeps tools clean and in good working condition, restocks paper, mixes paints, and provides needed materials for special processes.

- *Plant and flower monitor.* Waters and feeds plants. Arranges bouquets, changes water, and discards flowers.

- *Locker/cloakroom monitor.* Checks for and follows through on getting children to hang outer garments, clip boots together with clothes pins, and stuff mittens into pockets when they are dried.

- *Wastepaper monitor.* Empties room basket when it is full.

- *Dusting monitor.* Dusts room and returns scattered items.

- *Corrected papers monitor.* Passes back all corrected papers.

- *Roll call monitor.* Takes daily attendance.

- *Window and shade monitor.* Opens or closes windows and adjusts shades.

- *Light and door monitor.* Switches lights. Opens and closes classroom doors.

- *Chalkboard and eraser monitor(s).* Cleans board and claps erasers.
- *Desk monitor.* Inspects desks for reasonable neatness.
- *Flag monitor.* Leads group in saying the Pledge of Allegiance.

A for Art, B for Bulletin Board, C for Children

Everyone knows you do nice bulletin boards; everyone knows you're busy. Everyone does not realize that students from the fourth grade up can create and mount some striking boards. One approach: Choose a theme and elicit design and caption ideas from the class. Suggest they search further in magazines, and, more important, talk it over at family dinner time. Each student with an idea makes a simple pencil sketch. You may alter, refine, or simplify . . . students never seem to mind. Select a winner.

Execution: Winner names one or two classmates as co-workers. Advise the winner in advance that you must ratify his choice; thus he should select cooperative friends who will stay on target. Usually it's prudent for you to work at your desk while they are cutting, measuring, mounting; beyond that, expect to stay out of it. Naturally, you'd add a word if they're in a tight spot. Please do try your class several times before you pass judgment; by the third time, you'll be thrilled. This project markedly leavens a group pride in "our room."

"I Did My Best Today" Button

Make a large supply of stringed tags or buttons which read I DID MY BEST TODAY. Distribute these during the last ten minutes of school. At first be generous. Give one to almost everyone. After a few days raise your standards gradually. By this time the child will be questioned when he comes home without a tag.

Guest Lecturer in Another Classroom

This privilege plum is rather a natural if a student has done a particularly nice job on a project or report. It's also an effective strategy to reward a troublesome child who is coming around the corner.

Ending a Well-Spent Day

Rainy, steamy days make it harder to hold to diligence. You might announce to the class: Those who feel proud of their work today—you who think you've done your best in spite of the weather—may get your coats first this afternoon. Sometimes an imp will try to weasel his way with the forerunners, but the class will boo him back into the seat. Occasionally, a child will be overly severe in judging himself, and you'll need to intercede.

Everyone Has a Best!

Surprise children one day with an ego-stroking display. Take a set of creative writing papers, and on each child's story underline your favorite sentence or idea. Make no other comments or marking. Mount papers on a bulletin board, one for each class member. Add a large caption such as *Look at My Best.* Then sit back and watch joy light the children's eyes when they realize what's happened.

Tempting as it might be to exhibit only the group's best work when it's your turn to fill the lobby display case, remember that way is terribly traditional. Your teachmanship and not your showmanship got you your post originally. Now, if you show only the best student work, you'll be letting showmanship and a touch of personal vanity rule your decision. Surely by listening to your intuition and tapping your professional skill you'll find more inclusive standards. Perhaps make your display choices of the most cooperative students or the most polite-to-their-classmates youngsters' work. Place a small sign in the display announcing this fact. Parents and children alike appreciate the sign. This notice may get you off the hook if your principal would react to a public display of mediocre work with a "Ye gods, what will that teacher in 103 do next!"

RECOGNITIONS FOR
SLOWER STUDENTS

Praise them. Praise them. Praise them. How many times have you heard it? Yet how, exactly, is the best way to praise? When? What is best to single out for compliments?

Praising a child in glowing, sweeping remarks, "Jenny, you're an angel, an unmatchable jewel," may scare Jenny. She innately knows she doesn't deserve unlimited star billing, and she's afraid of it, so she'll intentionally try to blow it. Reduce the praise scope to, "Jenny, you were an angel for giving up your Easter basket to your homebound classmate," and you'll make Jenny comfortably happy. This second bouquet calls for no further action or proof. So obviously, the first point in praising is *be specific* and then leave no dragging ribbons or strings on which Jenny could, or thinks she could, trip.

What to praise? Naturally, at times a comment like, "Jenny, that's a might pretty blouse you're wearing," will be just the thing. Often it's better to praise an act rather than flatter an appearance. Compliment the child on her actions—especially when she has shown worthy motives—*without moralizing.* Earmark her actions which strengthen her individuality, independent thinking, kindness to an equal, truth-telling. These can mean more to her personal development than her classroom helpfulness to a teacher, which sometimes stems from docile conformity or even servility. Spotlighting attention on Jenny's worthy motive and/or spirited actions means focusing on aspects over which Jenny has conscious control, and she knows it.

When to praise? Who doesn't like to have his virtues hailed in front of his most cherished friends.

Let's consider several indirect ways in which a teacher can praise—e.g., by actions such as placing trust, by accepting a youngster's action or suggestion as having real merit, even by taking his advice. Again, letting the child's peers know of her strengths adds a resonant dimension to her improved feelings of self-worth. The following suggestions were offered by expert teachers who enjoy exceptional rapport and success with slow students.

Quiz Maker—Not Quiz Taker

Low average students get a particular thrill from having their questions used in a quiz. Often while the class is taking the test, you'll hear a young voice quietly squeal, "Ooooh, that's my question she used."

Announce a quiz two days ahead. Everyone who composes a good quiz with correct answers will automatically get a grade check and be excused from the classroom test. These questions go into a pool from which you draw in compiling the quiz. As you introduce this arrangement, a few students will mutter, "There's a catch here somewhere. What is it?" There are no tricks involved. The purpose of a quiz is to get students to study, and if they pore over the unit carefully enough to compose good questions, they will have reviewed the material thoroughly enough to satisfy requirements.

One More R—Reliability

She is accurate and responsible . . . let her know it. Having her record grades in a supplementary marking book informs the group of her standing. If you plan to rotate this privilege, inform the student before she starts the assignment, thus closing the door to possible hurt feelings.

Rank Hath Power and Privilege

Usually upperclassmen enjoy listening to first graders read orally, on a one-to-one basis. Of course, make arrangements via the big brown desk, but start your program on a schedule of one twenty-minute period per week. Expand as you deem prudent. Little ones are thrilled with praise from anyone as cosmopolitan and discerning as a sixth grader. Older children, particularly slow students, feel grateful and much stronger for the experience.

Mi Amigo Simpático

Occasionally, the most fitting child in a room to help a poor reader is a mediocre reader. Although poor students tend to have low frustration points, many of them relish the more relaxed feeling, are more willing to chance a mistake, while being observed by a less than brilliant classmate.

One Swipe of the Eraser . . . and It's Gone

Let a child call the order of this week's spelling word test. Choose a captain, perhaps the student who made the biggest improvement this week in your current promotion campaign, be it neatness, not butting in line, or staying in assigned seat. Send him to the board on which you've written this week's words. He erases a word and then the class must write it. After the class has learned the game, he may erase words in any order he elects.

Author's note: This strategy is a real winner among youngsters.

"Listen My Children and You Shall Hear . . ."

If you maintain a chart for credit on library books read, include the nonreader, too. Give him the same amount of credit if he listens attentively to a classmate reading the book aloud. The reading child gets his much needed oral reading practice and the slow student gets a check for doing his best.

Classic Status Symbols

Gold stars may be old-fashioned and pedestrian to you, but they put sparkle in the eyes of low level math students. Give them stars for 100 percent papers. Poorer students haven't received many awards at school so they treasure the pure gold and pure silver. (Better students enjoy the surprise of imaginative decals.) It's best not to use stars every day—save them for more difficult assignments.

English Once Looked Like Swahili

Slow readers are overwhelmed with the many words they can't read on a page, but they often forget how far they have progressed. If a student seems discouraged, show him a book written in a foreign language and ask him to start reading. Of course, he won't be able to read a word. Then show him his current reader and have him count all the words he knows on one page. Remind him that, just a year or two ago, the book in English looked as formidable as the foreign text does now.

Sighting Through His Periscope

Though a student may have fallen short of your expectations, still he has gained in knowledge. Emphasize this growth by grading on a plus system rather than a minus schedule. Mark correct answers and then give him a + 8 on the page top for eight problems well done. A variation: Many math teachers grade papers on a 24/36 system: the 24 stands for correct answers and the 36 represents the total number assigned. Actually, this gives the student a most precise picture.

Slower Students With a Handwriting Flair

We habitually give academically gifted students special creative writing assignments and talented art students drawing projects. Consider this. If you have a poor or mediocre student with a promising, graceful stroke in penmanship, call her aside. Explain that with more practice she could have the best handwriting in the room. Ask her if she would like extra practice lessons to do at home. Invariably, you will receive a grateful "Yes."

The Power Behind the Throne

Choose partners consisting of one reliable and one teetering student for each major subject. Ask each duo to plan a one day's lesson. If you undertake this well into the year, you'll find students unconsciously pattern your style, thus other children won't be thrown a curve. Low average students greatly appreciate this honor and they have an amazing sense of appropriateness. Add intrigue by making these assignments privately with no general announcement of the planners' identities: word spreads and news from the underground is more interesting. A moderated schedule for giving these lessons is having a student-planned social studies lesson on Monday, science on Tuesday, and so on through the week. Scamps and teetering students, when they are chosen, are usually flabbergasted and delighted.

One Minute of Glory

If a public address system in your assembly is available, ask permission to let your reading class use it. Individuals enjoy microphone experience tremendously. Slow students probably will never have the opportunity again, while they are in school, anyway.

Directions: Announce the event ahead of time. Ask children to choose one-minute readings. Interest zooms. Students weigh and consider material like there's no tomorrow. If they ask to practice and time their selections, and they will, let them use a tape recorder. Before taking them to the assembly hall, announce you will issue microphone call in random order; a pupil who does not respond the first time his name is announced, misses out.

Spider Tracks Across the Page

Another perennial. Any student work, whether creative writing or a routine assignment, looks more impressive, more accomplished in print, and many clumsy students despair of their own gawky penmanship. Treat them to the pleasure of seeing their efforts neatly typed and mounted for all the world to view. It'll warm the cockles of your heart to witness their reactions.

Performance Packets Made Public

At all times display at least one work product for each class member. The traditional practice of showing only the best neglects helping children who most need effort-put-forth recognition and stimulation. Since gifted kids become accustomed to having their papers mounted and made public (and so often the task was accomplished with minimum anxiety and effort), it's no big deal to them if one more sample is posted. Less promising children, finding their assignments are never displayed, slowly, through the years, lose ambition. Insidiously, they become aware they'll never get the coveted A's and B's, so what's the point of listening to the cant "try a little harder"?

After mediocre work has been posted, you may ask a student to redo it. Generally, he'll jump at the opportunity. Please don't be afraid this display scope will lower group attainment. IT WON'T. It brings up morale and cultivates more of an "our room" spirit, and a below-the-surface momentum is accelerated.

Double Set of Books

Daily, record students' successes in making a genuine effort. Maintain a special marking book for the purpose. One day grade each child on correct paper heading. The second day, give each a grade on penmanship. On the third day, give each child a grade on overall neatness. The fourth day, issue a mark on preparedness, or text, paper, pen, notebook, and so on. Your students know these marks will never reach the central office, but they are still very enthusiastic about the system. Lagging students from ghetto schools to those in affluent suburbs— all enjoy these small affirmations of their accomplishment.

Another Tour of Duty

If any child must repeat a grade, assign a veteran status to him. Explain the role and importance of reenlistees in the armed forces: they know the ropes best. Ask your veteran to help rookies learn the room rules.

May I Quote You?

We've all seen calendars that identify birthdays or carry quotes of famous people. Revamped for Room 103, this idea promotes a good room climate by highlighting individual student comments. After eliciting ideas from the class, either prepare a ditto master and insert suggestions yourself or prepare an outline month on posterboard and let students inscribe their contributions. (Figure 7-1 shows a sample calendar.)

Figure 7-1

GOING-TO-SCHOOL SKILLS IN ROOM 103

October

M	T	W	Th	F	S	S
1 Be friendly Joy	2	3 Use pencil sharpener before school Jerry	4	5 Put your books where they belong Gloria	6	7
8	9 Do all your homework Peter	10	11 Take only the paper you need Josie	12	13	14
15	16	17 Don't copy Paula	18	19 Line up quietly Nancy	20	21
22 Close lockers quietly John	23	24	25 Play fair at recess Donell	26	27	28
29	30	31 Go right home after school Chris				

CONCLUSION

Recognize means to *know again* or to *show appreciation.* As we acclaim a student's worth as an individual, we're doing much for ourselves as well. Our awareness of his efforts and motives—our enriched sincerity and insight in publicizing his strengths—adds to our stature, too.

When a child expresses aspirations which soar and reach for the stars . . . please don't cut her down. Our pragmatic views may blunt or stunt ambitions without considering an unseen dimension. Instead, let's guide her in intelligent discussion. Tactfully weave into the chat values and habits needed for her selected role and stress the importance of beginning to cultivate these traits, today. Striving for excellence and fine craftsmanship is enjoying a nationwide resurgence; our efforts to promote these qualities will be more appreciated than ever.

A scholastic pyramid with a few stars at the peak is the old-fashioned idea of a good classroom. It engenders mediocrity, because it emphasizes a concept of limited good, the belief that only a small proportion of students can really make their mark. Its dulling influence lingers today. A more modern concept is of the classroom as a high plateau where, in one personal asset or another, students can really achieve and be considered outstanding. Honor rolls and other traditional customs can be made more inclusive and morale-effective by adding an expansive or topical touch.

Many modern teachers have ingenious ways of showing students that they are cherished for their individuality. Some basics glimmer through:

1. Each child needs, and can earn, respect for constructive personality qualities and attitudes which he can contribute to the class scene. Joy, consideration, reliability, responsiveness, sharing, or cooperation are essential to any outstanding classroom; but it doesn't take academic aptitude to express these. A slow student can excel in one or more of these. Usually he will work hard to express a particular trait if the teacher directs his attention to his innate ability to fill the role and to the class's need for a model.

2. Each child has a continually rising best. She's more impressed with *her* best being acknowledged and displayed than she is with the papers of an academic elite.

3. Nothing activates a child's self-respect more than his knowledge—and a teacher's recognition—that he has accomplished a solid day's progress in school lessons and in the art of self-control. Being credited with this progress leads to the greatest asset of all, his own broadening and deepening identity.

Eight

DEVELOPING STUDENTS' WORK AND STUDY HABITS

Motivation. Would you like to take an educated guess on how many educators have expounded on the topic? Simply stated, a motivated student is a girl or a boy with a purpose; *purpose* means *being concerned about accomplishing something.* An individual's purpose is developed only as he becomes aware of new values which promise to make life richer than it was previously. Moreover, accomplishment of a goal must seem attainable before he will work for it.

This chapter addresses the topic of improving work and study habits by first considering the qualities of a good student. This is followed by strategies for sharpening direction-following skills and for smoothing transitions. Next, negatives such as dawdling, incomplete supplies, nameless papers, and messy work are considered, along with correctional remedies. This chapter also touches on lack of study for tests and apathetic student attitudes toward recitation.

Many lousy students have little interest in anything beyond life's basics. In this state they are bored and boring people. As a trained teacher you know the power of friendly, understanding chats. To ferret out information about the students' present interests, however limited, try asking them to bring in newspaper clippings that they find appealing. It's a start. Sometimes an interest inventory (see Figure 5-2) will reveal latent possibilities.

Some poor students use indifference as protective armor to mask fears of failure. Honest praise for a specific piece of their work, a specific talent, or a specific character trait starts cutting through this armor. Praise them in front of their friends. Some mediocre students are apathetic because they carry the oppressive burden of a false conviction that they "just don't have it" in the world of school.

In our concern for helping poor students become better students—indeed in many cases, good students—let's consider the qualities necessary for a good student.

1. **Perception—of what can be discerned by the senses, including the subtle, small, or apparently insignificant.**

As we think about this, we realize there are also nonacademic ways in which a student can work on this trait. Sharpness of attention to nuances adds grace to social life, touch to playing or singing music, and finesse to acting.

2. **Reason—to calculate, to think, the power of comprehending, especially in orderly, rational ways.**

We can help students marshal facts, look for patterns, and slot items into major and minor categories without ever mentioning we're helping them reason. A few nonacademic topics are: wardrobe building, professional athletics, pop music trends.

3. **Memory—the power of recall.**

A most important ingredient of a good memory is interest in the information. Experience teaches us that we forget those things which mean little or nothing to us. The opposite? Here one thinks of enticing TV ads with quotable lines and clever jingles from children's poetry that capture interest because they are amusing. Asking mediocre students to memorize these loosens their false conviction of an inability to memorize.

4. **Application—is the act of putting information to use.**
A most important factor here is an inclination to give close attention. A good demonstration lesson is taking a current song favorite done by three different groups and taping segments of each on a single cassette. Play it in the classroom and compliment slow students when they identify the differences.

5. **Judgment—the process of, or skill in, forming an opinion, or evaluating, by discerning or comparing.**
This, of course, is an ultimate goal of real education.

Let's move on to the immediate application of daily details. None of the following points is of earthshaking importance in itself, but in the aggregate they make a tremendous difference in the way the final score reads. Combined, they bring greater habits of order, coherence, and completeness—attributes which lead toward success in any department or station in life.

Although not an end in itself, order is a tool which will serve the child well. Start building for order and coherence with larger factors: complete room supplies, moderately neat desks (of teacher and pupil) and organized notebooks. Making a child redo a paper because it has blotches on it when his desk and notebook are in colossal, chronic chaos is similar to putting a silk dress on a goat. Ideally, teaching a child reasonably systematic desk procedure comes first, but sometimes this is impossible. The next choice is to work on both aspects simultaneously, but there are times when this can't be done either. In some cases our concern must be narrowed to teaching him to improve his papers, while never forgetting that an easy order promotes growth, and our ultimate goal is success, not order.

FOLLOWING DIRECTIONS

Learning to follow instructions explicitly is the easiest way for a student to add to his success painlessly. Teachers like his sincere effort. Always they feel, he's "trying" even when he isn't expending much energy. Sometimes we need to reassure a student that he's not compromising his individuality by following instructions—individuality and nonconformity are definitely not interchangeable terms.

Occasionally, a student ignores or disobeys specific directions as a device for defying the adult world. If we find this widespread in our classroom, we are wise to reexamine the tone and wording of our directions. However, if it's an isolated case, try telling such a youngster, "It's just as easy to conform on inconsequential matters as to nonconform. And it eliminates dumb hassles. Save your nonconforming, your rearing up on your hind legs, for occasions when you really have something at stake." Another tack for a willfully balky student: tell him how many of his fellow students have raised grade, test, and IQ scores over brighter pals by carefully following directions; he's going to leave himself behind needlessly. Who is he going to hurt but himself?

If you sense a deeper rebelliousness, or a touch of personal antagonism, you might remind him of the minutiae-laden directions and obligations required in your job. And in the principal's post. This gets to kids. The fact that the school faculty must adhere to standards imposed from on high, pleases students. Resistance melts.

When giving directions, by all means start with a clear statement of goal. Follow with a general route or method, and then give specific details. If the class is following directions poorly, ask yourself: "Am I concise? Do I keep it simple? Do I omit extraneous comments and details?" For every teacher who fails to give adequate instructions, there must be fifty who just talk too much.

Certainly, intensified direction-following practice improves student skill. Short sessions are great for the times when the group needs a five-minute pace change or break. Here are some suggestions which teachers offered to share.

And the Next Voice You Hear . . .

Switch on a tape recorder. Give explicit directions for a lesson. Ask one or two children to repeat. Then have the class listen.

Just in Our Room

Study skills booklets often contain exercises in following directions, but to make the lesson more concrete, more interesting, develop a list of twenty directions which apply only to Room 103. Read the directions orally, just once. Here are a few:

1. Put your name in the upper right-hand corner and the principal's name directly under it.
2. Draw the same number of windows that our room has.
3. Put an X in the window drawing representing the window closest to you.
4. Draw the pumpkin on the front table.
5. Turn it into a jack-o'-lantern.

With Duly Impressive Ceremony

Use familiar workbook pages for practice in improving the direction-following skills of a class. If this is repeated four or five times before an important, standardized test, students will be far more comfortable on the big day. This strategy pulls the class into a feeling of oneness, which the children love.

Make it a formal occasion. (1) Clear desk tops. (2) Separate desks. (3) Two sharp pencils and an eraser on each desk. (4) No talking. (5) Set timer. (6) Read directions aloud twice. (7) Release timer and Go! Without the pressure of a "for-real" test, children enjoy the click, click, click atmosphere.

Let Me Think . . . What Did He Say?

Ask each student to develop a written set of directions with three, four, or five steps. (Everyone writes the same number.) Example: (1) Go to globe and point to Arctic Ocean. (2) Write your middle name on the board. (3) Give your brown bag lunch to the teacher. Jane calls on Peter and orally gives him directions *once*. If Peter completes the tasks without stumbling, he reads his directions and calls on Chris. Whenever a student makes a mistake, the teacher selects the next candidate, thus assuring that those who most need drill will receive practice.

Good Listeners Club

Everyone belongs in this club. Officers are a president, a vice-president, and a secretary. The club roster has a ditto sheet picture of each member, which the member has colored to look like himself. Cut-out faces are placed on a bulletin board with tacks. If a student errs in not listening while another is talking, refuses to follow directions, or talks while another is talking, an officer removes the offender's picture and gives it to him for the school day. Just before dismissal a club officer gathers all faces from the desks and displays them again. Visiting teachers find this device a big help in maintaining a good tempo while they are teaching special lessons.

MAKING THE TRANSITION
BETWEEN SUBJECTS

You're sorry to interrupt busy children—sorrier than they realize. But you must. It's the school pattern to have schedules, but then much of school enjoyment is doing things in groups.

In promoting smoother transitions, a first step is putting your ear to the ground. Acquire a sensitivity to class tenor by being quiet and mentally listening. Eye your top average students. As they are completing a lesson, announce a few more minutes for others. Offering students structured steps for closing a lesson is effective and considerate: (1) A monitor will collect papers. (2) Return supplementary texts to the bookcase. (3) Clear your desks. (4) Take out your math workbooks.

Some teachers ask paper passers to distribute the next lesson's ditto a few minutes prior to agenda time, but they don't interrupt the students until switching time. Other teachers have identified a special hand or sound signal which is a natural for their group. Splendid.

Still others have smoothed transitions by using the stimulus of a variety of signals. The options are open, but ALWAYS STAND when introducing the next subject.

Here are techniques which a few thoughtful, effective teachers use.

Names of the Elect Are . . .

Write on the board names of students who are ready for the next subject or who otherwise followed directions. As you are writing, you will be asked, "Why are their names up there?" When classmates learn the reason, they hasten to comply.

Pansy Purple, Pink, Green

Children enjoy direction signals which involve color. This strategy also improves their listening attentiveness and helps to quiet the room (without a direct admonition).

Example: Ask children to take out a speller and two pencils when you announce the word "yellow." In full, firm voice start naming other colors and gradually lower the tone of your voice. The room becomes hushed. When the noise level is at a good point and their attention focused, call "yellow."

"Stars and Stripes" Will Do Nicely

Another old-timer but very good. Play a few bars of a moderate tempo tune on the piano—same tune each time, of course.

Eins, Zwei, Drei . . . Fünfzig

Teach your class to count to fifty in a foreign language. Even before they've mastered the task, you may use the numbers to time them. Example: Everyone is to put away his math book and take out his crayons. Give directions and start counting; students will count along with you, but they will also speed up. Counting in a foreign tongue makes a game. This technique may be used often; it doesn't wear out quickly.

Which Side Is Winning?

Divide class and perhaps give each team a name. Draw two boxes on the board. During the day put check marks for the team that is ready first. Prizes? Winning group goes for drinks first, or leaves to get wraps first.

Idle Hands . . .

"Make good use of your spare time." A trifle ambiguous, isn't it? After having a group discussion clarifying specific activities and why they are viable, try mounting a student-decorated wall chart reinforcing and reminding them of their options. Figure 8-1 gives sample text for the chart.

Figure 8-1

WHEN I AM FINISHED WITH MY WORK, I WILL:

–Check my lesson for possible errors
–Complete other unfinished work
–Do my monitor job
–Read a book from the library table
–Work at the science or art center

DAWDLING

Many children live in an enchanting land, a never-never-kingdom, where time stands still. Charmingly free from adult concerns, they love it. Thus it's difficult to impress them with our bells and schedules. Putting time to work for us is an important lesson. If it's deferred too long, the lesson becomes harder.

You have your work cut out for you, teacher. You're to teach the importance of living today and in the same breath, the simultaneous need of preparing for the tomorrows. Focus on the word—perspective.

Just like adults, youngsters need goals and due dates. When the class is nibbling on their pencils and gazing at the walls, deadlines add a sharpness which cuts into the apathy. Although undue speed cuts into quality, moderate speed actually improves efficiency. Meeting a challenge within a specified time brings a feeling of accomplishment, self-respect, and power over oneself.

Heeding background factors is important, but a large portion of the task is simply training youngsters into recognizing that clock hands move relentlessly. In a word, improving habits. Here are some constructive suggestions teachers offered.

Lap One, Lap Two, Lap Three

Divide Slow Sammie's assignment into thirds. Ask him to tell you when he finishes the first section; give him a star. The second section brings another star. Naturally, he'll get a third star when he completes the task. In some classes you'll find that amusing decals are more cherished than stars.

Crossing the Finish Line

Post correct finished work of the first ten students on the bulletin board in the order of completion.

A Fellow in the Royal Snail Watchers

Sometimes a student looks like he's working, but actually he's accomplishing nothing, just diddling. Try persuasion first. Then stop at his desk and say, "I want to see you do five problems in the next three minutes." Later, stop again, comment on completed work and say, "Now I want to see you do eight more problems in three minutes." Again, stop, comment on completed tasks, and add, "Please finish your paper in ten minutes and bring it to my desk."

It Seems Time Stands Still

Have your dawdling friend take his work to an ordinary table. Direct him to *stand* there and work until he finishes. It's uncomfortable, but not miserable, to stand and write. He'll get busy and complete his tasks.

Time Stands Still Throughout the Room

A whole class is dragging. The room is not too warm, and they haven't had too much sedentary work; the class simply has the blahs. Use the biggest, noisiest test timer available. Place it on your desk. Select a period of time, say twenty minutes. Ask each child to decide how much he will accomplish, and jot it down. His success is measured by how close he comes to his estimate. Results are remarkable in both quantity and quality.

Hunger Makes a Faster Worker

Have Dawdling Dannie stay at noon and finish his work before he leaves for lunch. Stay with him. When he complains he's hungry, assure him you're hungry, too. (If he goes home for lunch, be sure to advise his parent ahead of time, please.)

Loafing by Yourself Is No Fun

When a dawdler becomes an idler and accomplishes virtually nothing all morning, send him home at noon to spend the balance of the day. Tell him that by refusing to work, he has lost the privilege of coming to school. Don't use the word "suspend"—this makes him a hero in a negative way. Ask his mother to keep him in the house but not to punish him. You might suggest allowing him to play with his toys, but she is to avoid giving him companionship herself. Usually, it's good to let him go out and play at his normal arrival home time.

Poker Chip Peter

Peter was a problem child, a sensitive stinker, with a very short interest span. The teacher and a social worker decided on an incentive plan. Peter received a poker chip for every twenty minutes he worked hard. When he accumulated twenty chips, the two adults took him to lunch. While eating they praised his progress and growth, and in acknowlegment, they increased the time span to thirty minutes. Again, when he accumulated twenty chips, they took him to lunch. Once more, growth earned a time-span increase. So the pattern went until he reached an hour. By this time he no longer needed help to stay on-task.

She's Going to Blow Me a Kiss!

Sometimes children, especially small children, can be teased into a degree of diligence. Tell them, "If you finish your work, I'll blow you a kiss. If you don't complete your tasks, I'll blow you ten kisses."

INCOMPLETE SUPPLIES

Students without proper supplies are rocks in the stream of class progress. No teacher needs to be told that they are diverting the flow of attention from the task at hand.

Some homes are completely disorganized, and it's not the child's fault that she is without needed items. Other homes are unaware, because the child simply hasn't told them of her school needs. Usually, you must start with her elders. Most often a child could well have everything she needs if just one member of her family knew of its importance to her school progress.

As we reflect, we realize that hers is not a correctional problem as much as a growth-of-responsibility need. A child must feel mild discomfort in her carefree disregard of her own interests. You can stretch her into accepting the day's demands.

Again, here are suggestions of practicing teachers who want very much to help these children.

Do Not Enter!

Post a sign on the classroom door window. "Do not enter the room without a pencil and paper." Stick to it. If neglect is widespread, be lenient about tardiness the first few days if it seems due to obtaining or borrowing the needed items.

Her Name Is Now Pawn Shop Nellie

When you lend supplies, you rarely get them back. Right? Ask each student for a deposit . . . a book, a shoe, an ID card. Hold these objects until you get your pen back. Students love this approach.

Snafued Supply Safari

Your spritely friend never has the right books or her colored pencils when she needs them. Sit down with her and make a list. If students are allowed to go to lockers three times a day, divide the list in three:

First Trip	Second Trip	Third Trip
1. Speller	1. Music instrument	1. Art project
2. Notebook, compass, pen	2. Flash cards	2. Smock
3. Math workbook and text	3. Reader	3. Library book
4. Gym shoes	4. Lunch	4. Etc.

Tape one copy of this list inside her desk and another inside her locker.

Only If You'll Lend Me Sunglasses

When, against your warnings, a child persists in using wildly colored ink for assignments, don't grouse. Tell him with tongue-in-cheek exaggeration that the color so pains your eyes you can't even look at his paper, much less grade it.

Where Is Your Slate?

No pencil or paper again? Don't fret, friendly teacher. Sell the needed paper—one sheet for one cent; pens rent for one cent a period. Let students borrow from a classmate if they're short of cash, or let them run a tab. Students enjoy this arrangement. Evidently paying removes an implied need to be grateful for a personal favor. It's a nice intermediate step between buying a packet of paper ahead of time and depending on dole during class.

PAPERS WITHOUT NAMES

This perennial annoyance can be eliminated pleasantly. Teaching a forgetful child to sign his papers is actually reminding him that consideration and courtesy are a two-way street. He learns to be mindful of a teacher's problems—in this case stacks of papers she must grade and record. This lesson also helps him realize he is one member of a group, no more, no less.

Most teachers first warn the students and then either accommodate them by learning individual handwriting, or discomfit them by discarding unsigned papers. Here are several in-between steps.

Johnny, AKA

Select a famous name . . . Peter Cottontail, Paul Revere, Carl Lewis, E.T., and write it on the child's paper in felt marker printing. Never again will he forget to sign his work. The surprise has a shock effect. This technique is good for any age level.

After You Sign Your Name

Distribute ditto lesson. Ask children to place their names on their papers. After they've done this, they are to stand and hold papers under their chins. Repeat for a few days.

Hardest Working Monkey in Our School

Hang a large, stuffed monkey on a bulletin board and have children name him. When you get an unsigned paper, put the monkey's name on it. Post a good unsigned paper on the bulletin board; tuck a poor one in a desk drawer. If a child doesn't get his paper back, he knows he can look in two places.

Over and Over and Over

For the first occurrence, warn the forgetful student. The second time, have him sign his papers twice. If he forgets again, increase the number of signatures to five, ten, or twenty.

Every Time in the Same Corner

Having a uniform position for the student's name on all papers is helpful. In other words, avoid having him put his name at the top for one lesson and on the bottom for the next.

INCOMPLETE WORK

Incompleteness is a habit and a state of thinking. It should be corrected in a child's outlook as well as in his assignments. Usually, all his activities suffer; rare is the child who does a half-baked job on his schoolwork and yet finishes other projects. Learning to budget time in work and play, and practicing stick-to-itiveness are required.

As teacher, you set a pace, provide a role model. If you find student incomplete work widespread in your room, look around at your own projects. Reset target dates for finishing pet extras. By that date, do them or eliminate them entirely.

Every time a student shows a glint of increased perserverance, laud it. If he finishes a task, no matter how messily, don't make him redo it. Firmly establish a pattern of completing jobs. Later on, tackle teaching him tidier habits—pride in a task not only done, but well done.

If this habit isn't broken in a reasonably short time, delve deeper into causes.

It's More Than Smiles of Lady Luck

You know better, I know better. But lower echelon students often conclude that good students are simply lucky. Since

poor students have never absorbed the importance of intermediate steps, they are, at best, mystified. And often frustrated.
First, lead a class discussion on characteristics contributing to
successful school work, emphasizing qualities of diligence, persistence, completeness, rechecking work, and of meeting deadlines. Then, pair off your children, a good student and a poor
one. Ask each duo to prepare jointly a list of attributes which
lead to better grades. Together, they are also to pinpoint one
list item on which they will concentrate during the coming
week. On Friday they will compare progress.

Three-Day Limit

Strangely, a normally good student turns in almost no
work, or very poor work, three days in a row. Tell the child
you plan to call her home. When you call, ask her mother if
anything at school or at home is troubling her daughter. Then
report the unsatisfactory progress.

Play Early—Pay Later

The form note in Figure 8-2 clarifies matters when a child
must complete classroom assignments at home. It helps avoid
scolding during school hours.

Figure 8-2

Date _____

Dear _____,

    I talked and played in school and disturbed others.
Now I am to do my work during my playtime.

Signed _____

Parent's signature _____

MESSY WORK

Try writing with your toes. It'll refresh your memory: learning to write is hard work. Probably you won't continue your efforts in toe writing long enough to acquire a Palmer stroke, but you'll grow in your desire to be gentle with little hamfisted students.

If your district has a standards manual for English, get it out. Explain the book to the students. Read the points you plan to stress this year. No longer will the items, major or minor, appear as pet idiosyncrasies of yours; the book makes it impersonal. The students will live with these rules all their school years. Even if, or especially if, you think some rules are fussy, consider the fact that you'll be doing the child a favor if you teach him these. Surely, this is preferable to letting him learn the rules from a teacher who thinks mechanical standards so important that she chops down well-earned grades on subject matter.

One day, while you're spieling about neat work, explain the term "halo effect" and its impact on teachers and on almost everyone. Show the students concrete examples of how general appearance has an impact and heightens credibility of the thoughts presented, without touching the thoughts.

Here are some steps kind and earnest teachers suggested to help children overcome the crippling appearance of sloppiness.

Quicker, Too

Permit students to cross out mistakes with one line. If a child deletes mistakes with many scratches and curls, grade the paper but withhold credit until he recopies it. Or, you can record a grade in your book but not indicate it on his paper until he recopies the assignment. Usually, once or possibly twice is all you'll have to do this.

With That Teacher's Handwriting?

Good handwriting has an artistic flow. If your own penmanship is, hmmm, relaxed and yet you must teach handwriting, try this. Explain that class members who write better than you habitually do, will receive automatic A's. You will continue to mark their papers for closed o's, proper slant, and so on, so they may perfect their skill—but they will receive their A's.

Two Grades on Every Spelling Test

Put both a spelling grade and a penmanship/neatness grade on every test. Use a standardized handwriting guide sheet for evaluation. Consider this double grading for science and social studies, too.

Pride Can Come After a Fall

Tell students who have turned in mediocre work that you're thinking of displaying the assignment. You're considering their work, too. Don't ask them to redo the papers, even though the work is messy. Instead, ask them, "Your ideas are good, do you think your friends will notice the blotches and scratches?" Invariably, students willingly and gratefully redo the papers.

Call the Game "Ouch"

Neater, faster penmanship is the goal. The lesson time limit is fifteen minutes. Distribute four sheets of school paper and a penmanship book to each student. Select one or two check points such as: holding pen properly, sitting straight, correct paper angle, digging in paper, drawing letters. Put chosen points on board.

Start the class on a routine assignment. As you notice a child commit an error of the day, call his name. He must start over on the next sheet of paper. If he's far down the first sheet, he'll give you a pained expression. These pained looks inspired the name of the game. Children tremendously enjoy this lesson.

MAKE-UP WORK

Make-up work is more important than the lessons made up. As we know, every day on which a child is absent brings a continuity gap. Perhaps he didn't miss consequential material, but he's not aware of this fact, and he fears that unknown quantity. Usually, he doesn't know quite how to inquire about his concerns. For the sake of his self-confidence, it's wise to hold him to most class work missed—or its equivalent. It's as important for bright students as for average or slow students to know that they know. Of course, your reputation for fairness is enhanced when everyone makes up missed assignments.

If yours is a self-contained classroom and you elect to update back assignments and records during class time, or if time constrictions of departmental periods force using class time, please give the group an unexpected, fresh lesson meanwhile. The surprise element jogs diligence even when a teacher's attention is elsewhere.

Forgot to Do the Homework? Let's See . . .

If Charley goofs on home assignments, warn him the first time. On the second occasion have him spend recess writing on the topic of, what else, homework. Before he starts writing, explain to him that homework reinforces daytime lessons, shows when he understands concepts thoroughly, gives the teacher feedback on the group, and helps in grading.

He is to write his parents a letter; one page of composition does nicely. It is to carry an explanation of why students receive homework, who gets hurt when it is neglected, and what he anticipates in parental reaction to his ignoring this responsibility. Keep the letter and arrange an alternate due date for the missing assignment. The third time he drops the ball, have him write a fresh, second letter. Then staple both letters together and send them home for a parent countersignature.

No Homework Done? Delayed Deadline

Let's say Maria has previously failed to do Monday's assigned homework. It's happened again. On Tuesday have her write a letter outlining a schedule for completing it. Maria herself decides the deadlines. This letter should not contain excuses for the original lapse; this tempts fabricating reasons.

Instead, Maria is to state: the math problems will be on your desk Wednesday morning, the map work will be in Thursday noon, and the story essay will be ready on Friday. (She does have to combine the make-up work with her daily homework.) Keep the letter. If Maria assumes her responsibilities as promised, destroy the note. If she fails a second time, send the letter home for a parent countersignature.

LACK OF STUDY FOR
DISCUSSION AND TESTS

Ever since the great flood, some good-natured youngsters have been riding through school doing as little work as possible and cloaking it with a *mañana* casualness. Basically, most of these students are not hostile, repressed, rebellious, sly, or even lazy—they're human. No need reminding that when this condition is in its contagious stage, it virtually eliminates preparatory study, and renders discussions worthless.

Using the following ideas for bolstering student efforts has a great advantage in that you, as teacher, need not admonish. Why not try some of these approaches? Normally, you'll see a real change. And, if you don't see improvement, check other factors.

Leading Steps

Use ditto worksheet of sentences, paragraphs, and statistics on the material studied. Leave key words blank. Ask your class to fill in about two-thirds before class, any two-thirds of the questions and blanks. Tell them not to fret or lose sleep on anything they find too challenging.

When they arrive in class, immediately give them a ✓/O grade on having the two-thirds done. Students who worked seriously appreciate this. Then review the sheet orally with the group. The combination of some work beforehand, reading aloud, contributing answers, and writing produces an atmosphere they all enjoy.

There's a Long, Long List Awaiting

Judged by past performance, the group will know nothing about today's assignment. Develop and ditto a list of terms and definitions, leaving space after each entry for writing. Ask each student to pick two or three terms and think about them briefly. Rotating around the room, *let each student select the term he wants to explain or define.* Usually the student defines the term orally and classmates may write as he talks. Orderly rotation provides stability; discussing terms at random brings a surprise element. Allowing each child to choose lets him put his best foot forward. You'll gain his gratitude as well as fewer wrong answers. This is not a deep learning process, but it will shake a group out of a "gather-ye-rosebuds-while-ye-may" outlook. And, more important, slow students really enjoy this procedure.

Science Bowl

Patterned after College Bowl, this strategy or game was developed for students who refused to study for tests. *Caution:* The first time, it'll probably be a dud. Second time, it'll be a success. Later times, it'll be so successful and the students will try so hard, you'll get an accurate reading of how much they know without giving the exam.

Example: Divide the class into two groups. Each child writes five questions pertaining to the unit and puts answers on back of his paper. He may develop more questions if he desires, and many do. During the game ask a question once. If you get an incorrect answer, put the question aside and proceed to the next question. In a Lightning Round include all questions the children missed earlier. In this last round if a child pauses mid-answer, someone else on his team may complete it.

Surface Skimming, Then Plunging

Your class keeps coming without having studied. When you prepare thoughtful discussion questions, earmark some specific objective points or data. Next compose a surprise quiz on the specifics—hard, but not sneaky hard. Ditto and distribute it to the group on their arrival. Ask them to take the quiz, exchange papers, and grade. They will do poorly.

Next stage. Remind the class that your first concern is their learning; if, as a group, they can pool enough ideas and pertinent comments for today's discussion, or if they ask stimulating questions of each other so a good thing gets rolling, you'll not record the quiz grades. During the discussion you'll notice a shift of effort. You won't be tugging to extract responses; the students will be offering information and volunteering to do their share.

Handouts for Everyone, None Alike

You're quite sure no one will arrive prepared for today. Using a different question for each class member, put one question on each sheet of paper. Give one to each student, and ask him to write an answer without using the text. Next, each student passes his paper to a classmate. This person is to write a good answer using the text. Sometimes you may elect to have the second student put a ν+, ν, ν-, 0, other times not. In any case, return papers to the original writers, and allow the class a few minutes for chatter among themselves. You'll hear, "What one did she hand you?" "Listen to the one I got." "What's wrong with this answer?"

Party of the First Part Asks . . .

. . . and party of the second part answers. Have each student put her name on two sheets of paper. Next, ask students to compose three good quiz questions on the day's assignment, open book. On the second sheet of paper students are to write good, normal answers to the three questions. They keep the answer sheet and turn the questions in to you.

You redistribute the questions. The next student writes his answers. At deadline time, have each student give his answer to the author who will grade it by comparing it with his own answer. He will then return to the quiz taker the graded paper and his original answer. Collect papers. Normally, don't record grades, at least the first time or two.

These strategies can be described as pump-priming. As interest continues to awaken and an awareness of the need to study begins to sink in, you'll find a few more students coming prepared each day. These devices are also effective for reviewing.

CHEATING

A child who cheats needs help. Regardless of how you handle the immediate situation, the long-term solution is seeing he gets help. And handle the immediate situation you must— the other students need affirmation of your basic fairness.

In talking with the errant child, explain that cheating is a sign of weakness. You want her to develop or show more strength. She may need help in learning how to study more efficiently. Or she may have more subject mastery than she realizes and only lacks self-confidence. Perhaps she simply needs someone to ride herd on her buckling down to study. A fourth possibility may be a tendency to be a leaner.

After you've caught her cheating and she has paid the price, forget the incident. Almost. When an occasion arises, put her in a position where she can show trustworthiness. Please commend her when she lives up to your restored trust.

Here are some immediate steps which considerate teachers have offered.

Answers (A), (B), and (C)

Many times it's hard to pinpoint copying; here's a clever cure. Develop your test, let's say twenty-five multiple-choice questions. The *questions are the same for everyone.* However, unannounced to the group, on one-third of the papers the correct answer will be (a); on one-third of the papers the correct answer will be (b); and on the last third, the correct answer will be (c). It's extra work for the teacher, but she need do it only once.

Credit Where Credit Is Due

If you discover a child copying during a minor test, have him put his classmate's name after the answer he copied. This seems an especially humane and courteous way of handling cheating for the first or second offense. It alerts the erring student to the fact that he's been seen chiseling, but the sanction is mild.

Cooperating During Exams Is Out!

It's called cheating. And the solution is simple. Stand in the rear of the room during testing. Either the students' laxity or your suspicions will disappear. If a student raises his hand, have him come to you: don't leave your post.

CONCLUSION

We've considered a few facets of study and work habit improvement to lead poor students into mediocrity and mediocre students into excellence. The basic qualities of thinking for a good student are: perception, reason, memory, application, and judgment. Every student in school can work on these in some fashion. Then there's a call for orderly, coherent, and unified actions, first in the larger elements of the students' experience and then in details.

The negatives considered in this chapter, such as incomplete supplies and lack of study, are important because they indicate a mind-set. Occasionally, improvement in work and study habits will be dramatic; a youngster suddenly comes to grips with the school life scenario. More often, the change is a gradually rising standard and accompanying it is a greater enthusiasm for schools, teachers and students alike.

Measuring results is a precious activity to educators; measuring perceived causes is also important to them. Let's turn to teacher performance in the classroom. What do they see as obstacles interfering with their progress? The NEA research charts in Figures 8-3 and 8-4 should help you see how your cozy classroom in a corner of the building and your peculiar problems fit into the nationwide picture.

Figure 8-3

What in your present position as a teacher hinders you most in rendering the best service of which you are capable?

	GRAND TOTAL	STRATUM			REGION				RACIAL GROUP	
		25,000 or More (Large)	3,000–24,999 (Med.)	1–2,999 (Sml.)	North East	South East	Middle	West	Non-White	White
	1	2	3	4	5	6	7	8	9	10
Discipline/Negative Attitudes of Students	210	69	83	58	48	44	61	57	16	191
%	18.2	26.0	14.6	18.1	17.9	18.0	19.9	17.1	19.3	17.9
Heavy Workload/Extra Responsibilities	239	65	121	52	60	55	48	75	24	214
%	20.7	24.5	21.3	16.2	22.4	22.4	15.6	22.5	28.0	20.1
Lack of Preparation/Planning Time	42	5	23	13	6	10	12	14	1	41
%	3.6	2.3	4.1	4.0	2.2	4.1	3.9	4.2	1.2	3.8
Lack of Time to Teach/Classroom Interruptions	81	18	39	24	16	16	24	25	7	74
%	7.0	6.8	6.9	7.5	6.0	6.5	7.8	7.5	8.4	6.9
Negative Attitudes of Public/Parents	136	25	73	37	33	25	39	38	4	131
%	11.8	9.4	12.9	11.5	12.3	10.2	12.7	11.4	4.8	12.3
Lack of Funds/Decent Salary	99	9	59	31	25	22	28	24	4	95
%	8.6	3.4	10.4	9.7	9.3	9.0	9.1	7.2	4.8	8.9

Figure 8-3 (Cont'd)

	GRAND TOTAL	STRATUM			REGION				RACIAL GROUP	
		25,000 or More (Large)	3,000–24,999 (Med.)	1–2,999 (Sml.)	North East	South East	Middle	West	Non-White	White
	1	2	3	4	5	6	7	8	9	10
Incompetent/Uncooperative Administrators	205	43	98	63	45	40	50	60	14	191
%	17.7	16.2	17.3	19.6	16.8	16.3	19.2	18.0	16.9	17.9
Lack of Materials/Resources/Facilities	64	14	32	13	15	17	16	16	10	54
%	5.5	5.3	5.6	5.6	5.6	6.9	5.2	4.8	12.0	5.1
Assigned Outside Field of Training/Inexperience	5	...	2	3	...	1	2	2	...	5
%	.4	...	.4	.9	...	.4	.7	.6	...	.5
Lack of Teacher Cooperation/Unprofessional Teachers	33	5	17	11	10	3	9	11	1	31
%	2.9	1.9	3.0	3.4	3.7	1.2	2.9	3.3	1.2	2.9
Other	42	11	20	11	10	12	9	11	2	40
%	3.6	4.2	3.5	3.4	3.7	4.9	2.9	3.3	2.4	3.7
Total	1,156	265	567	321	268	245	307	333	83	1,067
%	100.0	100.0	100.0	99.9	99.9	99.9	99.9	99.9	99.9	100.0
No Response	170	39	77	53	30	37	40	53	28	137

Source: National Education Association Research, 1981

Figure 8-4

What in your present position as a teacher hinders you most in rendering the best service of which you are capable?

| | GRAND TOTAL | AGE | | | | SEX | | CURRENT TEACHING LEVEL | | | |
| | | Less Than 30 | 30–39 | 40–49 | 50 or Older | Male | Female | Elem | Middle/ Jr Hi | Sr Hi | Comb Sec |
	11	12	13	14	15	16	17	18	19	20	21
Discipline/Negative Attitudes of Students	210	34	86	35	51	65	142	85	63	74	126
%	18.2	16.4	18.7	13.7	23.1	17.4	18.3	15.0	21.8	19.4	20.5
Heavy Workload/Extra Responsibilities	239	48	86	60	41	58	178	145	40	60	97
%	20.7	23.2	18.7	23.4	18.6	15.5	23.0	25.6	13.8	5.7	15.7
Lack of Preparation/Planning Time	42	6	18	13	4	9	33	25	8	13	19
%	3.6	2.9	8.9	5.1	1.8	2.4	4.3	4.4	2.8	3.4	3.1
Lack of Time to Teach/Classroom Interruptions	81	13	21	25	21	27	54	45	16	26	38
%	7.0	6.3	4.6	9.8	9.5	7.2	7.0	7.0	5.5	6.8	6.2
Negative Attitudes of Public/Parents	136	21	56	28	30	43	93	67	44	32	70
%	11.8	10.1	12.2	10.8	13.6	11.5	12.0	11.8	15.2	8.4	11.4
Lack of Funds/Decent Salary	99	25	49	15	10	54	44	32	34	48	72
%	9.6	12.1	10.7	5.9	4.5	14.4	5.7	5.6	11.8	12.6	11.7

Figure 8-4 (Cont'd)

	GRAND TOTAL	AGE				SEX		CURRENT TEACHING LEVEL			
		Less Than 30	30–39	40–49	50 or Older	Male	Female	Elem	Middle/ Jr Hi	Sr Hi	Comb Sec
	11	12	13	14	15	16	17	18	19	20	21
Incompetent/Uncooperative Administrators	205	31	99	50	34	76	129	97	51	73	115
%	17.7	15.0	19.3	19.5	15.4	20.3	16.7	17.1	17.6	19.1	18.7
Lack of Materials/Resources/ Facilities	64	16	18	15	15	16	48	29	18	24	37
%	5.5	7.7	3.9	5.9	6.8	4.3	6.2	5.1	6.2	6.3	6.0
Assigned Outside Field of Training/Inexperience	5	...	1	2	2	2	3	3	...	2	2
%	.4	...	.2	.8	.9	.5	.4	.5	...	.5	.3
Lack of Teacher Cooperation/ Unprofessional Teachers	33	5	19	5	4	11	22	17	11	12	20
%	2.9	2.4	4.1	2.0	1.9	2.9	2.8	3.0	3.8	3.1	3.2
Other	42	8	17	8	9	13	28	22	4	18	20
%	3.6	3.9	3.7	3.1	4.1	3.5	3.6	3.9	1.4	4.7	3.2
Total	1,156	207	460	256	221	374	774	567	289	382	616
%	100.0	100.0	100.0	100.1	100.1	99.9	100.0	99.9	99.9	100.0	100.0
No Response	170	37	50	47	33	62	106	82	45	53	89

Source: National Education Association Research, 1981

And, if you feel overworked, you have lots and lots of company, On the positive side, these statistics indicate that remarkably few teachers are asked to teach outside of their certification. And most faculty members apparently get along well with their colleagues.

Getting back to students, the immediate effects of better work and study habits often, but not always, show up indirectly via better grades. As professionals we know that the genuine, long-range benefits will stay with children for years to come through their strengthened ability to think more cogently and to act with greater self-assurance.

Measuring results is a precious activity to educators. Children like to measure results, too, but statistics leave them cold. They enjoy rewards for their efforts, not in the sweet by and by, but now. If your class improves greatly and the ethos of your room changes, why not give them a treat; explain to them they've *earned* it because they've done a great job in becoming better little scholars.

Nine

CARING FOR
SCHOOL PROPERTY
AND SUPPLIES

Anytime, anywhere, taking good care of property is an active form of appreciation. It's a sign of maturity and generosity. The students' heroes and heroines all do it; astronauts take precise care of their instruments and equipment; so do speedcar drivers, dress designers, nurses, and dentists. It's not a sign of sissiness; it's a sign of manhood, womanhood. It's a technique of life.

The real importance of teaching youngsters property care reaches beyond the intrinsic value of the involved equipment to cultivating a more appreciative and caring attitude toward their fellow student, an emerging sense of community. In school, perhaps more than in most places, it's a sign of generosity. The pupil's younger brothers and sisters will be passing through this building, too. Let's keep it nice for them.

Children learn property care by precept, example, and/or experience. It's a normal, natural facet of their training, every-

183

one's training. If the home and community are doing their job properly, teachers have little trouble with vandalism. But if home and community have slipped or defaulted on the task, it falls to the classroom teacher to squeeze in this lesson. Care of one's tools and environment is part of the road to success *in almost any definition of "success."*

A full-time home economist for the New York Housing Authority commented, "It is not enough just to give people better housing. You can take a person from the slums but it is as important to take the slums out of a person's thinking. That will require more teaching, training, and orientation than anything we've done so far."

Wanting and knowing how to care for things is an acquired skill, not an innate talent. Though children seem to have a destructive streak, most lapses are due to ignorance or a careless environment, or to hidden personal problems which no child should have to bear, and which the child himself may not recognize.

CARE OF SCHOOL PROPERTY

It's well to remember that, when students don't appreciate what is done for them in modern, convenient, efficient, handsome school surroundings, it's because they have no measuring stick with which to compare here and there, past and present. Learning about the immense changes in school facilities since grandmother's day is a real eye opener to them. A citizenship meeting is a good setting for this discovery, or it could be a project during orientation training while you're emphasizing class and building procedures.

Example: THEN AND NOW—A lesson toward appreciation. Prepare the way by discussing the abundance and affluence of American life. Have them mention comforts and luxuries the simplest family has today which even the carriage classes of 100 years ago didn't expect: central heating, running hot and cold water, electric lights, refrigeration, telephones, TV, self-operating elevators, fruits and spices from the world over, the year around. The list, of course, can be more extensive in middle- and upper-class neighborhoods. Then ask each student to bring a picture from a magazine of, for example, a little red school, a kerosene lamp, an outdoor pump, a slate, a potbellied stove, an old-fashioned car or a horse and carriage. Perhaps an ancient textbook can be passed around.

A day or two later, when children have brought these in, distribute ditto sheets of the format illustrated in Figure 9-1. Put the same format on the board. As different children make contributions, ask them also to fill spaces on the board. (Others fill in blanks at their desks.) Some groups will surprise you with how much they contribute about the schools of yesteryear, but in some classes you'll have to supply much information.

Dramatize the scene a bit with your descriptions of a dunce hat and stool and a hickory stick. You might want to add that formerly in England, when a child misbehaved, the master called in a building assistant, the thrasher, who gave the youngster a

Figure 9-1

Item	Then	Now	How to Show Our Appreciation
Transportation	On foot, street cars, buggies	Bus, bike, car in bad weather	Lock bike in rack. Thank driver
Bell	Big... loud bell, rang anytime	Buzzer, electrically controlled	Come in when you hear it
Desks	Bolted, one size, sometimes gouged	Moveable. Adjustable, easy-clean, smooth tops, etc.	Don't jump on them. Don't play with bolts, etc.
Writing Tools	Slates, ink pens, quill pens, bottles of ink, blotters	Ball points, long pencils, felt pens	Keep track of them; use covers, etc.
Books	Used for years and years, small print, etc.	Big clear print, attractive pictures, changed often	Use covers. Leave them at school in wet weather, etc.
Lunchroom	In gym, behind boiler or empty room	Cafeteria, hot food, etc.	Eat, don't throw food, etc.
Resource Center or Library	Resource Center didn't exist. Library seldom used	Movies, slides, strips, computers, etc.	Handle books and equipment with care. Help others

whipping. He was paid fourpence for each thrashing. And years ago in this country, some rural schoolmasters would put a naughty student in a large basket and string it from the ceiling.

Wind up the lesson. After the chart is completed, question them on how today's changes reflect our overall higher standard of living and schooling. Why do parents (and the school) provide milk? Orange juice? Vegetables? Hot dogs? Along the way you'll pick up the summarizing answer—good, healthy bodies. Then ask, Why does the community provide school movies and a projector? A good gym? Maps? Lab supplies? Computer terminals? Again, you'll pick up a summarizing answer— so children can grow into adulthood literate and able to think, strong and healthy in their minds.

Speaking of thinking, many boys regard removing their hats on entering the building as school rules nonsense, while they accept a clean shoe requirement because it's a reinforcing of home training. "Wipe your feet CLEAN," insists one principal. He demands mudless feet before students enter his handsome school. The rule is intended to care for public property, and a visible dividend is cleaner hall floors.

More important, however, this simple act helps to change the tone of the children's demeanor from outdoor freedom to indoor courtesy. They slow up from the romping pace and become quieter naturally, without the faculty resorting to formal class line-ups. In many neighborhoods this amounts to superfluous regimentation.

DEFACEMENT AND DESTRUCTION

Destructiveness and creativity are opposed forces in the life of man. To create is to construct, and to construct cooperatively is to lay the foundations of a peaceful community.
—Sylvia Ashton-Warner, *Teacher*

Since property defacement indicates the destroyers' lack of belonging feeling, lack of responsiveness to neighborhood welfare, its mood is more serious than the property damage involved—although the cash cost may be substantial. It's a short step from a general destructive attitude to a self-destructive one.

Students venting their negative feelings against school is a reaction as old as Montaigne, but the destructive student is still missing the mark. He won't affect the school seriously. His actions rarely touch the matters which need changing or even the things he thinks need changing. And the really sorry aspect is: the defacement won't even help his frustrations, except on a fleeting basis.

Anyone's frustration is within himself. It's not in the situation—regardless of how incredibly difficult it is. The origins of his frustrations may be so obscured that he doesn't know the source or how to define his problem, but his dilemma is never a problem without a solution. A solution exists. He may not recognize it, or perhaps he won't accept it; whether he should have to accept it is for the social engineers of society to determine. We are simply teachers.

Meanwhile, getting back to avenues open to a frustrated person or student right now—the snarls can be corrected only in his own thinking and actions, or reactions; he himself has to do the changing. He alone must handle his frustration and the rage which caused him to strike out. First, he must develop a more expanded, more understanding outlook, and then an attitude of greater responsibility toward himself and others. Understanding a situation is the best means of initiating an escape. The schools, specialists, teachers can assist, but that's all.

Occasionally, a child's home atmosphere is rife with frustrated thinking by every family member. He arrives at school like a water bucket filled to the brim. A cupful of any discord or disappointment and he overflows. An incident follows. Many times this involves property destruction.

When you speak with him about it, you'll usually encounter defiance. Be quiet. Listen carefully after you get the child talking, and keep him talking. Listen some more. Usually, you'll soon learn the defiance is a relatively thin layer covering a thick sense of defeat. Then, when it's your time to comment and while you are talking, you might compose a pencil list in your handwriting of his specific accomplishments and concrete, small victories. Let him keep the list. Only then take correctional steps concerning the incident.

If the fact surfaces that he feels his scholarship efforts have been permanently neutralized by his poor general behavior, fortify him with sustaining, contrary facts. Offer to speak with teachers he feels are prejudiced because of his lousy record. You may not dent the teacher's feeling, but you'll do much to convince the student he has an adult friend, one who will go to bat for him. This alone can be a pivotal point.

Still, any property damage calls for restitution. He must, of course, make some amends. If school laws and funds permit, hire and pay him for work covering the costs. If laws don't permit paying him and the school must absorb the loss, have him work a prescribed number of hours anyway. You might ask the student what the going rate for odd jobs is and calculate accordingly. Especially fitting is a job assignment where he can assist a cordial teacher daily, for example, washing seats and desks in her room. The casual friendliness can be a strong counteracting influence or preventative. One school principal helps solve damage incidents by allowing the culprits to sweep halls or wash windows.

Occasionally, if the student doesn't make actual financial restitution when the vandalism involves lab equipment or books, it can be a natural move to require him to use the broken, defaced equipment. But not for too long. If his emotional problem is being solved, there's no point in reminding him of his misdemeanor forever.

The above comments are a synthesis of suggestions and ideas various teachers and administrators offered when I questioned them. Now for a few more which, I hope, a teacher may use or imaginatively build on, should the need arise.

$3 Down and $2 a Week

If serious damage has occurred, arrange a conference with the principal, the student and his parents, and yourself. After assessing the total cost, have the child start paying. Even if he can pay cold cash—say, from a savings account—weekly payments from current income are a better arrangement. The lesson of taking responsibility for one's actions and respect for public property will be more indelibly fused in the kid's mind if he has a series of friendly payment meetings with you or the principal.

Fresh Air, Sunshine, and the Birds Are Chirping

If you're short on suitable tasks for making damage restitution, have the student take a wastebasket and fill it with litter from the school yard. Obviously, he shouldn't be outside unaccompanied so this may have to be done during his recess playtime.

Many Hands Make Light Work

If, in spite of your warning, the class tends to be slipshod in caring for school supplies have them pick up playground scraps for a series of days. Tell them this activity will continue until they learn to take reasonable care of items in the classroom.

PERSONAL PROPERTY

The challenge of working to acquire or keep possessions, whether of spirit or property, makes them more precious to the possessor. Great and powerful men often have tremendous respect for humility, while the obscure man places little value on it because the world's temptations haven't tried to decrease his. Public figures and celebrities usually value privacy in their personal lives above almost anything else. As a rule middle income adults respect property acquirement because it represents planning, goals, and successful hard work. Poor people value respect for their dignity and character, because so many would deny or overlook it.

When a student needs better habits in caring for personal property, let her expend effort in relation to it. Even a search for teacher-hidden playground balls compels effort. If she carelessly loses a book, let her work it off at going rates for odd job helpers.

Here are a few suggestions offered by interviewed teachers,

which may provide useful guidelines for your own way of correcting thoughtless indifference to equipment or supplies.

Storage Box Brings Storage Fees

Stray objects are placed in a locked storage box. Then, when a student is missing a possession or leaves a school-issued text on the playground, he may ask if it is in the box. The first time he leaves a belonging out, he may retrieve it after one day; the second time, after two days, and so on. Storage costs accrue at 10 cents a day with the collected cash going to the Red Cross or the room treasury.

A Treasure Hunt . . . The Treasure?

Sometimes the treasure is the student's own gym clothes. If a child leaves her gym clothes out, warn her. Second time, hide them. She's not allowed to search for them until her classmates are almost ready for gym. If the gym teacher makes her sit on the sidelines for being late, it will simply reinforce the lesson.

Snitch Those School Bags

The first time a student leaves her school bag out, warn her. Second time, put it in a closet and she must ask you for its return. Third time, she must write a note home which you will sign. When she brings it back, countersigned, return her property.

PENCIL SHARPENING

Imagine each of your thirty students equipped with a quill pen and a sharpening knife (not a pocketknife), a bottle of India ink and blotting sand . . . how's that for the old-fashioned schoolmaster's nightmare? Makes the inconvenience of a slate dull by comparison. And it makes a blunt or broken pencil point seem trivial. Still, one of a student's most important personal tools, and the only one over which he has decided quality control, is his pencil.

When writing with a keen-edged pencil, haven't you felt the enjoyment that comes from using a well-sharpened tool? Moreover, hasn't it strengthened your confidence in the preciseness of what you are writing?

Worldwide, any noisy school pencil sharpener has a siren lure. Until students' desks come equipped with silent sharpeners, students will feel the magnetic pull of the RRRR at the windowsill.

Since it's normal for kids to want to move about, and sitting still can pall even for the most docile, try providing several other valid reasons for students to leave their seats occasionally: getting fresh paper, crayons, a book. Even an honest count-to-twenty gazing at the hamsters would be better than faked pencil-sharpening expeditions.

Also, the children instinctively know this is a good way to tease or test a teacher. Trying out a teacher on pencil sharpening is one of the safest ways a child has to check out a teacher's reactions. Our whole democratic system is founded on the constant testing of regulations and authority—so love your youngsters' spunkiness even while you nip their little games. Please, whatever rules function in your classroom on pencil sharpening, be sure to adhere to them yourself. Don't pull rank. Living according to this highly visible single standard is an excellent nonverbal mode of conveying the fact that rules are rules.

Who Has the Sharpest Pencil?

Another name for this frolic is, "How many of us will she let go to the pencil sharpener?" Stop and ask class a few brief questions. "Why can't I let you play this game? It's fun, isn't it?" The children will offer some good answers.

If I Break the Point Myself . . .

Maybe she'll let me go to the pencil sharpener . . . and maybe she won't. In this case, you might hand the broken pencil to a nearby student and let him perform the honors.

A Lackluster Cache of Stubs

Keep a coffer of well-sharpened pencils, medium length or short. When you lend, extract a promise of return. The percentage of returns is high. Medium and short pencils aren't as much fun to use as long ones with good erasers. The difference prompts students to get their own sharpened at the permitted times.

Captain Grinder

Daily, one child in each row keeps all the pencils sharpened. He may go to the pencil sharpener anytime. Rotate this role, perhaps seat one on Monday, seat two on Tuesday, and so on.

RRRR Goes the Sharpener

Often one youngster sets off a chain reaction and . . . Stop everyone. Mention the need for good judgment. Have they used it? No one is to sharpen a pencil for a while. You'll let them know when you think they've learned their lesson. Wait fifteen minutes. Try their judgment again. Repeat several times, if necessary. Denial of a privilege and restoration in a short time is a good technique in guiding self-control and judgment development.

"I FOUND IT"

One of childhood's most deliciously wide-eyed, vacuous, who-me? explanations is, "I found it." While assuming the pose of a choir boy's innocence, a youngster offers it to cover embarrassing moments. As long as adults are permitted to ease facts in diplomacy's name, surely we should not be surprised when students find their own evasions. Occasionally, a child uses these words the way an adult would—he actually did find it.

Of course, you'll attend to the actions which brought on need for evading the truth. Generally, it's wise to let exact words fade into the background and concentrate on helping the child learn to speak with greater straightforwardness. First, let him know that you place extremely high priority on honesty, so when anyone levels with you, he has not only your respect, but you always try to lessen the punishment. And then do just that, after he tells you the truth. For instance, you might say, "Ordinarily, I would ask a student to write a page essay for having taken the miniature shrunken head out of Willy's desk, but since you admitted the whole story without my pressuring you, I'll just have you . . . ."

Do you value a child's property rights more than his other rights? Of course not. Do you value one child's property rights more than the class's other rights? Again, no way. Then try to save discussion on a belongings hassle until it doesn't interfere with the group's rights. A good room climate is more important to each individual member than is the immediate settling of an ownership dispute over a pickled frog. Thus oral lessons would not be disrupted nor would your professional duty to individual tutoring and group needs during study period be diverted.

Some teachers start each September with a blanket rule. Any "found" money with hazy ownership claims goes automatically to Oxfam. Interviewing gifted teachers on various topics brought to light that most of them treated minor "I found it" items with courteous but brief dismissal. Here are a few suggestions.

Where on the Agenda? Later

You have a good discussion going. A quiet squabble over a small object develops. Place the disputed object on or, better still, in your desk. At a free moment or at passing time call the two children up for a brief talk. Among your questions you might ask, "Where did you find it?" and "Why do you think you should keep it?"

Two, One, Zero

Two students, one disputed object, and no decision seems quite right. Take school funds or your own and duplicate the item.

Fibbers' Memories Fade

Keep the disputed object at your desk for a day or two. Almost invariably the false claimant will drop the matter. The real owner will ask about it later.

A Collection Basket for the Needy

Choose a basket with a top handle. All loose crayons, pencils, pens, and erasers go into the basket. Then when a child complains he doesn't have a green crayon because his cat ate it, perhaps one is in the basket.

All Roads Lead to Rome . . .

. . . and all lost items in Room 103 go into a pot. Crayons, athletic cards, money, all of them. Money is placed in an envelope, dated, finder named, but total cash is not recorded. At the end of two weeks any unclaimed items revert to the finder.

TEACHING A NEW
DISTRIBUTION METHOD

Efficient handling of these tasks can add fifteen minutes to an ordinary classroom and thirty minutes or more to a poorly organized one. Maintaining an even-flowing tempo is as important as the time saved, for it's during brief periods of minor confusion in passing supplies that chattering and pranks erupt. Joey whacking Harry with a book, for example. When all is calm and orderly, Joey knows for sure he'll be caught; but during moderate disorder he gleefully is willing to chance it. No matter how skillfully and tactfully the incident is resolved, still it has diverted group attention and teacher time, energy, and patience.

A serene atmosphere helps the insecure child, and a well-taught routine lends its own kind of stability. Just as a kind, bland person can be very comforting at times, so a benign, predictable climate can be most welcome between demanding or exciting lessons. Paradoxically, routine for routine's sake has a deadening cast, but routine with a worthwhile purpose in mind can be energizing. Children enjoy a certain amount. It's economical.

Simplicity dictates distributing supplies according to the order you would like students to tackle different lessons. Rarely, if ever, offer younger children an order choice in which to complete tasks. A child's security rests in a sturdy framework, and knowing what is expected of him at a given time helps, not hinders, his growth. Provided, of course, your motives and manners are not domination but consideration. As children grow older, extend a limited choice: "You may do your math or your spelling first, whichever you prefer." Then, as they prove themselves in this, expand into a three-way, or wider, choice.

For tedious, necessary detail, a well-taught pattern promotes freedom in the long run, since it releases time and concern for better purposes. Many classes would welcome discovering that a teacher really has their interests at heart when she asks for rather strict conforming on mundane, trivial matters.

A Working Model

It's easier to teach five children than twenty-five. Then let the five show the class how it's done. Although at first glance, this approach might appear time wasting, it's actually an efficient mode for introducing a new procedure and a tremendous future time-saver.

Example: Select one row. Give supplementary textbook passing directions to a captain. Repeat the instructions to the entire row. Ask class to watch model row perform. Choose a second row. Give directions to a captain, and again instructions to the entire row. Does the second row catch on as easily as the first? Which row thinks it could do a better job? A quicker job? Finally, have the entire class go through the procedure.

When the Clock Strikes . . .

Put morning's agenda on board. Include starting time for each subject. Instruct paper passers to distribute fresh paper at specified times without waiting for your signal. If the group is working reasonably well, you probably wouldn't insist that all youngsters immediately stop one task and begin the next. However, if the class is working halfheartedly and you realize the lesson was close to a flop, it's a good out for everyone if you announce, "Let's start the next lesson together."

First at Work, First in Privilege

Let the first student who settles down in the morning pass out the first set of papers.

School Supplies, Buffet Service

Organize your room into supply centers. Various papers and pencils in one location, workbooks in another, outside reading books in a third. Permitting students a brief respite by allowing them momentarily to leave their seats reduces the squirms and promotes a more relaxed room climate.

Mischievous Minority

Have you three or four rather dedicated discipline imps in your room? At least once a day let each pass a packet of papers or arrange one piece of equipment. More than this? Be careful. Well-behaved kids lose heart if their rowdy buddies get too many plums.

Returning to Sanctum Sanctorum

As your class returns from library or gym have two students stand at the door and distribute items needed for the ensuing lesson. Select students ahead of time and have them place supplies in readiness.

First the Complicated

If a lesson includes an involved worksheet, start the lesson by explaining it. Then use a second worksheet that needs little or no explanation. When the class is settled and quietly writing on the first paper, walk around and slip the second sheet on or into their desks.

On a Clear Day

Place work folders for completed assignments on a window counter. This gives kids a brief, appreciated leg stretch when they place their completed papers—and a peek at the "real world."

A Visiting Teacher's Rules

One traveling art teacher applies three basic rules regardless of the classroom rules; they could easily be adapted to other subjects. She discusses the following rules thoroughly with the class and then, from day one, she enforces them.

1. When the teacher talks, students stop talking.
2. Exact supply limits are set: if the student messes, he's out. No seconds. (Usually, this means he has had two opportunities, each side of the paper.)
3. Clean-up time is announced in advance. When the signal is given, if a child ignores it, he loses the privilege of participating in the next art session.

Circumventing Clean-up Capers

Art, science, or social studies projects often require a clean-up period. No one need tell you that activity seems to be stirred with a spoon at the time. Some classes are prone to pad the time period by diddling and fiddling. Thus the teacher has a two-forked management situation: getting kids to clean at a good tempo and keeping others who have completed their chores free from temptation while they wait.

One teacher arranged chairs in a semicircle and directed students to sit there when they finished. Then she wrote the names and time of the first five on the board. When the earliest arriver sat down, she was to start singing a song of her choice; the second, third, and so on, joined her. When they finished the first song, the second picked a song and everybody sang. The group kept on singing until the teacher could join them.

CONCLUSION

Learning care for school property is a first step in helping a youngster develop a community feeling with those outside her immediate circle. Her enriched sense of identity is worth far more than the preserved property—important as that is. She's enlarging her sense of responsibility for her own acts. In many neighborhoods children and adults feel like helpless pawns of their environment. Eventually, every student resents it when too much is done for her without providing her the opportunity to show her strength or developing ability. By demonstrating to students that they do have an ability, a control—however small—over a few material things, we are sharing a glimmer of how it feels to be somewhat independent of circumstances.

To understand why property, whether personal or communal, must be cared for one must first recognize its value. A graphic way of learning the worth of possessions is to compare life with and without them. This is not moralizing, but simply acknowledging how the facts read. In this chapter we've included a sample lesson in appreciation of school equipment.

Of course the causes underlying destruction and defacement of property or supplies are often deeply rooted; but sometimes these incidents occur merely because kids enjoy stirring up some excitement, or want to get away with something. A perverted sense of adventure may be the propelling cause. While never losing sight of the goal of the student's understanding her own environment, we must be constantly teaching her control over her own actions.

A common sense method of shaking a child out of carelessness for her belongings is requiring effort on her part to regain them.

Although handling pencil sharpening needs during the day may seem irritatingly monotonous and trivial, a pencil point is as important to a student as a well-adjusted microphone is to a public speaker. Pencil sharpening offers children a safe avenue for testing a teacher's mood and control. Smooth passing and gathering of supplies and papers in an easy, predictable manner increases a sense of natural control and cooperation so vital to an active learning climate.

As the children are constantly testing us on our authority, so we have the privilege of constantly testing them on their readiness to make more decisions and take more responsibility. Stretching . . . and growing. In teaching the care and maintenance of property we are also trying to protect the child's happiness, now and later.

Ten

DEALING WITH CONDUCT AND NUISANCE PROBLEMS

There once lived a scholarly, cosmopolitan fellow named Erasmus (1467–1536), who enjoyed meditating. He spent much of his life in contemplation and, for a cloistered gentleman of the Renaissance, he came to some amazing conclusions.

He believed in universal education, rich and poor, men and women; the only limit would be the individual's ability. The next surprise: he advised using stories, games, pictures, and objects as good teaching method—and that was almost five centuries ago. He expressed little patience with grammar teachers who wasted precious years yammering and hammering rules into children. Since he believed in appealing to interest, it's not surprising that he felt "teaching by beating is not a liberal education, and the schoolmaster should not indulge in too strong and too frequent language of blame." Strange, isn't it, that appealing to children's natural interests is still considered a contemporary approach.

In this chapter we'll consider something of a blend of typical physical behavior problems: squirming, out of seats, stealing, fighting, throwing objects, and gum chewing. A few of these antics stem from buoyancy and high spirits, but still students are well aware that teachers should not be indulging them. And teachers, quite properly, may insist there be no exceptions to general rules. As always, the teacher's tone and attitude are pivotal points. So is her promptness.

Squirming often stems from physical discomfort or mild fatigue, and thus a change of pace brings welcome relief. If you notice a consistent restlessness, you may want to reexamine your lesson scheduling to confirm you're *alternating sedentary assignments with tasks allowing for some physical movement.* Or, you might provide students with valid reasons for leaving their seats briefly—getting paper, writing at board, visiting the library corner. Also having the group stand in a circle for an art or science demonstration is a healthy change. Later in this chapter you'll find specific strategies.

Possessions such as weapons and toys are usually best handled by pleasantly enforcing the impersonal rules of room and school. Often students need to learn that the guidelines are real, not just paper rules.

Closely related to this topic is stealing, and the interviewed teachers offered an abundance of ideas on how they have handled various situations. Most teachers don't encounter this problem as often as one might expect, but they place great importance on resolving matters thoughtfully and considerately.

Then we'll touch on fighting, including how it varies from neighborhood to neighborhood, and offer guidelines to help teachers develop their own ways of coping with this difficulty.

Flying objects, except for paper airplanes, are almost nonexistent in some schools and quite an annoyance in others. Misbehaving with them appears to be particularly contagious.

More needless claptrap ensues over old-fashioned gum chewing than any other single school rule—and it's the easiest matter of all to correct with tactful or surprising action.

TAKING A BREAK

When a normally relaxed class becomes squirmy and a bit inattentive, or anytime a lesson lasts longer than thirty minutes, adroit classroom management requires that a teacher provide some relief. Lots of times teachers whose classes are well under control may say simply, "Take a short break." However, many circumstances can prohibit this liberty—the group doesn't yet know how to monitor itself, the principal would disapprove of students standing or wandering a trifle, a few scamps are apt to start a mêlée, or the teacher is not sure of herself.

Included here are a few suggestions which teachers offered to share, ideas which they feel would make life more comfortable for other teachers and students on those restless days.

Dress Rehearsal for a Fire Drill

Announce shortly ahead of time that Room 103 will have a practice fire drill at 2:00 P.M. Then at 2:00 have the class form lines, turn off lights, close doors, whatever your fire rules include. With no buzzer sounding, the children tend to be less agitated. March the students to your fire drill exit. Stop. Turn around. Return to the classroom. You understand your principal well enough to know whether you should mention this expedition to him beforehand.

Seventh Inning Stretch

Call it. You might let a child explain this custom to the class so that everybody understands. Let the group stand at their desks and wiggle a bit.

Around the World

This almost classic learning game makes a good ten-minute boredom or blahs break. It can be played with math or vowel cards. Many times children will opt to play it during indoor recess.

Directions: Give a student some math flash cards. He shows one to the first child. If she answers incorrectly, she remains seated. If she answers correctly, she stands, takes the pack, and shows a card to the classmate sitting behind her. The pack changes hands with each correct answer. Continue around the room.

Sit Your Hands Still

Children usually sit still when their hands are not moving. This device is great when the whole class is antsy and you're not going to try to keep them perfectly still, yet you do need their undivided attention for a few minutes. Please don't ask pupils to fold their hands on their desk tops, not now. Instead, ask them (1) to place their hands on top of their heads; (2) to sit on their hands; (3) to hold their own wrists; (4) to use one hand to hold a wrist and with their second hand touch their nose. The students participate gleefully, but they also listen attentively to the next directions.

Drop It on Them

This strategy, a real boredom shaker, is wonderful for conveying the art of communication without speech; it should make students more alert to subliminal language. It's useful for regaining or retaining the attention of a youngster who is resisting words by tuning the teacher out. The first time, this approach comes as a shock. Moreover, it can be repeated, as often as once a week, and not grow stale. (Demonstrations in science can be adapted to this device.)

Good example: Give a fifteen-minute penmanship exercise in sign language. Have your supplies in readiness or get them organized without comment to class. Tell one child by pointing and signs to pass the booklets. Tell another by signs to pass writing paper. Tell pupils to take their pencils out—without using words. Put right and wrong samples on the board . . . everything without a sound. If a student asks a question, put your finger to your lips and shake your head.

RESISTANCE, INCLUDING
STAYING SEATED

Several teachers informed me the children most likely to resist directions are those who are allowed to do exactly as they please at home. After a few classroom correction tries, the teacher probably should contact the mother. If parents are aware of how much more effective they could make their child's schooling by lessening their own permissiveness, most of them adjust gladly . . . often they don't realize they are more lenient than other parents. (Their in-laws have long been thinking it, but do you think they are going to say anything?)

Here are steps some teachers take when faced with balkiness.

Either . . . Or

Offer him a choice. "Either quit fidgeting in reading group or sit on the stool in back of my desk." This face-saving option is not fundamentally corrective, but often it's better than holding up the entire group's progress at that moment. Also, when offering the choice, extend an open invitation to him to rejoin the session anytime he is willing to wholeheartedly cooperate.

Now this leads us into the related problem—the child who refuses to sit in his seat. Often merely bad habit. You might try these corrections, or something similar, a few times; if the penchant isn't nullified, you'd better delve deeper into the whole matter.

No Stool at the Counter

A child persists in bouncing around out of his seat. Require him to clean his desk, take all his books, notebooks, papers, and belongings and place them on the counter or a table. At first it rather amazes the child, but it isn't too inconvenient. After he completes one or two written assignments while standing, check to learn whether he's ready to modify his behavior.

Seats Are Made for . . . Looking at

Don't bother mentioning sitting down even one more time. Have the youngster stand next to his desk until the lesson's end. Usually, he'll feel uncomfortably conspicuous.

All Eyes Are on ME!

If a child keeps falling or getting out of his seat for attention, take the chair away from him for a while. In about ten minutes ask him if he has learned his lesson.

Author's note: Personally, I am at odds with the idea of asking a child to sit on the floor as part of any correction, although many otherwise fine teachers do. At those moments when we're emphasizing more grown-up behavior, it would seem almost a return to nursery school standards to even permit him to do so.

Fasten Your Seat Belt

This strategy must be handled with very good judgment; it can be most effective, but it can also thud. In a friendly voice tell the student that today he can pretend he's a pilot. The first thing pilots do when they sit in the cockpit is fasten their seat belts. Tie two pieces of string/rope to the chair and direct him to fasten his "seat belt."

WEAPONS AND TOYS

Evidently children learn quickly to follow rules when their treasures are in jeopardy, because the interviewed teachers did not offer much on this subject.

One school, which has a diverse student body, has about eliminated this problem. The all-school rules state there will be no toys, squirt guns, Boy Scout knives, and so on, in the building. The first violation brings a warning from the teacher; the second violation brings a trip to the office. There the principal speaks with him and sends a letter to parents.

With Rubber Bands, Who Needs Toys?

David brought a sack of rubber bands to school, and he equipped his friends with all they thought they needed. Later, when the teacher discovered the source, David was required to sit at a wastebasket in front of the class. Then he was asked to cut each band in three pieces. While he was snipping, everyone who had received part of his largess was invited to step forward and "let" David cut those bands, too. Needless to say, a quiet gala was in the air! Every classmate who had any sort of rubber band brought it up in a spirit of glee. The more our friend muttered, the harder his buddies scoured their desks.

Obviously, if a child brought an undue supply of tacks or pins to school, it would be easy to develop an alternate procedure. Stand on a chair and make a border across the top of a bulletin board? Spell out ROOM 103 in tacks?

STEALING

"Who steals my purse, steals trash . . ." And if it's all the same to you, we'll have the trash back, thank you. Since your students have heard numerous parental admonitions about stealing property, why not give your remedial spiel a different slant? First, you might mention stealing in good fun—as in a ball game. Or, with older students perhaps comment on "midnight requisitions" (taking school and office supplies for legitimate purposes without filling out proper forms). Then ease into a discussion of indirect stealing, such as slander or wasting an employer's time. If the discussion has been brief enough to hold everyone's interest, it should deepen the children's sense of right. More than merely refraining from swiping, they learn respect for our moral obligations to others.

Over and over, teachers I interviewed mentioned the importance of building an atmosphere of trust. They advise, "Expect honesty." A surprising number felt free to leave their handbags out and never had any trouble. Those who found it necessary to lock things, did so very quietly, almost without negative comment.

As I talked with them, they offered to share these suggestions. If you need guidance on a stealing incident, I hope these will be helpful.

29 Plus 1 Equals 30 Letters

Some rare old English coins were passed around the room. One disappeared. Angrily, the teacher announced that the whole class must stay after school until the missing coin reappeared. At 3:35 she was perched on a swaying limb; the culprit had not summoned the nerve to announce his guilt publicly; mothers would be worrying.

The teacher explained that she couldn't keep the class any longer, although she knew it wasn't fair to let the guilty go scot-free. She was sure he was sorry for his actions. Were there any suggestions?

One girl offered this idea. Have each student write a note. The guilty one was to write, "I did take it, and I'm sorry" and sign his name. The others were to write "I didn't take it" and sign. The teacher's role in the pact was to let the offender remain anonymous that day and to settle with him later. It worked like a charm.

Within These Walls

Weekly dues of 10 cents are appropriate if you have a room treasury. Then if a book-clip, a good pen, or some such item disappears, direct the class treasurer to buy a replacement from the funds. One can readily see this would promote a sense of group responsibility.

Suspect Assigned the Role of Sherlock

Brian, who had a good record, took a paint box from the room and was caught redhanded on the playground. He insisted another boy had given him the box.

His teacher wrote a note asking other teachers to check their paint supplies; Brian had to take it to every room. On his rounds, Brian was to look over the classes to see if he could identify the alleged donor. Since he was a sensitive boy who would feel pangs of regret, his teacher didn't try to obtain his confession; she felt carrying the note was enough. Later on, he did confess of his own accord.

Trust You? Of Course I Do

After you've corrected a stealing incident, take an early opportunity to show the child you trust him. Have him carry money in an envelope to the office—ask him to fetch your purse or to lock the desk drawer.

No Invisible Ink, Either

No marker? No graded papers! Occasionally colored pencils or felt markers will disappear from a teacher's desk. You might try, "I'm sorry, but I can't mark any papers until I find my marking pen." Almost invariably some child will find it, usually before the day is out.

Safety in a Neutral Zone

A wallet has disappeared. Tell students you're sure the thief must regret yielding to temptation; if this wallet, intact, is returned within twenty-four hours, you'll not investigate further. Choose a deposit receptacle into which the thief may slip the wallet. Nearly always it will be returned. Afterward, let the class discuss the long-range benefits of *honesty*, taking care not to cast innuendoes.

If He Cares . . . If He Doesn't Care

When a child, sensitive to law, has been caught stealing, even getting caught is a punishment. Additional sanctions can be mild and still be effective. Perhaps returning the item is enough.

When a rather brazen child, indifferent to law, has been caught, he views getting caught merely as an occupational hazard, not as a punishment. Have him write an essay? Could be. Probably both the office and his parents should be involved.

I'm Sorry Plus

Gary prized his set of presidential statues. Billy stole them. Later Billy returned them, apologized, and felt such remorse for his actions that he offered voluntarily to make a special gift for Gary. This teacher has handled many incidents of stealing along the same strategy: restitution, apology, and an extra act of friendliness on the thief's part. If no hostility exists in the culprit's thought, he's glad to make amends concretely to show he really meant it when he said, "I'm sorry."

Information Wanted—No Reward

A theft has occurred, and you need information. Pass out lined paper and instruct children to print, not write, any knowledge they have. Have children who know nothing say so and ask them to continue printing by adding their views about cooperating with authorities. (This way, everyone in the room is printing, not just those who have relevant facts.) Explain that classmates who report information are not tattling; they are doing the culprit a favor, since you're almost sure to catch him later, and it will be rougher then. Reassure the class that no scene will ensue; you'll speak privately with the thief. Almost always, someone saw the act or missing article, or has a lead.

Please, Just Ask

For years one teacher has been extending an offer, and still no takers. She tells students she doesn't want to see them tempted. If anything in the room attracts them so much they might be tempted to take it, let her know. She'll give it to them. Incidentally, there's no stealing in her room.

FIGHTING

In the children's minds, there's fighting and then there's fighting . . . and still other fighting. Puppy-dog wrestling and pummeling a classmate are not fighting. "Honest, we weren't. He was having fun, too." Scrappiness doesn't always mean a student is swimming in hostility. Sometimes, it's a sharp competitiveness, sometimes the pleasure of pitting one's strength, sometimes it's mere habit. Often it reflects home and community standards. Historically, rural settlements have prized great physical strength, especially among boys; this influence lingers today. Other parents teach their boys to fight; they are proud of a youngster who can "lick every kid on the block."

Many teachers know only too well that physical force is a dominant fact of life in some areas from remote villages to crowded high rise apartments, thus community mores have a decided, if unspoken, influence on the acceptability of fighting. But, if fun fighting is permitted at school, the ice is getting thin, for other types of fighting are close behind—the kinds that degenerate into personalities and bitterness.

Any school yard referee must first raise her thought above personalities to principles—rules of fairness, consideration. In supervising playing children there's a difference between realistic caring and anxious caution. Caring stems from a positive base, appreciation of a person or thing's worth. Excessive caution means acting from a base of fear. *Carefulness* and *caution* are two words whose meanings diverge only slightly at the start, but a definite angle is set.

One gentle, effective teacher told me that when she has fights to settle, she always asks the youngsters after they've calmed down, "Whatever it is, is it worth fighting for?" She maintains that in her classroom any child who is stealing, fighting, lying, or name-calling is not ready for school. He's better off at home. On the next natural schedule break she phones the home and sends the child home for the day. May I add that her class enrollment consists of students from every conceivable background?

City or suburb, often you can prevent more fights by chatting with parents than by any other step. Casually and gently try directing their attention to the fact that most "middle-class" parents teach children to avoid most fights. If you've been tactful, they won't answer you directly, but they'll take a hint. You'll know it, because Junior Jones's skirmishes will drop in number, often dramatically.

Coping with the little viking himself is another story. If he finds that others pick on him often, he may just be asking for it. You may try explaining the difference between being aggressive and being assertive, and then compare these with being passive. You, of course, might counsel him on how to avoid troublemakers without making it obvious and how to develop constructive, closer friends. Sometimes, though, he's got a reputation to live down before he sees real results. In conclusion, advise him that fighting is but one way to resolve matters, and tell him,

"Don't give up your right to decide for yourself whether a difference is going to be settled in a grown-up way."

If there's been scapegoating, you know how to handle it as a form of bullying, a special kind of fighting. Every bully has had his life warped in some way. And, for the record, nagging is an adult form of bullying, or so I am told.

In talking a situation over with a bully fighter, a private, three-way conversation with parents, child, and teacher is suggested. Require the child to face what he's done. Let him state his position—this weakens his defensiveness. Let him explain why he's done nothing wrong if he's still thinking that way. Certainly, extreme cases should be routed through the office; sometimes they are corrected by letting or forcing a child to transfer schools.

Any mental atmosphere is contagious, and aggression can be highly contagious. It must be nipped.

Excellent comments and suggestions came abundantly when I questioned teachers about fighting. Here are a few for your consideration.

Locking the Barn Door Before . . .

Stage a mock fight with role-playing by structuring an incident of fighting. Ask about eight children to participate. Select a pair to scuffle. The others are bystanders. Afterward, have a group discussion on the causes of fighting and various types of fights: with fists, words, nasty looks, and so on. Suggest available alternatives to fighting if the class doesn't spontaneously offer them. These alternatives may be included:

1. Tell the offender to cut it out
2. Tell the teacher or playground supervisor
3. Walk away from impending fights—this takes a strong person

One Large Needle and a Long Thread

If a student rips another's clothes, have him repair the damage with needle and thread. Obviously, it won't be satisfactory, but it will help him learn more responsibility for his actions. He'll remember the task.

Well, Mom, It Was Like This

A scrappy imp has not responded to warnings. Stop his next fight. As soon as convenient, take him to the office and dial his home. When his mother answers, explain to her the boy has been in another fracas. Now you'll let him tell her the whole story. You stand next to him as he talks. This way, a parent gets a straight story. Also, this method gives the mother time, before the child arrives home, to consider how she wants to handle the incident.

We Stick Together

In persistent cases of fighting make the two students involved do everything together for two days or so. They'll get so tired of each other's company that they won't even want to fight.

A Playground Is Not an Arena

A pugnacious child is ruining playground happiness so deny him the privilege of using it. Specify an exact number of days and whether the denial is before and/or after school. This approach requires follow-through on your part: (1) You'll need to inform the home, and (2) You or another adult must be outside during the stated times. If it's a morning denial, send the child inside immediately on his arrival and give him work. If it's an afternoon restriction, someone must see the child goes directly home.

Not Even a Bully Can Fight by Himself

When dismissing the class, leave the bully in the room while you walk students to the dismissal door. By the time you return, two minutes will have elapsed. A long time in an empty classroom. He'll have felt the separation. Let him go with only brief remarks, not a scolding.

I'd Like to Have You Meet . . .

If you're quite sure the loser of a fight was not the provoker, have the bully winner meet the loser's parents for a conference. This gets through a tough shell. Generally speaking, clear this meeting with your principal—you may even pick up support.

Visiting Hours

If one student's fight injuries are serious enough to hospitalize him, take the winner to the room and let him personally view the results.

And in This Corner

Separate fighting students. Speak firmly and briefly. Let the sureness of your voice inform them of outside control. At the moment don't reason with them about their actions or motives. When you notice changed expressions, talk to each child separately. Using a warm voice tone explain your earlier abruptness, and tell them you'd always rather talk and reason with children.

FLYING OBJECTS

Most children love to test their throwing agility for the same reason they like to wiggle their toes in wet sand. It feels good. The pleasure of communicating by hitting another with a flying object (yet with no intention to hurt) is hard for a child to relinquish once he has discovered it.

Discovery and creativity. Which came first? Rather come and go together, don't they? Connecting these clarion calls of modern education with the perennial childish fondness for paper airplanes and paper wads, we discover another challenge.

Discovering is one thing, acting is another. We teach art to students. We teach them physical coordination in gym. Yet when they combine art talents and coordinated arm muscle control by communicating with Identified Flying Objects, we exclaim, "This will never do!" But what of the new challenge?

Almost any teacher who has taught in both city and suburbs has noticed that in suburban schools paper airplanes of various sorts are not uncommon, but paper wads and spitballs are quite rare; the ratio is reversed in industrial neighborhoods. If I return to city teaching and find myself confronted with the nuisance of paper wads and spitballs, I believe I'll take art lesson time and teach those children how to make interesting paper airplanes.

When interviewing teachers on paper wads and airplanes, I received rather routine answers, with a few exceptions. I was much impressed with those few.

Plain Planes? Passé!

If you have many students folding these deuced little annoyances, here's a great correction. Plan a special art lesson on creative folding of paper. Then, if after all this imagination stimulation, you still have a few old-style airplanes sailing around, invite a small cluster of children for an after-school session.

The Natives Have Their Own Art Forms

Paper airplanes were a real nuisance in one school. The teachers gave an airplane unit-in-study, but it didn't help. Then they became radical. A book on folding paper airplanes was brought into classrooms and everyone was asked to make folded planes, the fancier the folding, the better. The next move was to have every child fly these creations each morning for about five minutes, and then the planes were put in the cabinet. These practice sessions lasted for three weeks and were leading to a grand finale, a contest on the playground one sunny morning. After this, the children were glad to forget them.

Bull's-Eye Benny

Invite your paper wad devotee or your spitball-maker expert to return after school. When he arrives, have his atelier ready. It'll consist of a desk with a huge stack of manila paper and a wastebasket placed at an interesting, challenging distance. Then direct him to sit down and start creating more paper wads (or spitballs) and shoot each one into the basket. All the while he's not to leave his seat for any reason. At first this is fun. As he continues, he'll be increasingly aware this is cutting into his own time and his mouth may be getting dry. Soon he'll be giving an evil eye to the remaining manila paper. This is your cue to consider letting him go home.

Chalk Missiles and Soaring Erasers

Eraser and chalk throwing had become a problem and though many were involved, the teacher caught only two pupils redhanded. The next morning, while the room was still clean, she named these two as sole members of a committee responsible for the appearance of the entire room. They were to pick up every chalk and paper fragment before they could leave for their next class.

They complained bitterly about the unfairness and inhumanity of the universe in general and this teacher in particular. She advised them that if they couldn't persuade classmates not to throw objects, the committeemen were to report unruly students. Also, she added, though this arrangement wasn't instantly fair, many times on this planet a few suffer for the sins of the multitude.

GUM CHEWING

The chicle tree is native to semitropical regions of Central and South America. Have you ever visited a chicle plantation? The owners' appearance is right out of central casting for Latin American gentry, broad-brimmed panama hats, white guayabera shirts, glistening gold jewelry and watches. In actuality they are amazingly wealthy men, but this fact shouldn't surprise any American schoolteacher.

Gum chewing isn't serious, but if there's an all-school rule against it, or if gum crackling grits your nerves, there are many good-natured ways of convincing students to cooperate willingly. Here's a nice selection of suggestions; I hope you'll discover a fresh one to try.

If I Have Five Pieces of Gum

One math teacher, tired of mentioning the all-school, no-gum-chewing rule, took action. Just prior to class she stuffed five sticks in her mouth. During class she chewed and chewed.

Simultaneously, she presented a new concept—orally. Lots of snickering rippled among the students, but never again was gum chewing a problem with her group.

"To Each According to His Needs"

If a student is chewing gum, insist he give you two pieces. If he protests, tell him you *need* two pieces because your mouth is twice as large as his.

When Students Enter Hallowed Halls

Prior to the bell, stand at the door. As students enter, hand out small bits of paper, saying only, "For your gum." Quietly courteous, this method eliminates time-consuming, spotlight processions to the wastebasket.

Where There's Gum, There Are Wrappers

Gum chewing is rampant so cancel morning recess. After the other rooms have enjoyed theirs, take your class out and require them to pick up candy and gum wrappers in the yard.

Bubble, Bubble, Double Trouble

Let's make bubble gum chewing in class costly. Fine the child 10 cents and put the dime into the class kitty. If the student doesn't have a dime, keep the class after school until some-one lends him hard cash. Extracted fines may be used toward a party.

Gum and Chums

Once a month plan a gum-chewing party which lasts about thirty minutes; this should be combined with a semirecreational project. During the party everyone must chew gum and join in the games. The highlight is a contest, and the champion making the biggest bubble wins a foolish prize. Close the party by passing the wastebasket, and everyone discards his gum.

CHANGING CONDUCT CONTOURS

Isolation, or a sense of isolation, long has been a chipped facet in teachers' professional lives; they do feel a schism. Especially in learning exactly how their classrooms, their students, compare with others, it's hard for them to obtain an accurate reading. Statistical studies serve as a very narrow bridge to a better perspective: figures abound in most aspects of American education, except discipline. Rhetoric on discipline is plentiful, percentage figures scarce.

As today's teachers use the word, it refers to everything relating to student demeanor; what the public calls school discipline could be more precisely identified as student attitudes toward authority and education in general, going-to-school skills (or lack thereof), courtesy, and cooperativeness in the role society has thrust on youngsters.

Discipline is a harsh word that for centuries often has touched a raw nerve; it apparently affects adults' deepest self-concepts: If I can't get that little squirt to do what I ask, what's wrong with me? So, when people today get up-tight on the topic, it should come as no surprise. Neither should we ascribe behavior problems to contemporary influences. Perhaps they are compounding factors, but no more.

The NEA research studies on student discipline and how

various school districts are addressing the matter show that even though educators (alarmists and publicity seekers aside) don't enjoy making public statements on the severity of the problem, administrators and teachers are coming to grips with it. And they're making headway. (See Figure 10-1.)

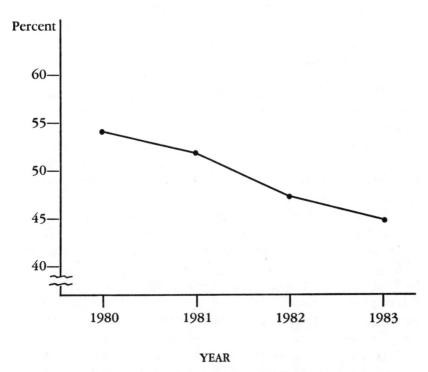

Figure 10-1

PERCENT OF ALL TEACHERS REPORTING THAT STUDENT MISBEHAVIOR INTERFERES A "GREAT" OR "MODERATE EXTENT" WITH THEIR TEACHING, 1980–1983

YEAR

The percent of all teachers reporting that student misbehavior interferes a "great" or "moderate extent" with their teaching has *decreased 9 percentage points in the past three years,* from 54 percent in 1980 to 45 percent in 1983.

Source: National Education Association, 1983

Exact percentage figures do vary from one formal study to another but they all hover in the span which finds that 85 percent to 95 percent of classrooms have small to moderate discipline problems. How various individuals define "moderate" is an unanswered question. As for serious or major discipline problems, most experts seem to cite a figure of 7 percent of classrooms and schools.

Anyone who has grown up in a village will not find the data in Figure 10-2 surprising. Most of these youngsters have home, church, community, and school all working together. If a kid gets into a fracas in the morning, everyone knows about it before the child gets home that day.

The conduct problems, and the strategies, techniques, and insights for coping with them which are discussed earlier in this chapter apply primarily to the schools which report small to moderate discipline deviations. Needless to say, some ideas are effective in chaotic conditions.

The author of the widely acclaimed reform book entitled *Horace's Compromise*, Dr. Theodore R. Sizer, comments, "First, excellent schools absolutely depend on excellent teachers." The purpose of this book, *Classroom Discipline*, is to offer individual teachers pragmatic help, nuts and bolts methods for becoming more adept in the classroom because that's where the whole show starts.

The context of a single classroom is important, isn't it? Yes, indeed, but the variables are simply too great to take in the entire school, district, and region. These do carry a profound influence, but this kind of scope, handled in pragmatic detail, becomes unmanageable . . . at least in a single text. Though it is rather viewing the scene through a scrim, the Survey of School Programs and Practices does enhance a better understanding of nationwide trends.

Do note on Figure 10-2 that the smallest point spreads between regions and between region, hamlet and city, seem to be in writing a strict discipline code, establishing broader provision for suspension, and in giving teachers greater authority to handle problems. Aha, but look at the chart again. The very smallest point spread from community to community comes under the category of making parents more responsible for the discipline of their children.

The widest differences in approach between regions and between communities are in providing special schools for chronic offenders, in providing special staff training, and in creating special classes for the chronically disruptive.

Although these NEA charts don't identify school administrators' concerns, they have been quoted as finding their most serious general problems to be apathy, insubordination, defiance, and profanity. A more detailed delving into their opinions, we can be sure, would bring to light their troubles in handling vandalism and theft of school property.

CONCLUSION

In this chapter we have discussed behavior problems that basically involve physical movement. There were suggestions for correcting squirming when it comes from fatigue or the blahs. Then we considered that peculiar resistance which finds expression in a student's unwillingness to stay seated.

Apparently weapon and toy problems are quite minor and uniform enforcement of all-school rules is simple. Interviewed teachers offered a variety of strategies for handling stealing incidents, but without exception they emphasized the importance of also nurturing a climate of trust. Another facet of stealing was clarified: stealing is not limited to physical objects.

Next we moved on to consider fighting among students and why it's more prevalent in some neighborhoods. Teachers offered a variety of techniques on this topic.

The students' penchant for paper airplanes provides a grand opener for combining a nuisance with the children's budding creativity. And your local paper wad king was mentioned.

Instead of a gaggle over chewing gum, some teachers reduce this problem to a normal perspective. Although little concerns such as pencil sharpening or gum chewing are miniscule in your roster of duties, it's on this type of rule that most

Figure 10-2

SURVEY OF SCHOOL PROGRAMS AND PRACTICES

Questions/Answers	Total	REGION				STRATUM		
		North-east	South-east	Middle	West	300–2999	3000–24,999	25,000 or more
What has your school system done to help schools and teachers with their student discipline problems? (Percent responding; percents may add to more than 100.)								
Nothing specific	7	8	1	8	8	15	3	2
Provided more work-study opportunities	44	55	47	46	42	29	50	55
Provided more extensive vocational programs	51	44	63	55	49	35	59	61
Required at least some schools to provide more traditional curricula and classroom organization	15	13	18	13	14	8	15	23
Provided special staff training on how to handle student misbehavior	50	38	54	49	52	29	50	77
Hired more paraprofessionals to work with teachers	31	26	30	31	34	24	33	38
Made parents more responsible for the discipline of their children	35	38	38	32	34	37	31	37
Hired more counselors and other specialists to work with problem students	27	29	22	28	24	15	27	41
Reduced class sizes in problem schools	14	13	11	13	15	12	11	23
Written strict discipline codes	42	46	51	38	46	35	43	49
Hired security personnel in problem schools	18	19	20	12	26	2	14	45
Given teachers more authority to handle discipline problems	25	23	18	19	29	29	21	25
Provided special school(s) for students who are chronic problems	31	26	37	26	34	8	28	66

Figure 10-2 (Cont'd)

Questions/Answers	Total	REGION North-east	REGION South-east	REGION Middle	REGION West	STRATUM 300–2999	STRATUM 3000–24,999	STRATUM 25,000 or more
Provided for special classes in some schools for students who are chronic problems	38	31	43	38	39	17	38	65
Allowed limited corporal punishment	39	15	49	43	48	36	39	45
Established broader provisions for suspensions	32	26	34	36	32	34	30	33
Established broader provisions for expulsion	21	14	28	22	24	16	21	27
In general, to what extent is student discipline a problem in your school system? (Percent responding.)								
Major problem	3	3	5	1	5	0	1	8
Moderate problem	39	26	59	36	36	25	39	58
Small problem	51	59	31	56	52	60	56	33
No problem	7	12	5	7	7	15	5	2
What percent of your schools would you estimate as having SERIOUS student discipline problems? (Percent responding.)								
5 percent or less	63	59	46	66	72	81	54	57
6 to 14 percent	24	26	26	31	16	13	29	28
15 to 29 percent	9	15	15	3	6	3	12	12
30 to 49 percent	3	0	9	0	6	0	5	4
50 percent or more	1	0	4	0	0	3	0	0
Mean percent	7	6	12	5	7	6	8	8
Median percent	5	5	10	5	5	3	8	5

Source: National Education Association Research, 1980

students make up their minds about a teacher's instinctive fairness. Also, they use such rules for testing to learn whether she will hold the line or is the friendly, neighborhood pushover. They don't try to judge her on the far-out cases. Maybe we shouldn't either until we know more of the facts.

Eleven

PREPARING FOR EXCURSIONS INSIDE AND OUTSIDE THE BUILDING

Enrichment is a phase of schooling which needs to be handled gingerly. Yes, alert, curious, ambitious students and classes must have their abilities considered, but it's a two-sided coin. Pulling children from class too often and interrupting a healthy schedule cadence can sap the overall school program. Obviously, the complete picture should be carefully analyzed before undertaking the exceptional.

As we know, many classroom teachers are scheduled to be once-a-week librarians or biweekly assembly supervisors. Normally, these teachers have reasonable classroom management control, but sometimes students are less amenable outside their native habitat. This changed demeanor is often even more pronounced on excursions beyond school walls.

The first section of this chapter, on libraries and resource centers, starts with ideas for enrichment library book reading

225

in the classroom. Next, rules are presented which were contributed by library, resource center, and computer personnel. These provide an idea base from which to adapt new, tailor-made guidelines for your situation. Following this are suggestions on methods of paying for lost or stolen property and for defacement of materials. (Also see Chapter 4.)

The second section includes preventative and corrective measures which relate to irksome student conduct in assembly.

And finally, we will discuss preparatory steps and en route strategies which make a field trip more memorable and happier for all involved—teachers, parent chaperons, students, and the bus driver.

ROOM LIBRARY

The morale-building features of the following suggestions are stronger than they might appear. The teachers who offered them are highly successful in developing spirited, harder-working pupils.

Money aside, children, even wee ones, need the self-respect and strength which come from contributing to the well-being of others. The project below has been especially successful in deprived neighborhoods. Correcting a recognizable shortage of books is one factor, but only one factor. A dearth of material possessions and assets causes many people to forget the need everyone has, the poor included, to reap the satisfaction of being able to give material objects.

Even Carnegie Started With Only a Dime

Students may fund a classroom library from allowances or from doing chores. As teacher, you may match the total, no more. It is important to avoid parental dollars. After accumulating some cash, one adult and several students form a committee to choose and purchase books. Here it's a nice touch to invite a well-liked speech or gym teacher to be the adult member; it won't take much of her time. The pilot committee sets lending and fines rules, too.

They may decide to buy a rubber stamp reading "This book

belongs to Room 103 library'' to pinpoint the book's origin. However, they might consider a charming commercial paper book plate and having a talented student or willing art teacher inscribe the same message.

Control by Book Cart

When bringing a cart of library books to the classroom, a teacher need not disclose her reason, which could be one of several. A surprise treat. Or, she wants the class to browse and read on a particular topic, but going to the school library will result in many students' being distracted by current magazines and fiction. Third, disruptive class members make group control difficult in a familiar setting; the library scene will increase their rowdiness.

A librarian or an adult volunteer might be willing to assemble the books, other times a teacher must do it herself, but the extra effort pays off. Students, once they've experienced this type of classroom free read, are delighted when they walk into class and spot a book cart. A student may visit the cart several times during the period; however, each time she may take only three books back to her desk. This restriction promotes a good flow of materials.

Book Reports—Out of Print

Rich or poor, skinny or fat, clumsy or agile, children dread writing book reports; they're a dull finale to a good show. Taping, puppets, or pictures are good alternatives but they take time and planning. Here's a form (see Figure 11-1) which is an intermediate position between old-style essays and asking students to list titles of books they've read on cards . . . with its attending temptation to cheat.

At the Starting Post Before the Gun

If your group gets a bad library conduct report, make your reprimand short. Save your breath. Immediately prior to their next library visit, have a discussion and role-playing session. Seat a few pupils around a table and have them read story

Figure 11-1

Name _____

Title _____

Author _____

What is the book about? _____

_____

_____

The part I like best _____

_____

_____

_____

Instructions to student: After you've completed this
side, add on the back a pen, pencil, or crayon sketch of
the part you like best.

---

books. Save one chair. As children are demonstrating purpose-
ful conduct, have a troublemaking Merry Andrew sit in the
empty seat and start disrupting the scene. Follow his performance with another short discussion. Let a second group play
these roles? Perhaps.

If you know your students well, consider this. Ask your
naughtiest child to play the troublemaker. He will be stunned.
Often, he will be so self-conscious that he won't be able to
match his habitual standards, and his subsequent behavior will
be better, much better.

LIBRARY, RESOURCE, AND
COMPUTER CENTERS

Initiative and curiosity, many studies have shown, seem to
be stifled during students' middle years of elementary schooling. This gradual, unnecessary atrophy can be reversed when

children work with congenial age-mates in a discovery climate of new devices and fascinating, fresh topics of a good resource center. And now computers in schools are opening entire new frontiers for experimentation and imagination.

When you send students to the resource room to work, you'll sense which children need directional goals. For others, Figure 11-2 completed in duplicate, makes a good chart. You retain one copy, and the second goes to the center's attendant. If you and the youngster complete the form together, it helps him focus his attention and reminds him, without admonition, that he's on his way to discover, search for answers, and work.

Figure 11-2

RESOURCE LEARNING CENTER

Name _____   Teacher _____

Date _____   Time _____ to _____

Prescribed Activity   *Self-Selected Activity*

Reading _____ Level _____

Math _____ Level _____

Science Topic _____   Science Topic _____

_____   _____

Social Studies _____   Social Studies _____

_____   _____

Creative Writing _____   Creative Writing _____

_____   _____

Art_____   Art_____

Computer Activity_____   Computer Activity_____

_____   _____

Other _____

Suggested Material or Equipment _____

_____

Since browsing in a library is by nature flexible and un-structured, framework rules for conduct are even more essential. Almost everyone advocates: Be firm in controls and relax them gradually as students prove themselves, and a good climate exists. Sound reasoning underlies this advice. Students find security within sturdy guidelines, considerately administered. When a child has learned what is expected of him in behavior, he is free to proceed to other learning. Most teachers have sensible rules which fit the classroom milieu, but a library session is really quite different; adjusted rules are mandatory.

Whether you are assigned library duty on a scheduled basis or simply take your class occasionally, consistent guidelines are important. After rules are firmly ensconced, then comes the time to make intelligent exceptions. Here is a good foundation.

1. Ask students to sit three to a six-chair table, four to an eight-chair table, and in alternate chairs at a round table. (See Figure 11-3.) Your reason, if asked? You want students to have oodles of room for books.

Figure 11-3

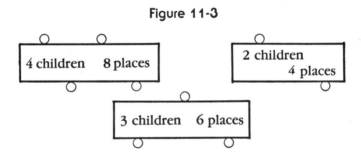

2. Friends may sit with friends until they prove they're not ready for the privilege.
3. Special permission is rarely given to make an exception to the general seating rules.
4. Students take their seats immediately on entering the library.
5. Make necessary announcements.
6. Extend permission to go to the shelves.

7. Issue a warning call a few minutes prior to the bell. All books must be signed out or returned to shelves.

8. Students then reseat themselves at tables before dismissal.

Occasionally, you might check fifteen minutes before the bell to learn how many students will be signing out books. If they are numerous, have just a few come to the check-out counter at a time.

Let's Not Crowd

Stationed at the entrance, the teacher directs children to various tables as they come through the door. "Carlos, over here . . . Lester, near the window. Ann, over there . . . Betsy, near the display, please."

On Leaving, Don't Slam the Door!

Sometimes the politest, most effective move is quietly handing persistently talking students a *Disciplinary Pass*. (See Figure 11-4.) They know they've been breaking the rules.

Figure 11-4

Disciplinary Pass

Your talking is excessive. Therefore, you are NOT TO RETURN to the Center TODAY.

This is a pass to _____

Multilateral Pact

Figure 11-5 is useful for more severe cases of a badly misbehaving youngster. Asking for the student's signature has a salutary effect.

Figure 11-5

Student's Name _____   Date _____

This student was asked to leave the Resource Center because (s)he was making improper use of the center.

ID attached _____

No ID _____

_____
Signature—RC Staff

I understand I am not to return to the Resource Center until I see the Assistant Principal. During this time I am free to use the RC before and after school.

_____
Signature of Student

Student's name _____

Indicate status of student:

_____
Signature of Assistant Principal

To the administrator: Please return lower portion of form to the Resource Center.

MICROCOMPUTERS

Whether your school has a computer center or you're about to have one installed in the classroom, the basic equipment-handling rules are the same. Posting them next to each microcomputer establishes a natural reminder. Computer companies often recommend students be required to write the rules from memory before they are allowed to touch anything. Here are some suggested factors on which you may alert and drill your class.

1. *Always ground yourself* before touching any portion of the computer. (Grounding yourself means removing static electricity from your person.) An inherent, but remote, danger exists that static electricity will jump through the keys and damage some electronic components. Some computers have a special metal case for grounding in the back.

2. *Type gently.* Computer keys do not require pounding, and excessive force can shorten the computer's life.

3. *No candy, gum, food, or drink* is allowed near the computer. Liquid, even a little, spilled on the keyboard will certainly cause damage.

4. *Disks belong in the protective envelopes.* Lint and dust will diminish the life of a disk.

5. *Hold disks by the back edge.* Even a single fingerprint can interfere with information.

6. *Never insert or remove a disk from the disk drive while the computer is "on."*

7. *Never put a disk near a TV.* Don't lay diskettes on top of the TV or hold them near the screen. (The picture tube in your TV or monitor produces a magnetic field that can erase information.)

8. *Never write on or bend a disk.* Inscribe labels by writing on them before adhering them or use a felt tip pen. Any impression or kink in the soft material inside a diskette will probably cause information loss.

ASSEMBLY

The children are aglow! Today, there's an all-school assembly. Leading into this event requires preparing the class, getting them seated in the auditorium, and making provisions for possible scamp antics. Of course, the best deterrent against mischievous behavior is a good program, but as we well know, sometimes you and the class are painted into a corner, just stuck.

One or Two in Every Crowd

Schedule an audience conduct dress rehearsal by preparing your students for an assembly program with role-playing. Ask five or six kids to demonstrate good audience demeanor for an assembly, a movie, a play, a concert. Then instruct two other students to join them and add an imp element, doing everything they shouldn't. Follow this impromptu theatrical with a discussion by the class, eliciting ideas for sanctions.

Forearmed is Forewarned

Intrigue your group about an upcoming assembly with a sneak preview, and then prepare them on required conduct standards with a pep talk. Next, give explicit directions on expected self-management rules, writing something similar to the following on the board. Collect suggestions from the class.

1. Act like ____ graders. (We/you have earned this status, show it.)
2. No talking. (We/you have been together all morning so there's no need.)
3. No scuffling or fooling around.
4. Don't touch anyone's legs or feet.
5. Stay alert.
6. Obey another teacher without argument. (If you object to her directions, comply, and then talk to me later.)
7. One punishment brings another. (If another teacher needs to correct a class member, he may expect another sanction later because his antics have detracted from the room's reputation.)

May I Walk You to Assembly?

Eighth grade boys escort the girls, thus, walking in pairs, no formal line is needed. Initiate the selection by calling a boy's name. He in turn selects a girl. If a teacher chooses the oafs and shy boys first, they tend to pick the quieter girls. As a result the occasion doesn't become a social barometer. At first a teacher may hear mild protests, a bit of resistance, but if she observes carefully, she'll learn it's a surface objection only.

Boy, Girl, Boy, Girl

Clusters of boys sitting together—buoyant horseplay! Clusters of girls sitting together—giggling and gaggling! Direct your students to form two lines, boys and girls. Have them walk to the hall. In seating them, alternate boys and girls.

FIELD TRIPS

A solid, experience-expanding field trip needs the utmost in careful preparation and designing. Otherwise, it's a vivid learning activity on paper only: the students most accurately recall the hamburger stands, colas consumed, and the souvenir shop(s). Obviously, if students are well-primed on the day's framework, they'll see and learn much more. Finally, when they return, a review of events and sights is quite mandatory.

Setting a tone of learning inquiry rather than of festive outing can begin by directing the class's attention to university and government research teams in anthropology, oceanography, space; by discussing TV documentaries or how foreign correspondents gather information. Then ease into reinforcing the fact that the class, too, is going to acquire information from nonacademic, often informal sources; the trip is not a "whee, no classes today" ride through the country.

For your own sake, please be sure students are relaxed and calm when they board the buses. Unnaturally excited or agitated youngsters simply do not improve as the day progresses. If it's a trip which thrills them, it's a short step to becoming over-wound. How to calm them, you know best, but do insist the group be quite collected before leaving.

When students fly, food comes with airline service; when they motor, family car conduct rules are a known; however, children have little experience riding buses on field trips: they're not sure of what's in and what's out. Invariably students bring snack food, soda, and often brown bag lunches. Unless the kids are explicitly instructed to the contrary, they will thoughtlessly trash the area near their seats.

Here are a few suggestions for rounding out and ensuring a more successful field trip:

1. Thorough preview preparation. Some teachers hand students a simple worksheet, not burdensome, to help them focus discovery and learning goals on arrival. Others distribute colorful brochures en route.

2. Hand each child a brown paper bag as he boards. Shortly after departure, ask him to write his name on it with a felt marker. All his paper refuse, empty cans, and unfinished food, every dinky little scrap, should go into this sack. Later collect these brown bags in a green plastic bag.

3. Establish clear rules about staying in seats, including a provision for lavatory trips; surely, the first hour out, there should be no need.

4. Adult chaperons and teachers, in pairs if they prefer, sit in scattered locations throughout the bus. (So often they tend to cluster near the front.)

5. Mischievous students head for the rear of the bus so consider assigning seats to known imps. If they disregard rules or start horsing around, warn them twice and then relocate them near an adult.

If the class understands the above conditions, they'll still have great fun on the trip. They'll giggle. They'll squirm. They'll chatter and sing. But they won't make others miserable in the process. Another plus: if they've been observing clear conduct standards on the bus, they'll be more obedient when you arrive at your destination.

Usually, students do not know or recognize landmarks of the route. You can add greatly to their enjoyment of the trip by pointing out—sometimes with the driver's help—even the most mundane of sites, such as "Greener Pastures shopping mall" is on our left . . . in a few minutes we'll be passing the United States government testing labs" and so on.

Knotted Ropes

Divide the class into four or five squads and use four or five knotted ropes, each section with a teacher or adult in charge. Prior to the big day, let children choose partners and have each pair put their names on a tag which is tied to a knot. Then, when you're at the zoo or wherever, line-up time is greatly shortened and minor hassles avoided: the kids know exactly where they belong, and the missing can be identified immediately. (Lower grades.)

A School Pennant

You're at the United Nations or some other popular school field trip destination. Since you want to leave at 11:10, you've asked the group to reassemble at 11:00 under the big clock. Some will be late. Others will be prompt and then float away or ask special permission, which is reasonable to grant because you've allowed time leeway. Then, when you hold up the pennant, everyone must stay in the cluster, no exceptions. If this procedure is explained ahead of time, the students respond well, and it's much easier to adhere to the schedule. Obviously, if there are dozens of school groups milling around, holding up the pennant makes it easier for your students to locate their groups.

CONCLUSION

Library periods, resource centers, assemblies, and field trips take a small portion of school time. By comparison with daily classroom routine, they are unstructured, or at the very least, restructured. Since this enrichment is frosting on the cake, it should be affable and relaxed—without crumbling to pieces. The best time to establish clear conduct requirements for these events is before the fact, not during or afterward.

Twelve

BUILDING
RAPPORT WITH
PARENTS

Parents and teachers are partners. A natural lead for teachers in establishing a good rapport is to pointedly express respect for the job of parenting. A little book which emphasizes normalcy, naturalness, consistency, in the joint venture of training youngsters is *How to Get Your Children to Be Good Students—How to Get Your Students to Be Good Children* by Bernard Schwartz and James Pugh. It is well worth examining carefully. Among other topics, it tackles the guilt trip many parents have been given by curbstone psychologists.

As we know, most professional educators have earned advanced degrees, sometimes multiple advanced diplomas. Since they are also armed with test scores, statistics on behavior, court rulings, and a clientele who usually are assigned by law, well-trained teachers are especially alert to protecting parents' sense of dignity. They also must guard against unwittingly seeming to promote their views with too much of the "something" which often accompanies the bullying effect of peremptory facts and specialization.

Members of other professions thrive, falter, or fail according to the number of clients they attract and serve well. Obviously teachers are in a Catch-22 in relation to some of their "clients"; they don't want to be served well, and yet the teacher can't dismiss them or resign from the case. But a wise teacher still makes the effort to ensure parents understand and value her services, thus increasing the number who would select her again if they had a free choice.

In this chapter we'll consider informal contacts with the home and home visits. Parent conferences at school are of two types, the Open House and the special/problem conference. Concerning strategies, these two rather overlap. Finally, there's a short section on general faculty, student, and family socializing.

We all understand that harmony is built in part on mutually agreeable relationships and charitable good will. Moreover, true charity does not overlook errors, or make semivalid, conjectural excuses—only false charity does that.

Any sensitive teacher can listen carefully when a parent speaks, not only to words he is uttering or muttering, but for underlying values and trends he's holding in esteem. Somewhere, viewpoints are bound to coincide; and, many or few, these points make the only valid starting base.

Basic security for the child is essential, regardless of whether a child's parents agree with you and the school. Insisting on a reasonable climate in the classroom and meeting basic curriculum standards are mandatory. Certain skills a child must have if he's to survive in today's world, and chaotic individualism interferes with acquiring them.

Chaos always breeds insecurity, which in turn paralyzes creativity and hobbles routine learning, so the child has lost out on both counts. Creativity requires self-control and a wholesome sense of self-direction which knows when to conform and when to refuse to conform.

Most parents approve of moderate study requirements at home; perhaps, among other reasons, they feel more in touch with school life and the curriculum. Good homework assignments can be a great soft sell promoting your effectiveness as a teacher. Why not designate a portion of your most imaginative, clever worksheets as homework—and try to winnow out the mundane.

Frequently, parents ask, "How can I best help my child become a better student, be more successful?" One's thought flashes instinctively to a good lamp, a dictionary, a desk in a quiet corner. Far more vital in promoting a child's progress is the home's attitude toward the genuine value of education and genuine respect for the child's day-to-day achievements. (Incredible as it may seem, some parents are jealous of a child's scholastic success and his affection for various faculty members. Perhaps they see competition weakening family power and ties. Who knows what other reasons exist, but they do.)

Some parents unwisely criticize a child's school or teachers in his presence. This erodes his respect for some or all concerned, divides his loyalties, hobbles his progress. Occasionally, harmony may be restored by reminding parents that a child is encouraged and reassured by a feeling of oneness in educational purpose between home and classroom. Suggest that you have tried to eliminate hair-splitting criticism of students (if you have). Then, if necessary, gently ask parents to examine their motives and carefully weigh the importance of their comments to actually improving conditions.

Thus, they could probably eliminate carping criticism and nitpicking at the staff and curriculum by confining their complaints to matters which really count—and make their displeased remarks to the school personnel, not to the child. This isn't asking for pretense that whatever the school does is right; certainly you'll be glad to meet with parents who feel they are at moderate or serious variance with you. No matter from which direction it comes, petty criticism acts like termites, silently undermining support until suddenly someone's foot goes through the floor.

Then, how about reminding parents of the power of their good example? Suggest to them that they, personally, make a concerted effort to express the qualities they see as weak in the child—alertness, remembering, diligence, completing tasks, neatness, punctuality, courtesy, and so on. One aside: Anyone working hard to improve his own shortcomings is not prone to nagging others for the same failing.

INFORMAL CONTACTS WITH THE HOME

An excellent way of building innate understanding with parents is to visit the student's home to discuss his progress, without waiting for an incident to trigger the event. Naturally, telephone first to arrange the appointment. Generally, you'll feel a grateful welcome, especially in more humble homes. Frequently, you'll acquire many insights in a few minutes because the family is relaxed. So few teachers make this effort that immediately you will have earmarked yourself as exceptionally conscientious. Even dedicated?

Different teachers will take quite different tacks in preparing for these home visits. Again, it's more congenial to compose a list of points and questions, think it over carefully, then leave the list on your desk to avoid any possibility of a monitoring appearance. One teacher might gain the most helpful insights by asking parents about the child's persistence, curiosity, responsibilities at home. Another might inquire into his reading habits and the student's feelings about school. A third may prefer to inquire into his general interests or his reactions when he's challenged.

At troubled times in school consider making a casual, not a "high noon," call to parents. Usually, it's most appreciated. Let's say Charley suddenly becomes rambunctious in class. A phone call may quickly uncover a contributory difficulty. Gracefully approach the question by asking, "Is there anything at school which is bothering Charley?" Once in a while you'll learn of a snag at school, but most often the parent will volunteer information of home turmoil. Then you can not only act accordingly, but the parents will be alerted to how deeply affected the child is.

And speaking of affecting people deeply, try calling the parents when Charley does unusually well on a particular project or test. It's extremely thoughtful and considerate—not to mention unusual—for teachers to call on a glowing occasion, and parents will love you for it.

Here are some other avenues and bridges which practicing teachers have used with marked success.

For Information, Dial . . .

Calls to students' homes on a routine basis yield a treasure trove of pertinent background facts. Most teachers, particularly inner city teachers who call each child's home several times a semester, enthusiastically report splendid discoveries. Initiating calls when all is normal is an excellent way of establishing stronger relationship. Let's remember, in any neighborhood mothers are hesitant to phone a child's teacher for a casual chat. While they respect a teacher's time and schedule, parents also wonder if they'll be considered meddlers. Other cases involve garden variety parental shyness.

Yes, it takes time, but it's time that will come back to you in pleasanter school days; you'll go home less exhausted. Satisfying calls with about five or six homes will take about half an hour. Avoid alphabetical or date patterns for calls. Thus, judgment day can come anytime in a student's life, so he tries harder to keep himself in a state of comparative grace.

Instead of Ex Post Facto

One foresighted way to maintain good feeling with the parents is to send out—about halfway through the quarter—a progress letter. (See Figure 12-1.) Timing should be early enough in the marking period to permit the child and his family to boost a poor or mediocre grade.

"If You Don't Get a Letter . . ."

Parents must be informed if they're going to cooperate wisely. A form letter sent weekly can be most effective. If everyone gets one, then it's much harder for an individual child to feel "she has it in for me." Also, it gives parents early feedback on their corrective efforts. You might initiate the process with an introductory letter and continue it with a weekly model. (See Figure 12-2.)

Challenging a Lack of Change

Three of the above letters marked "unsatisfactory" bring a conference attended by the student, teacher, principal, and *both* parents. When family wage earners have to rearrange affairs to attend a school conference, it alerts them to the seriousness of the situation. The other side of the coin is that if a student seat in the classroom costs taxpayers $4,500 a year, three weeks has cost them about $375. What has the child gained worth $375 during the three weeks?

Figure 12-1

Date _____

Dear _____,

    Thus far this quarter we have taken _____ quizzes.

    Specifically, _____ got quiz grades of _____, _____, _____, _____, and _____. Therefore his present grade is approximately a/an _____.

    His grade is not final and is subject to change before or by the end of this quarter. In case this midquarter grade is unsatisfactory, there is still sufficient time to bring it up to an acceptable level.

                  Cordially yours,

                  Ben Gillie
                  Mathematics Instructor

Parent's Comments _____

_____

_____

_____

Figure 12-2

Sample Introductory Letter

Dear Parents,

We both realize that a good attitude is often the key to academic success. This year we plan to offer your child a wide variety of learning experiences. But all our plans are wasted unless your child is constantly encouraged to develop self-control. Thus we intend to ask your cooperation in our efforts toward fostering self-discipline.

Each Friday your child will bring home a deportment slip. If he has "very good" he has excelled in self-control. "Satisfactory" indicates a positive effort made by your child. "Improvement needed" indicates a lack of effort on your child's part. The last mark, "unsatisfactory," reflects a definite disregard for self-discipline.

Please sign this first deportment letter and have your child return it Monday. Thank you for your cooperation.

Sincerely yours,

Mrs. Elizabeth Arras

Sample Weekly Letter

VERY GOOD   SATISFACTORY
IMPROVEMENT NEEDED   UNSATISFACTORY

Dear Parents,

The above circled word indicates the conduct of your child for this week. "Very good" or "satisfactory" indicates definite progress in your child's conduct. "Improvement needed" indicates a definite lack of self-control. An "unsatisfactory" mark shows that your child's work this week has been greatly affected by his poor behavior in class. You need not sign this paper unless your child has received an "unsatisfactory" mark.

Sincerely yours,

Date   Mrs. Elizabeth Arras

One successful and ambitious teacher has developed the form letter shown in Figure 12-3. When he sends it home, he tries always to mark either positive comments alone or both positive and negative comments. His primary concern is correction.

Figure 12-3

Dear Parents,

I want to inform you when your child has done well at school or has made progress overcoming a problem. On the other hand, I believe you should know when your child is not conforming to regulations.

Thus, I have developed the following checklist. It includes an itemized list, a place for comment (teacher or parent), and a place for the parent signature. You are asked to return the slip to me. A repeated negative behavior occurrence will be followed up with a phone call; on the third occasion, either or both parents will be asked to come to school.

Outstanding Accomplishment or **Progress Solving a Problem**	**Not Following Rules**
School Grounds:	School Grounds:
Careful on playground	Runs
Careful of others	Pushes
Gets along well	Fights
Does not throw snowballs	Throws snowballs
Uses equipment carefully	Improper use of equipment
Halls:	Halls:
Walks carefully in hall	Runs
Is quiet in hall	Makes noise

Goes directly to
  destination
	Not going directly to
	  destination

Enters building when bell
  rings
	Enters building before
	  bell

Figure 12-3 (Cont'd)

Classroom:

    Completes work carefully
    Works quietly
    Shows special interest

Lunchroom:

    Speaks in soft voice
    Does not leave supervised
      area
    Does not disturb others
    Obeys person in charge

Classroom:

    Disturbs others
    Works carelessly
    Incomplete work

Lunchroom:

    Causes a disturbance
    Leaves a supervised
      area

Other: _____   Other: _____

COMMENTS: _____

_____

Parent's signature _____

Stationery Designed by . . .

Have the students create individualized writing paper with their own patterns and decorate the stationery with felt pens, charcoal, paint. Do have them craft their initials in the design somewhere. Use this paper to send positive notes to the home, probably twice a term for each child.

Time-consuming for the teacher? Of course it is. But it's a project that can be combined with watching TV one evening. You may want to keep a brief running log so that each family receives a variety of comments.

Bimonthly Newsletter

Everybody is sending out newsletters. Why not join the merry throng? If a teacher prepares a classroom newsletter for each home, of course she would mention special projects and study units. Then what? Even a list of the class duty roster makes pleasurable reading for parents. Certainly it gives them a conversational wedge at dinner a bit fresher than, "What did you learn in school today?"

May I Introduce Myself?

On your first phone call to a student's home, a wise early question is, "How is Pete reacting to school this year?" Another question to weave in shortly is, "How do you feel the school in general could be improved?" This second question probably won't bring an answer of any earthshaking value, but you will have opened a line of communication.

PARENT CONFERENCES

Most teachers view conferences with one clear, sparkling eye and one jaundiced eye. Probably the faculty has a slight edge on parents in enjoying Open House, although most parents would agree they need conference night more than the teacher does. If a teacher has a mild problem student, she has access to many avenues of help and advice; however, if a parent is besieged with doubts over a minor problem, or if he wants to check his own progress when all is relatively normal, there's no authoritative answer readily available. Hence, many parents regard school conferences as a barometer of their own success.

Understanding this fact, we can recognize why most parents may be a trifle ill at ease under a poised facade and casual questions. Since they're coming into our camp for the pow-wow, it's up to us to light a peace pipe of friendliness. Welcome them cordially. One teacher even served homemade cookies and brewed coffee on parents' night. A tremendous hit. Sharing light refreshments always seems to promote fellowship. (If you try this, do get advance clearance from the office.)

Curiously, in widely separated schools several teachers with rather urbane manners offered identical points as the most important in setting a conducive tone. Foremost, they said, if you really feel you and the parents are partners, sit around a table as equals. Or, even at two student desks *if the parents fit comfortably.* These teachers did concede that an insecure teacher might need the prop of her desk and books. A few of her college texts mixed in with curriculum texts wouldn't hurt: other professionals such as attorneys, with their book-filled offices, use this nonverbal credential sales point. Another exception might be in meeting with a blood-in-his-eye parent—then sometimes, it's wise for a teacher to keep a professional desk between the parent and herself.

Nonetheless, most conferences would be at a table. And to promote idea flow and casualness, the interviewed teachers emphasize having no official records on this table, not even a grade book. The student's card and folder should be available but not visible, at least during the initial stages of the meeting. And please, they suggested, avoid writing anything in front of the parent. If you simply must jot memos, invite your guest to do likewise and offer him a card and a pencil. Most important, of course, is your friendly spirit—all the mechanics mean nothing without that.

In order to turn on a parent's fluency, one adroit English teacher, a Mr. Gerald, explained his approach. He begins by posing a question, "How is Rob doing in English?" The startled parent responds in effect, "Yikes, you're the English teacher. You're asking me?" Mr. Gerald explains that certainly he knows what's transpiring in class, but he's interested in the interpretation the child is carrying home. From that point on, the parent begins divulging information.

If Rob likes the class, the parent usually offers positive remarks or recalls incidents Rob has mentioned. Parental hesitancy often indicates the child doesn't like English this year. Obviously, clarifying questioning is needed to expose the roots of the dislike. Sometimes a parent admits, "I don't know how Rob feels about English. He doesn't tell me much about any of his subjects." Naturally, further delving is delicate on the normal conversation collapse within the home.

Another teacher often sets the tone by opening with a remark such as, "Susan is having trouble in English," and then waiting for a parental expression or explanation. While making such a statement, voice inflection is of paramount importance. Let it be gentle, friendly, patient.

A rejoicing parent! When, during fall Open House a departmental teacher recalls a moment or personality characteristic which obliquely proves she knows the child as an individual, a parent is amazed, happily so. A self-contained classroom teacher won't quite so stun a parent, but she will delight him. You could even make a crib including names and unique features . . . Atticus, the puppy's name; the kid's love of soy sauce; his favorite poem; his druthers on almost anything. Once you've prepared the list, you probably won't have to refer to it; you'll remember.

Comes the time when you must ask for a special conference, an unhappy one. Several outstanding teachers advised me they consider the following moves important: After preliminary discussion with parents, (1) offer one to two constructive steps for the home to take. It's wiser to offer a limited number of ideas than to run the risk of overwhelming the parents. Also, (2) inform them on the specific steps you plan to take. Then, (3) *offer* to phone a month later with a progress report. If they agree, immediately mark the phoning date on your calendar. Finally, (4) as you phone on the promised date, you'll hear parents thrilled with your attitude and sense of professional responsibility. Now, if not before, the parents realize that you do care.

Several tactful faculty members suggested the following points as having contributed to their own successful meetings with parents.

Ask . . . Don't Wait to Be Told

Take an initiative and ask parents, "Is any child in the room making your child uncomfortable?" A mild situation may exist which the parents hesitate to report. If you are aware of an undertow, you can act in quiet ways to help both children.

Positive, Negative, Positive

Always start an appointment with a positive comment about little Dilbert. Please suggest a remedy or a constructive step to try for every negative point. Finally, save at least one garland of praise for ending the interview. This balance is easy if the student is essentially an asset to the scene; it takes serious prior thought if his presence contributes to the negative.

What Will Really Happen?

Many students are apprehensive of parent/teacher conferences and view them about as adults react to a notice from the IRS. The prospective meeting can portend the ominous. Try explaining the whys and details of the conference, including agenda points. Then have the youngsters evaluate themselves before you meet with parents.

Together We Will Consider

Some considerate teachers send each home a letter listing the points the scheduled conference will cover so that parents will be informed and prepared, and realize there is a definite structure to the meeting. A few friendly introductory statements may be followed by an agenda such as:

1. Share positive qualities about student.
2. Read student's self-evaluation.
3. Discuss report card and sample work.
4. Discuss behavior and peer relationships.
5. Invite parental questions or concerns.
6. Wrap up with an overview of conference, and arrive at focused, united goals for coming months.

Learning and Socializing by Design

If you notice a wholesome, complementary friendship developing among two or three students, mention this to the parents. Feel them out on the convenience/inconvenience of your assigning the trio a joint project where they would work together after school. A skit? Read and discuss a book, then report to the class? Taking a survey which is related to a current study unit? Even if the parents must say no, they do appreciate your deeper interest in the children's rounded development.

Balanced Scales of Justice

Work toward spending an equal amount of time discussing positive and negative points in your visits with parents.

Co-Sponsor a Specific Point

Elicit from parents *their* plans to help Mary Lou this year. You may be able to join the home program by stressing or underscoring the same points at school.

Every Day Can Be Parent Conference Day

During a consultation mention that you are always as close as the telephone. Give them your number and invite them to call. Parents do not abuse this invitation. Families lacking extensive formal education are particularly appreciative; many of them have never outgrown a timidity or a reluctance to approach faculty members first. As an added dividend, when parents and teacher are in close communication, children lose the temptation to work both sides of the street.

Best Foot Forward

On Open House night leave several magazines on the waiting chairs outside your door. Among them place some professional periodicals. Since your parent guests are not apt to have seen these issues, they'll find some articles interesting. Also, the publications serve as a tactful reminder that teaching is a profession, and that your judgments stem from academic training.

Keeping Them Down on the Farm?

One nugget which a parent welcomes when he stops to consider its implications is: Don't limit your children by your experiences in school. The math-was-always-hard-for-me-too sympathy, though kindly intended, actually deprives a youngster. It introduces a hurdle before he gets into the race. The

parent may have had math hang-ups for reasons beyond aptitude: inadequately taught basics, foundational assignments
missed, or dull classes. Or the teaching may have been excellent
and the parent hobbled by the heredity superstition of grand-
ma's math-was-always-hard . . . Gently suggest to the parent
that he have modern expectations to match modern textbooks
and today's methods.

Let Him Fiddle With a Timer, Too

Frequently, parents of slow students are confronted with
their child's dawdling over homework. How can they correct
this and still not nag? Suggest a household timer. The parent
and child decide together, with the child leading the decision,
how much she will accomplish in thirty minutes. Then let the
child set the timer. Remind the parent to schedule rest periods
of five minutes if the homework load is heavy.

Come Again When You Can Stay Longer

A good conference conclusion is inviting the parent to
visit while class is in session. Suggest he make it a long visit to
get a feel for the room. A side note—during a short visit the
child is on her best behavior. Consequently, on a leisurely stay
the parent gets an accurate picture of how Ingrid fits in with
the class.

THE LATCHSTRING IS OUT

A rising concern and caterwauling about today's lack of
close knit families and parental supervision has gripped the
American public. Aided and abetted by the media, everyone
knows it's a major cause of discipline unrest in the school and
youth problems on the street. Working mothers. Traveling
fathers. Broken homes. Materialistic priorities. Deteriorating
moral values. Certainly, greater parental interest in school matters is a need of utmost urgency. Now in the good old days
when life was so different . . .

Here are a few faculty complaints:

"What farmer would employ a young man of twenty to care for his cattle at the barn and then neglect to visit his barn for a season?"

"What merchant would employ a clerk and fail, for three months, to make any examination of the state of his books?"

"Mr. _____ owns 200 sheep on a farm four miles from his house. He employs a faithful man to feed them, but also goes twice a week to examine 'the state of his flock.' In a school-house, one-half mile from his dwelling, he has six children who have been under the care of three or four teachers—yet, for several years he has not once visited the other flock."

A slightly stilted language style is a first clue. Yes, these words were written in 1852 and appear in the *Instructors' Manual: Lectures on School Keeping* by S.R. Hall. The author also decries the "want of parental supervision and watchful-ness" and the "indifference of voters" on common school matters.

Since the problem has been around for well over 100 years, it's obvious that the roots are far deeper than Women's Lib and jet-traveling fathers. In spite of school fairs, parent open houses, and the telephone, a sense of schism and separation lingers. In many school districts it would be most appropriate for faculty members to go the extra mile, to take additional initiative.

Having parents and teachers visit in groups of ten or twelve is a good cohesive move. It takes just one person to get the ball rolling. The aim is conversation deeper than a tea or cocktail party, yet less intense than a one-on-one visit. Meeting socially does imply a partnership, and a better sense of friendship develops; often the parties mushroom throughout the commu-nity. Guests enjoy themselves and at the same stroke, feel their time has been well-invested.

Dad Visits Junior's Office

Schedule a brown bag lunch for eleven. Plan the guest list to include a good mix of diverse backgrounds and outlooks. Ask five children in your class to invite their fathers to lunch at school. A surprisingly high percentage of men are able to arrange to make this lunch date, if they have advance notice. Everyone brings his own lunch. During the noon hour, let each child take his father on a building tour.

Saturday? Anywhere But the Matinee

A Saturday outing for twelve people is usually planned by a pair of teachers. Place? Anywhere that's fun—a dog show, a farm, a small airport, a circus. Each teacher invites two students and one of their parents each. Then she invites as her guest a child whom she knows needs more parental attention. And off goes the little pack.

Sunday Evening at 7:30

Originally, a busing program inspired this series of coffees; however, it fits the needs of school communities with a large influx of Asian or Hispanic students: adults who ordinarily don't mingle socially but who have one overriding common interest, the effective and wholesome education of their children. The school PTA president is the coordinator; she with her committee planned for parent groups to meet monthly in various homes. About ten parent members comprise the fixed membership of each group, and one or two teachers (not always the same ones) are present at each gathering. Periodically, the circle views slides or movies taken at school; however, since the parents' children belong to different classes, the projections should be all-school, or at least several classes. The main object of these parties is to cultivate friendly conversation with others of different racial or cultural backgrounds in a natural home setting.

CONCLUSION

Teacher initiative is of vital importance in establishing real understanding with a child's family. This move is dictated by professional ethics and a teacher's high sense of responsibility.

As a faculty member, her work is made easier and more effective by good rapport with the students' families; as a sympathetic friend of the youngsters, her influence for good is deeper and more far reaching. The time spent is "bread cast upon the waters."

Informal contacts by spontaneous phone calls and informative letters are greatly appreciated by parents. Often, timidly, they yearn for more information from the classroom and yet they pause before bothering a busy teacher—perhaps out of consideration for her time, and perhaps out of fear that their requests might boomerang on their child's welfare.

Almost every district has a carefully written manual on the mechanics and procedures for formal parent conferences. As I interviewed teachers I tried to ferret out supplementary aspects beyond the basic format—examples of thinking and actions which successful staff members considered likely to add a patina to these occasions. Their emphasis was on enhancing conferences by anticipating unvoiced questions, and then weaving comments around the information obtained from adroit feelers. Without exception, they urged meeting parents as equal partners, regardless of the parents' background.

A few teachers claim large rewards from additional socializing with students and/or their parents, usually in groups of ten or twelve.

In conclusion, a most precious element in today's schoolroom is the children's and teacher's time. Dr. Ernest Boyer avers that the core problem is not lengthening the school day, the school year, but making improved use of present time. And he's probably right. According to the *Digest of Education Statistics*, 1983–1984, the average teacher expends 7.3 hours per day in the building and a total of 46 hours a week on all teaching duties. Longer hours? There must be a better answer.

Today, many elementary teachers have scholastic credentials undreamed of sixty years ago when a typical teacher's training was closer to a brief normal school session or a sixty-hour certificate. Perhaps then it was wise for teachers to turn docilely to university dignitaries and administrators for learned revelations, but times have changed. Professionally, teachers have never been better equipped for embarking on independent pursuit of excellence in the classroom, including discipline, or for organizing individual grass roots programs of improvement by drawing on their natural and acquired talents. Study. Thinking. Initiative.

And a child's time is so incredibly valuable because these are the years which fix the set of his sails, not unalterably, but very strongly. Think of the countless childhood dreams for the future which would be better protected, the countless taxpayer dollars which would be more wisely spent, if teacher and student morale were improved by just 5 percent each year. Five years: 25 percent. Ten years: 50 percent. Almost unbelievable, isn't it.

IT'S TIME
TO CIRCLE THE
WAGONS

"Mr. Alexander, where did you go to college?" asked a kid sitting in the front row. The class in a New England village was having a spirited discussion about their future job possibilities.

"I was graduated from Harvard."

"Harvard?" The student paused, then frowned skeptically. "If you went to a college like Harvard, how come you're just a teacher?"

A second pause ensued. Then Mr. Alexander answered quietly. "Teaching is the most worthwhile, the most important thing I could do with my life." And he meant it.

Meanwhile on the West Coast a researcher from the Stanford Graduate School of Education was testifying before the California Commission on the Teaching Profession. "Our studies show that teachers overwhelmingly agreed that the factor contributing most to their sense of dissatisfaction was the general absence of respect and recognition for their work." He added that "a consistent theme in our interviews is that teachers believe the job they perform with students is very important, but find the failure of administrators, school board members and the general public to acknowledge their contribution in any meaningful way—especially higher salaries—is utterly demoralizing."

Though many Americans equate good salaries with prestige, it's worth remembering that in the teaching field outstanding private schools traditionally pay even less than public schools, good suburban systems pay less than large cities. Beyond long-recognized psychic rewards of a stimulating environment with fewer discipline and supply problems, there exists an incredibly basic fact. People like to win and it's human nature to enjoy being associated and identified with winners; witness the improved alumni contributions when coaches produce winning teams.

But salary issues make splendid headlines; every reader can follow the reasoning. Never mind the fact that most young adults go into teaching for altruistic reasons. For many it's first cousin to a calling which is combined with tenure and prospects of a full, balanced life between career and family.

National, state, county, district, and building reform projections and plans are vital, but this book is addressed to the options an individual teacher has in her classroom. Or, in some cases, by the knack of being a friendly pest, she can effect other changes. This epilogue discusses the results of several decades of virulent attacks on schools which have culminated in teacher demoralization. It also examines a few ideas for more forceful selling of an established fact: Teachers are professionals who are entitled to the responsibilities and amenities our culture offers other professionals.

THE RUSH TO
THE DOOR MARKED "OUT"

The reasons teachers offer for leaving a particular school, a district, or the field come by the baker's dozen, yet discipline problems are conspicuously omitted from official records. Quite obvious why, isn't it? Then, too, regardless of deplorable conditions which may be stacked against a teacher, overwork and overtight schedules which preclude attending fully to behavior snarls, wimpy or overworked administrators who fall short on effective backup, a teacher who has had troubled classroom management feels, and usually silently, a sense of personal failure. However, the teaching exodus is so pronounced and the statistics so clear, that if she has failed, so have thousands and thousands of others.

It's rather face saving to refer to potential candidates and experienced teachers who have moved on to industrial management, law, or medicine, but how about the thousands who prefer being waiters in posh restaurants, decorating ice cream cakes, or working in pizza box factories? Why did they find teaching so miserable?

Probably in first place is an exhaustion and guilt cycle from trying to meet unrealistic demands. Nothing is more demoralizing than an unachievable vision.

Statistics on different studies vary but they all hover around the projection that one-third of college graduates now entering teaching will leave within five years. Typical conditions for new teachers include an isolated, "sink-or-swim" orientation, inadequate supplies, being assigned a basement classroom in a school down by the vinegar works (or its figurative equivalent). Chaos often prevails and there's skimpy pragmatic help on the horizon. It's a no-win deal.

According to 1983 NEA studies only 12 percent of today's teachers expect to stay until mandatory retirement age. Of the 88 percent left, 39 percent plan to work until they reach retirement eligibility; in other words, their financial investment in a pension plan is a major factor inducing them to ride it out. Another 24 percent are hoping something better will come along, and 9 percent plan to leave teaching as soon as they can. This leaves 16 percent who are teaching mugwumps.

As we know, any mental condition is contagious and discontent or disaffection is no exception. Although self-centered student attitudes and lack of respect are integral to the problem, how can youngsters be buoyantly attracted to lilting "learning discovery" if almost nine of ten teachers would just as soon be elsewhere? The kids have a problem—and so does everyone else. Dr. John I. Goodlad comments on the current emotional classroom tone as "neither harsh and punitive nor warm and joyful; it might be described most accurately as flat."

Within public schools three top contenders cited by teachers as impediments to optimal professional performance are virtually tied—and have been for ten years: heavy work load and extra responsibilities, discipline and negative student attitudes, and incompetent or uncooperative administration. Quite self-evident, isn't it, that discipline concerns seep into the first and last reasons.

Since 51 percent of teachers hold masters' degrees and 69 percent have ten years' experience, turning to tweedy academia for more training comes close to being redundant. Perhaps looking to the corporate world and assimilating business leaders' motivation methods would bring in fresh breezes, or in some cases reinforce ideas some university professors have been trying to get across. Studies show that teachers with a masters tend to be better teachers, but is it because of the additional training or is it because energetic, ambitious personnel are most willing to pursue higher goals?

National leaders concur that a well-trained, enthusiastic teacher corps is the nucleus around which everything else in education must happen. Revitalization of teacher spirits, morale, enthusiasm, zest—call it what you will—is pivotal to success. Excellence at any level in church, school, civic affairs, business, sports, is a purely voluntary commitment. In *Passion for Excellence* the authors ascribe contempt as the number one killer of successful and productive symbiosis. The antonym for contempt is respect.

Now, as individual teachers, what can we use as counterfoil to reverse ill-conceived perceptions? Since *to educate* means *to lead*, what can we do to lift teachers into a more active leadership?

ADAPTING FROM OTHER
PROFESSIONAL WORLDS

Like student, like teacher. How do we counsel students who are slogging along in the doldrums? Let's take a page from our own book. First, we advise them to take small, consistent, incremental steps of improvement; concrete changes have it all over designing home runs on paper. Then, we admonish, work within the system, but don't let the system get to you. Finally, we direct them to cultivate an expectant, winning attitude.

For collecting winning ideas on improving our lot as teachers let's look beyond our building to outstanding schools; beyond our profession to other well-informed groups; beyond campus life to the worlds of advertising, business, and church.

Professionally speaking, teachers feel they have been mugged by the press, hostile segments of the public, and alarmist, sometimes sanctimonious "experts." To avoid physical mugging, crime teams advise: Stay alert. Eyes forward to where you are going. Walk briskly and confidently. Anticipate ambush situations. Using these actions, let's start grappling with potential professional attacks. As long as it is a national pastime to criticize schools and teachers—and it is—countermeasures are in order.

Madison Avenue is world famous for its emphasis on adroit persuasion and sophisticated packaging. As a group, teachers may well veer toward adopting dress styles more classically considered as reflecting management level. In the classroom? Although posters and handsome bulletin boards are occasionally deemed superficial, they dress the classroom setting and its aura. Cutting little purple construction paper frogs is not vital to any child's education, but the pride that induces teachers to make the extra effort is priceless. These two leadership techniques are really putting on a professional smile, especially important when we don't feel like smiling.

Constantly, in education periodicals and reports, teachers are compared with lawyers and doctors. (For comparison purposes what happened to other professionals: journalists, surveyors, the clergy, librarians, accountants, to name a few—or for that matter, education statisticians?) When we enter a dentists's or doctor's office, what do we first notice. Usually, the diplomas and state license. As teachers let's display our credentials publicly; our diplomas need a dusting and hanging.

Lawyers generate monumental stacks of papers yet effective attorneys have orderly, controlled desks. Volumes they used in last week's research are not piled around; they are returned to a bookcase. Again, a neat desk in itself is secondary, but the message it conveys is that the owner is on top of matters.

Attorneys, along with consultants, engineers on site, account executives, all keep logs of time spent on projects and use these hours as a basis for billing. Teachers on fixed salaries donate their extra hours, but there's no reason why they shouldn't collect due credit for the time. Any teacher can well keep a log and then bring it out at evaluation interviews or on parents' night. Neither administrators nor parents can appreciate the unseen hours of a hard-working teacher if they don't know. And who alone is able to inform them?

If every faculty member were to compile an accurate log of surplus hours expended, the collection of booklets would make an effective presentation at salary review negotiations.

Corporations have a developed system, formal or informal, of mentors; savvy young MBA's make sure they have one. Presently, reformers are investigating the idea of teaching principals and teacher mentor programs. But, as individuals, why wait? Anyone with a modicum of leadership initiative can quietly find a mentor of her own choosing. Since competition among faculty is almost nonexistent compared to most business scenes, a floundering teacher usually has a good selection base available. Experienced, excellent teachers acutely need recognition of their expertise; most would be flattered to be asked.

And, drawing from executive practices, counseling sessions could properly be conducted over business style lunches or dinners with the novice using her credit card. Tax deductible? It's a professional conference; in business it would be.

Thinking it over, isn't a mentor arrangement "individualized instruction" moved up from students to teachers? According to NEA polls on inservice training sessions and seminars, about 52 percent of faculty find these building group meetings less than satisfactory.

In other fields professionals use well-designed letterheads. Is there a teacher alive who hasn't sent notes to students' homes on ordinary notebook paper? A few staff members do use *From the desk of* . . . If the message is critically important, a teacher rummages through a bottom desk drawer and finds a school letterhead sheet which carries supervisors' names and titles. A wider teacher recognition, and quite inexpensive at that, is school stationery printed with the names of the principal and entire faculty, complete with B.A. and M.A. after each name, running down a left-hand column. Then, using this paper routinely for sending notes home and to outsiders, not just for state occasions, picks up a major key in successful advertising: repetition.

The corporate world is awash in video conferencing. American public schools are spending vast monies on equipment preparing students for a computer age world. How about permitting teachers to enter the telephone age? A telephone on every teacher's desk or the classroom wall? Stunned? A few teachers who have finger tip access to a telephone thoroughly appreciate the convenience, the time saving. Efficient executives carefully monitor even five- to ten-minute segments of their time. Teachers, too, like to be efficient.

When great-grandmother was a girl, many families received their calls at a neighbor's home or the corner candy store; now most homes have phones and extensions. But teachers? They're still expected to use the school version of a corner candy store, i.e., the nurse's, counselor's, or assistant principal's office. If this antiquity isn't a professional put-down, it surely is a cultural lag.

Teachers who are able to call parents immediately report it's a great deterrent to frisky students. Other benefits come to mind: facilitating field trip or outside speaker arrangements, checking on ordered films, contacting the curriculum center— the enrichments. In this age of working mothers, the option of really convenient telephone conferencing provides a splendid, considerate-to-everyone, bridge to better home and school communication. Finally, it's a time-saving device for administrators by differentiating between a warning parent/teacher/ administrator telephone conference and a this-is-it personal meeting in his office.

When teachers sign contracts, an unspoken agreement exists: they will put in many off-campus hours grading papers, preparing materials, developing new resources, and keeping records. Surely, if the school takes up their evenings, it's fair to allow them the courtesy of making and breaking a few personal appointments during school hours. Believe it or not, even today there are schools which permit faculty no personal calls during school; in business, who of professional or management status works under such kerosene lamp constrictions? Adept corporations have learned people are not widgets, and it's petty chafings or oversupervision which take a serious toll in demotivating employees.

Whether an overworked teacher uses her phone twice or a dozen times weekly, having the instrument at her fingertips is important. Obviously, it saves time, makes difficult calls possible, and often eliminates several aggravating trips to the office. Simultaneously, teachers feel a discretionary freedom and recognition of their management judgment rather lifting them above an outgrown technician status.

For many years Columbia University has annually awarded an outstanding journalism graduate a roving travel scholarship; no journalist anywhere underestimates the value of wide travel. Elementary teachers and journalists are both primarily people-oriented, not scholars. They need to be good generalists who, after obtaining a solid grip on craft aspects, must be alive, perceptive, curious, yes, adventurous personalities. Freshness in a teacher's thinking is going to reach out and touch the freshness in children's outlooks. Training by travel is a magnificent route to add fresh dash to faculty lives, to whet discovery talents, and to diminish provincialism.

A few schools give faculty professional growth credit and salary increments for travel; it makes sense.

In one district teachers may work among South American Indians or bus down to Tierra del Fuego, go snorkeling and examine marine life in the Caribbean, work on a kibbutz. The possibilities, here and abroad, are endless. It's entirely up to the teachers but they must file a report at summer's end.

Young Jeff, who had been in the school system for five years, asked his sixth grade teacher, "How much and how far did you travel before the school board would hire you?" All his previous teachers had liberally tapped on their travel experiences for anecdotes and illustrative examples, shared native music records and slides, and developed off-center lessons

RECENT INITIATIVES REPORTED BY STATES

Columns:
- Curriculum Reform
- Graduation Requirements
- College Admissions
- Student Evaluation/Testing
- Textbooks/Instructional Materials
- Academic Recognition Programs
- Instructional Time
- Longer School Day
- Longer School Year
- Specialized Schools
- Academic Enrichment Programs
- School Discipline
- Placement/Promotion Policies
- Extracurricular/Athletic Policies
- Teacher Preparation/Certification
- Salary Increases
- Master Teachers/Career Ladders
- Teacher Shortages
- Professional Development/Teachers
- Professional Development/Administrators

STATES:

- Alabama
- Alaska
- Arizona
- Arkansas
- California
- Colorado
- Connecticut
- Delaware
- District of Columbia
- Florida
- Georgia
- Hawaii
- Idaho
- Illinois
- Indiana
- Iowa
- Kansas
- Kentucky
- Louisiana
- Maine
- Maryland
- Massachusetts
- Michigan
- Minnesota
- Mississippi
- Missouri
- Montana
- Nebraska

Legend:
- ▨ Under Consideration or Proposed
- ■ Enacted or Approved

Columns (left to right):
1. Curriculum Reform
2. Graduation Requirements
3. College Admissions
4. Student Evaluation/Testing
5. Textbooks/Instructional Materials
6. Academic Recognition Programs
7. Instructional Time
8. Longer School Day
9. Longer School Year
10. Specialized Schools
11. Academic Enrichment Programs
12. School Discipline
13. Placement/Promotion Policies
14. Extracurricular/Athletic Policies
15. Teacher Preparation/Certification
16. Salary Increases
17. Master Teachers/Career Ladders
18. Teacher Shortages
19. Professional Development/Teachers
20. Professional Development/Administrators

STATES:
- Nevada
- New Hampshire
- New Jersey
- New Mexico
- New York
- North Carolina
- North Dakota
- Ohio
- Oklahoma
- Oregon
- Pennsylvania
- Rhode Island
- South Carolina
- South Dakota
- Tennessee
- Texas
- Utah
- Vermont
- Virginia
- Washington
- West Virginia
- Wisconsin
- Wyoming

TOTAL	Curriculum Reform	Graduation Requirements	College Admissions	Student Evaluation/Testing	Textbooks/Instructional Materials	Academic Recognition Programs	Instructional Time	Longer School Day	Longer School Year	Specialized Schools	Academic Enrichment Programs	School Discipline	Placement/Promotion Policies	Extracurricular/Athletic Policies	Teacher Preparation/Certification	Salary Increases	Master Teachers/Career Ladders	Teacher Shortages	Professional Development/Teachers	Professional Development/Administrators
TOTAL (Under Consideration or Proposed)	23	13	12	13	10	6	20	13	14	5	11	13	8	13	19	20	24	16	21	16
TOTAL (Enacted or Approved)	22	35	22	29	11	18	18	8	7	11	29	13	11	5	28	14	6	23	20	22
TOTAL	45	48	34	42	21	24	38	21	21	16	40	26	19	18	47	34	30	39	41	38

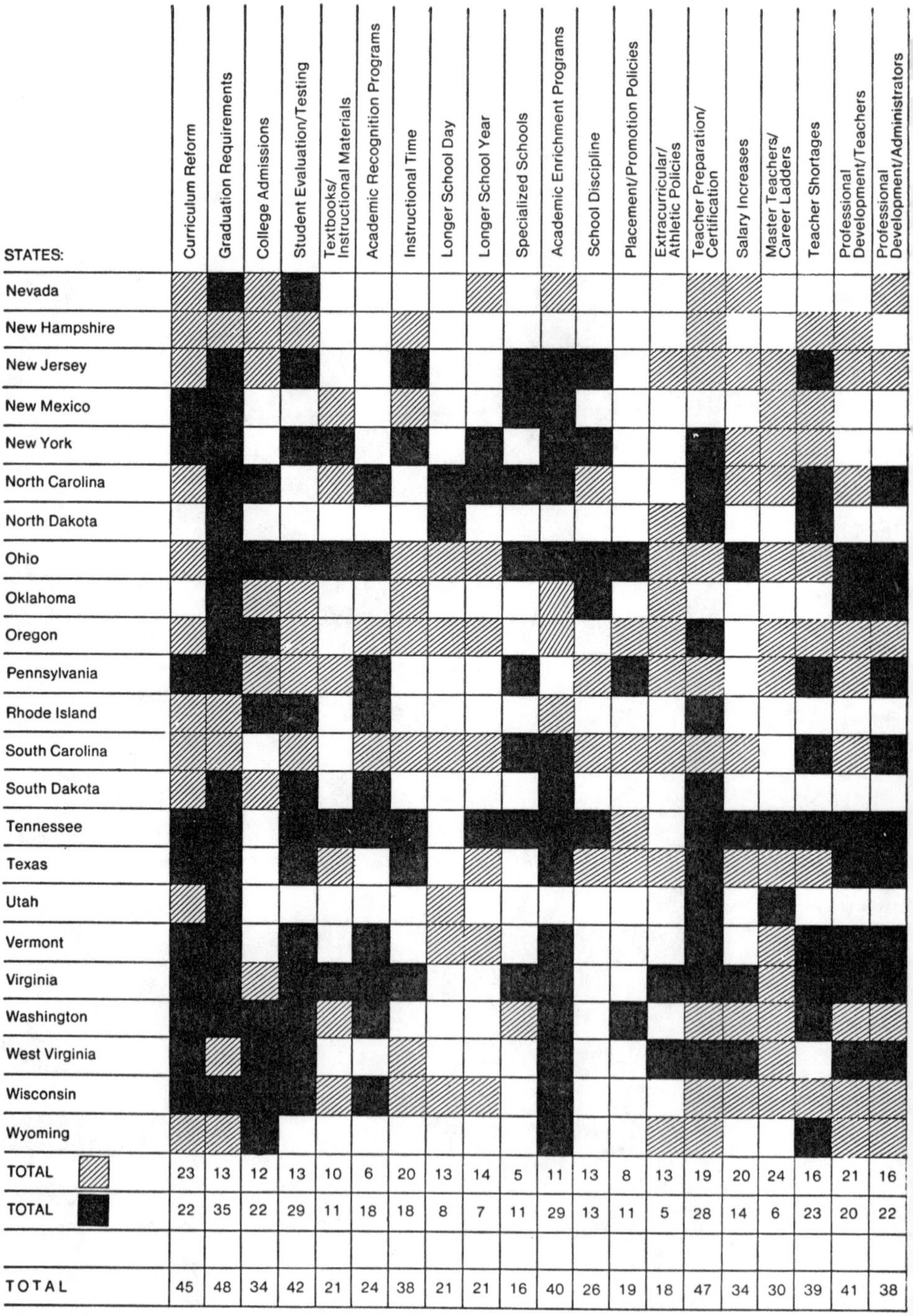

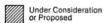

Under Consideration or Proposed   Enacted or Approved

Source: The Nation Responds, U.S. Department of Education, May, 1984.

with verve. In his mind teachers' lives were interesting—if not especially so during winter months, then certainly their summers were intriguing. Training by travel must be a genuine part of the deal from his view.

But still, professors and administrators are prone to collect teachers into summer seminars, preach to the choir for six weeks, and then pronounce them more learned—by six credits. Perhaps they are, but often these courses actually increase stolidity and divert teachers from their greatest needs: adventure and a sense of their growing uniqueness. Offbeat, not tourist-package, travel is a precious method to hone imagination, vivacity, a freewheeling spirit, and to motivate, revive, and keep teachers.

Many teachers now plan to take early retirement or quit, but these projections are not engraved in stone. We've all seen classrooms turn around, buildings turn around, districts do a metamorphosis. Training by travel adds a direly needed *je ne sais pas quoi* note to teacher preparation and professional growth; if it's to become a customary feature, it'll take a grass roots movement: the habit of speaking about the "whole child" is deeply entrenched; speaking about the "whole teacher" is ignored.

CONCLUSION

The American public gives the nation's educational systems strong support. According to Dr. Gallup "every major group in the population" placed education first in determining our country's future strength, "developing the most efficient industrial system in the world" came in second while "building the strongest military force in the world" came in third.

This endorsement may be similar to the public's approval of the Stars and Stripes, charity drives, and church, that is, many people who no longer attend church support the viability of organized religion.

The dichotomy of the public's stance is clear. Equally clear are the statistics which demonstrate teachers' chilling disenchantment with their chosen careers. En masse, if they are not turned off, they are indeed turned down to an ominous flickering.

Younger teachers are leaving; perhaps the 1970s produced a spunkier generation who—with wider options—are quicker to say, "Enough is enough."

Experts are offering repair and redesign plans for the education vehicle. Great! They're needed. And the project is vast. See Figure E-1, a graph that indicates the depth and scope of blueprints and laws either adopted or now under consideration nationwide. But a haunting silence still shrouds teacher problems of feeling a lack of esteem, working conditions, and student discipline in the current reform projections. And, nobody is going to travel very far, very fast, until the wobbling wheels are tightened.

Public schools, working through the system have taken long, evolutionary steps in correcting some formerly widespread teacher concerns such as inadequate planning time and needless meetings. This chapter has discussed strategies adapted from other professions to clarify and improve each teacher's individual sense of identity. Thus, when the general atmosphere is a white-man-speaks-with-forked-tongue, teachers can circle their wagons.

Bibliography

Charles, C.M., *Elementary Classroom Management*. New York, NY: Longman, Inc., 1983. The chapter on discipline gives a succinct description of nine systems which have become well known in recent years: Cantor, Dreikus, Glasser, et al.

Duke, Daniel L. (editor), *Helping Teachers Manage Classrooms*. Alexandria, VA: Association for Supervision and Curriculum Development, 1982. A collection of eight articles on the teacher's role shift from controller to manager. It is written especially for professionals who work with teachers: administrators, staff developers, curriculum specialists, and teacher educators.

Ekman, Paul, *Telling Lies: Clues to Deceit in the Marketplace, Politics, and Marriage*. New York, NY: W.W. Norton and Co., 1985. Although this book is written primarily for other professionals, attorneys, physicians, law enforcement officials, Chapters IV, V, and VI offer valuable information for educators and teachers.

Gardner, Howard, *Frames of Mind: The Theory of Multiple Intelligences*. New York, NY: Basic Books, Inc., 1983. The premise of this book expands perception of innate intelligence; it offers teachers schooled in traditional IQ theories an entire new way of viewing human intellectual capability, thus should be very helpful in raising classroom morale.

Gnagey, William, *Motivating Classroom Discipline*. New York, NY: Macmillan Publishing Co., 1981. Addresses the topic simply and to the point. Teachers doing independent study and research should find it a good reference.

Jones, Vernon F. and Jones, Louise S., *Responsible Classroom Discipline*. Boston, MA.: Allyn and Bacon, 1982. This book is divided into three major parts: theoretical foundation, preventative discipline, and corrective strategies. Balanced and informative.

Nighswander, James, *Planning for Better School Discipline*. Alexandria, VA: Association for Supervision and Curriculum Development, 1982. This is a text, four filmstrips, cassettes, and manual for a school and community-wide program to restore order when chaos prevails.

Peters, Thomas J. and Austin, Nancy K., *A Passion for Excellence*. New York, NY: Random House, Inc., 1985. Under Part V: Leadership, the chapter "Excellence in School Leadership" is alive with concrete information and a winning attitude.

Schwartz, Barnard and Pugh, James, *How to Get Your Children to Be Good Students—How to Get Your Students to Be Good Children*. Englewood Cliffs, NJ: Prentice-Hall, Inc., 1981. Advocates a united, single approach among teachers, administrators, and parents. Has excellent, specific material on teaching children the differences between passive, aggressive, and assertive social skills.

Weber, Wilford A. and Roff, Linda et al., *Classroom Management–Review of the Teachers' Education and Research Literature*. Houston, TX: University of Houston, 1973. Excellent and exhaustive overview. Authors identify 300 managerial strategies and systematically reduce this number into eight or nine categories. Each strategy identified also lists originators and dates they expressed approval of it. Although this study is dated, it should be invaluable to anyone writing a paper on the school discipline movement.

Index